# Welcome to Windows

Do you ever get frustrated with your PC? Is it running too slowly? Is there something you'd like to do but you can't quite remember how to do it? Well, Windows 7 can go a long way to solving those problems, and this is the guide you need to make the most of it.

It's written by a team of independent experts at PC Pro, who've been involved with the new operating system from its very beginnings. They use it every day and know it inside out. Think of this guide as a distillation of everything they've learned.

We've packed it full of step-by-step advice, insider tips and detail where detail is needed. This is no dull textbook, but a lively, full-colour guide written in language you're guaranteed to understand.

**FIRST STEPS** We start from the very beginning: how to choose the right version of Windows 7. Even if you already own a Windows 7 computer, you may be surprised to discover that you can upgrade to a superior version at any time simply by buying a new product code online. We explain how to do it and how much it will cost. If you haven't yet bought a copy of Windows 7, we reveal how you could save a lot of money when you do. And all this is in the first chapter!

But things get really exciting when we come to all the new features that Windows 7 has to offer, and how to take advantage of them. Maybe you want to edit home videos? Then meet Movie Maker on page 69, which makes it blissfully simple to produce professional-looking results. Perhaps you've got thousands of photos? We reveal how to quickly find the snaps you want courtesy of the new and improved photo organiser that now comes bundled with Windows.

If there are two or more computers in your house, but only one of them has a printer attached, we also explain how to use a brand new Windows feature called HomeGroup to share that printer with any computer that joins your network.

**SAFE AND SOUND** When it comes to security and stability, Microsoft has also concentrated on making this version of Windows the toughest yet, and we dedicate an entire chapter on how to stay safe on the internet. This covers everything from ensuring children don't visit sites they shouldn't, to how you can find and install anti-virus software for free.

And, if the very worst does come to pass, we explain how to rescue a computer that's been struck by a virus, suffered a hard disk failure or simply won't boot any more. (Though don't forget to follow our advice on backups on page 116, just in case all your resurrection attempts fail!)

In short, through thick and thin, bad times and good, this extensive guide to Windows 7 is here to be by your side throughout the life of your computer.

Tim Danton
Editor, PC Pro
editor@pcpro.co.uk

# Contents

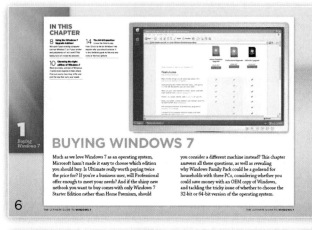

## BUYING WINDOWS 7

Much as we love Windows 7 as an operating system, Microsoft hasn't made it easy to choose which edition you should buy. Is Ultimate really worth paying twice the price for? If you're a business user, will Professional offer enough to meet your needs? And if the shiny new netbook you want to buy comes with only Windows 7 Starter Edition rather than Home Premium, should you consider a different machine instead? This chapter answers all these questions, as well as revealing why Windows Family Pack could be a godsend for households with three PCs, considering whether you could save money with an OEM copy of Windows, and tackling the tricky issue of whether to choose the 32-bit or 64-bit version of the operating system.

6

## INSTALLING WINDOWS 7

Windows 7's install process is a huge improvement on previous efforts. Gone are XP's ugly, intimidating text boxes and Vista's need for user input again and again throughout the process. Instead, Windows 7 asks you what you want up front, then goes away and takes care of everything itself. In this chapter, we guide you through the different install options available: either upgrade directly from Vista, replace your existing system with a clean install of Windows 7, or create a dual-boot setup in which you can continue to use your old Windows as well. Whichever you choose, it's easy to move the important files from your exiriting PC. Later, we'll also investigate the new option of installing Windows on a virtual disk: see page 60.

16

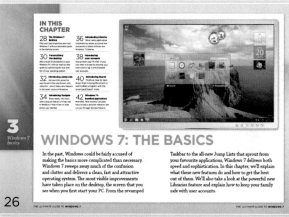

## WINDOWS 7: THE BASICS

In the past, Windows could be fairly accused of making the basics more complicated than necessary. Windows 7 sweeps away much of the confusion and clutter and delivers a clean, fast and attractive operating system. The most visible improvements have taken place on the desktop, the screen that you see when you first start your PC. From the revamped Taskbar to the all-new Jump Lists that sprout from your favourite applications, Windows 7 delivers both speed and sophistication. In this chapter, we'll explain what these new features do and how to get the best out of them. We'll also take a look at the powerful new Libraries feature and explain how to keep your family safe with user accounts.

26

## ADVANCED FEATURES

We've now covered the basics of Windows 7, but there's much more to it than a few tweaks. With just a little technical know-how, you can create virtual hard disks (and even install Windows 7 directly onto one), calibrate your monitor so that it displays colours more accurately, and speed up your day-to-day work in Windows with our pick of its keyboard shortcuts. We'll also reveal what the enhanced Aero interface has to offer, and it goes way beyond glossy effects – from shaking a window so that the others fall away, to instantly tiling windows and moving them between screens. And you'll discover exactly why so many people are getting excited about the new touchscreen technology built into Windows 7.

46

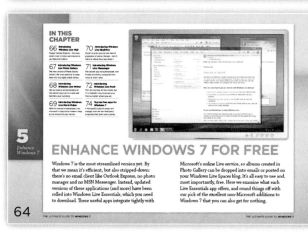

## ENHANCE WINDOWS 7 FOR FREE

Windows 7 is the most streamlined version yet. By that we mean it's efficient, but also stripped-down: there's no email client like Outlook Express, no photo manager and no MSN Messenger. Instead, updated versions of these applications (and more) have been rolled into Windows Live Essentials, which you need to download. These useful apps integrate tightly with Microsoft's online Live service, so albums created in Photo Gallery can be dropped into emails or posted on your Windows Live Spaces blog. It's all easy to use and, most importantly, free. Here we examine what each Live Essentials app offers, and round things off with our pick of the excellent non-Microsoft additions to Windows 7 that you can also get for nothing.

64

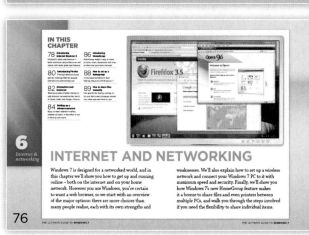

## INTERNET AND NETWORKING

Windows 7 is designed for a networked world, and in this chapter we'll show you how to get up and running online – both on the internet and on your home network. However you use Windows, you're certain to want a web browser, so we start with an overview of the major options: there are more choices than many people realise, each with its own strengths and weaknesses. We'll also explain how to set up a wireless network and connect your Windows 7 PC to it with maximum speed and security. Finally, we'll show you how Windows 7's new HomeGroup feature makes it a breeze to share files and even printers between multiple PCs, and walk you through the steps involved if you need the flexibility to share individual items.

76

# He deserves a birthday card as original as he is.

Not a problem.

Word 2007 makes it easy for your family to show their creative side.

Cards, photo albums, posters, invitations, flyers – with Word, they're all at your fingertips. The preformatted templates, themes and tools let you add a special touch to everything you do. It's all part of Microsoft® Office 2007.

Don't buy a new PC without it.
Office2007.co.uk

Real life tools.

# Contents

**7** *Windows 7 entertains*

## ENTERTAINMENT IN WINDOWS 7

All work and no play would make Windows a very dull place, but Microsoft's latest is also designed to please. In the Home Premium, Professional and Ultimate editions you'll discover the new and vastly improved Windows Media Center. Together with a TV tuner, this is the key to turning any PC or laptop into a fully featured cutting-edge home entertainment system.

Whether watching and recording TV, enjoying DVD movies or listening to your favourite music, it's the definitive hub for playing and managing all your digital media. In this chapter we delve into Media Center and show how to get it up and running with the minimum of hassle. For something a bit more interactive, we'll also take a tour of the games supplied with Windows 7.

90

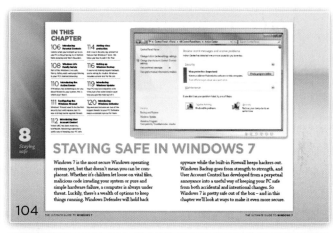

**8** *Staying safe*

## STAYING SAFE IN WINDOWS 7

Windows 7 is the most secure Windows operating system yet, but that doesn't mean you can be complacent. Whether it's children let loose on vital files, malicious code invading your system or pure and simple hardware failure, a computer is always under threat. Luckily, there's a wealth of options to keep things running. Windows Defender will hold back

spyware while the built-in Firewall keeps hackers out. Windows Backup goes from strength to strength, and User Account Control has developed from a perpetual annoyance into a useful way of keeping your PC safe from both accidental and intentional changes. So Windows 7 is pretty safe out of the box – and in this chapter we'll look at ways to make it even more secure.

104

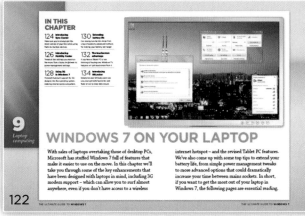

**9** *Laptop computing*

## WINDOWS 7 ON YOUR LAPTOP

With sales of laptops overtaking those of desktop PCs, Microsoft has stuffed Windows 7 full of features that make it easier to work on the move. In this chapter we'll take you through some of the key enhancements that have been designed with laptops in mind, including 3G modem support – which can allow you to surf almost anywhere, even if you don't have access to a wireless

internet hotspot – and the revised Tablet PC features. We've also come up with some top tips to extend your battery life, from simple power management tweaks to more advanced options that could dramatically increase your time between mains sockets. In short, if you want to get the most out of your laptop in Windows 7, the following pages are essential reading.

122

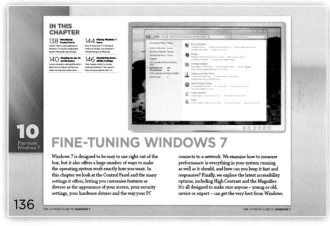

**10** *Fine-tune Windows 7*

## FINE-TUNING WINDOWS 7

Windows 7 is designed to be easy to use right out of the box, but it also offers a huge number of ways to make the operating system work exactly how you want. In this chapter we look at the Control Panel and the many settings it offers, letting you customise features as diverse as the appearance of your screens, your security settings, your hardware drivers and the way your PC

connects to a network. We examine how to measure performance: is everything in your system running as well as it should, and how can you keep it fast and responsive? Finally, we explore the latest accessibility options, including High Contrast and the Magnifier. It's all designed to make sure anyone – young or old, novice or expert – can get the very best from Windows.

136

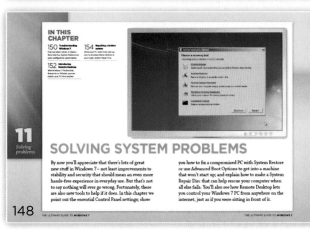

**11** *Solving problems*

## SOLVING SYSTEM PROBLEMS

By now you'll appreciate that there's lots of great new stuff in Windows 7 – not least improvements to stability and security that should mean an even more hassle-free experience in everyday use. But that's not to say nothing will ever go wrong. Fortunately, there are also new tools to help if it does. In this chapter we point out the essential Control Panel settings; show

you how to fix a compromised PC with System Restore or use Advanced Boot Options to get into a machine that won't start up; and explain how to make a System Repair Disc that can help rescue your computer when all else fails. You'll also see how Remote Desktop lets you control your Windows 7 PC from anywhere on the internet, just as if you were sitting in front of it.

148

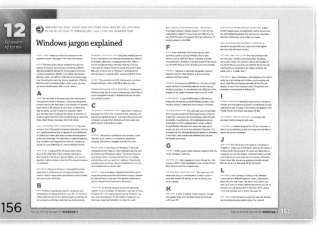

**12** *Glossary of terms*

## Windows jargon explained

156

## IN THIS CHAPTER

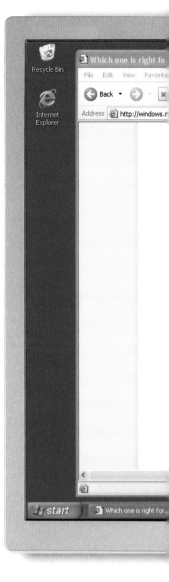

# 1
*Buying Windows 7*

# BUYING WINDOW

Much as we love Windows 7 as an operating system, Microsoft hasn't made it easy to choose which edition you should buy. Is Ultimate really worth paying twice the price for? If you're a business user, will Professional offer enough to meet your needs? And if the shiny new netbook you want to buy comes with only Windows 7 Starter edition rather than Home Premium, should

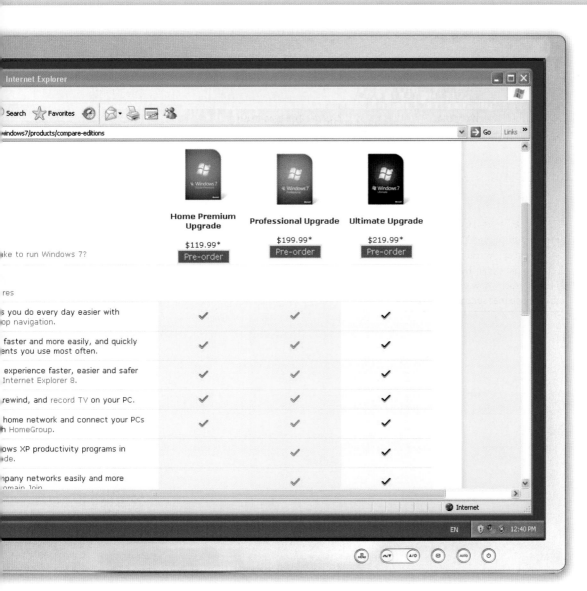

# S 7

you consider a different machine instead? This chapter answers all these questions, as well as revealing why Windows Family Pack could be a godsend for households with three PCs, whether you could save money with an OEM copy of Windows, and tackling the tricky issue of whether to choose the 32-bit or 64-bit version of the operating system.

# 1

## Buying Windows 7

**HOW LONG?**

Shouldn't take more than ten minutes, including the download.

**HOW HARD?**

Just about the easiest thing to do in this book: it's both quick and simple.

## *Tip*

Note that we tested an early version of the Upgrade Advisor. It may change slightly in appearance on its full release.

# HOW TO...
# USE UPGRADE ADVISOR

*Before you buy Windows 7, you need to make sure your computer can run it. Fortunately, the Windows 7 Upgrade Advisor is just a free download away.*

Chances are that if you're already running Vista, your computer will be plenty powerful enough to run Windows 7. After all, part of the appeal of the new operating system is that it runs snappily even on low-powered machines. But you'll want to be sure before shelling out, especially with an older computer – and then there are all your peripherals. A ten-year-old laser printer might have drivers that work fine in XP, but will it cope with Windows 7? And how about your scanner or fax?

You could spend ages poring through system requirements on manufacturers' websites, but there's a much easier solution: Windows 7 Upgrade Advisor. This is a simple software tool that you download from Microsoft's website. It's designed to analyse your system, look for weaknesses and problems with incompatibility, and warn you about any potential issues before you take the plunge and purchase Windows 7. We'd advise you to run it now.

**1  DOWNLOAD THE ADVISOR** Visit the Microsoft website and you may find it isn't immediately apparent where to get the Advisor. The best way to locate it is to search with Google or Bing. Enter "windows 7 upgrade advisor" and it will soon pop up at the top of the results list. Double-check that the linked page is within the microsoft.com site before clicking it.

**2  INSTALL THE SOFTWARE** Click the Download button and wait for the File Download box to pop up. It's only a small file, so even on a sluggish broadband connection it shouldn't take long to arrive. Click Run, then Run again when the Windows pop-up box appears asking "Do you want to run this software?" Click the Next button in the following box, accept the licence terms, click Next once again, and finally click Install. Click Close once the installation routine has run its course.

**3  FIRE IT UP** To launch the Upgrade Advisor in Vista, click the Start orb to open the Start menu, then select All Programs. Scroll down and you'll find the Advisor hiding away, just above Windows Calendar, Contacts, DVD Maker and so on. In XP, you'll find it in a similar location: click Start, then Program Files, and again you'll find it in the main part of this directory.

**(4) HOOK UP PERIPHERALS** Before you start the Windows Upgrade Advisor, make sure you've plugged in all of the peripherals you use on a regular basis. You want the utility to be able to look at, and assess, all of your accessories, in addition to your computer's internal components, to check whether they'll work or not. We're not just talking about printers and scanners here: you need to hook up everything, including mobile phones, MP3 players, external hard disks, digital cameras, scanners, graphics tablets and so on.

**(5) RUN THE ADVISOR** When the application window appears, click the "Start check" button in the bottom right-hand corner. At this point, Upgrade Advisor goes off and has a rummage around in your system to find out if it's up to the job of running the new operating system. The process will take a few minutes; the older your PC and the more accessories you have attached, the longer it will take, so be patient.

**(6) UPGRADE INFORMATION** The first screen you see will tell you all about your PC's ability to run Windows 7. You'll see in our screenshot (below right) that the Advisor presents a simple summary page with three main elements. The first of these gives advice on whether or not you can upgrade directly from your current Windows installation. Here it advises that we can, but in many cases you'll receive an alert advising that you

must "perform a custom installation" after backing up all your programs and documents. This means you have to install Windows 7 from scratch, known as a clean install, as we detail on p22. This isn't quite as simple as an upgrade, but you'll still be able to retain all of your existing files and settings if you wish.

**(7) PROGRAMS** Upgrade Advisor will also warn you if, by installing Windows 7, you're going to lose out on features that you may have enjoyed as part of your existing Vista or XP installation. Here it's telling us that Windows Mail, a basic email application included with Vista (and XP in the guise of Outlook Express), is no longer included with Windows 7. It's also warning us that the parental controls included as part of Windows Vista will no longer be available. Fortunately, both of these features can be added free as part of Windows Live Essentials, as we'll see in chapter 5.

**(8) OTHER SYSTEM REQUIREMENTS** At the bottom is a summary of more technical requirements. Click the link to expand this and you'll find out whether you have enough hard disk space, if your processor is up to scratch, and if you have enough RAM. You'll also see if your PC can run Aero effects such as transparent windows. Scroll down to find advice on whether software for your other hardware may need updating and if any programs aren't Windows 7-friendly.

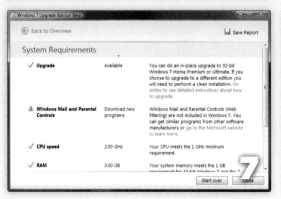

*Tip*

If you have an old PC that you're thinking of throwing out, it's well worth running Upgrade Advisor. Far from overloading an older machine, Windows 7 could be the new lease of life it's been waiting for: we've loaded it onto tired laptops and desktops with great success. As a rough guide, Microsoft says Windows 7 needs a 1GHz processor, 1GB of RAM, 16GB of hard disk space, and a graphics card that supports DirectX 9 (most cards released in the past five years will satisfy this).

THE NUMEROUS VERSIONS OF WINDOWS 7 MAY SEEM CONFUSING, BUT A LITTLE RESEARCH WILL REVEAL WHICH EDITION IS THE PERFECT ONE FOR YOU.

# Choosing the right edition

One of the biggest criticisms people had of Windows Vista was the sheer number of versions that Microsoft released: a total of seven, compared to the simplicity of Windows XP Home or Professional. Despite the gripes, Microsoft has stuck to its guns for the release of Windows 7, offering the new operating system in no fewer than eight editions, ranging from Windows 7 Starter and Home Basic to the more powerful Professional and Ultimate.

You don't have to wade through the pros and cons of every edition to find the right OS for you, though. Windows 7 Starter will only come preinstalled on low-power devices such as netbooks (also known as mini-laptops), and Windows 7 Home Basic won't be sold in the UK at all.

To satisfy the EU's monopoly watchdogs, Microsoft initially threatened to produce an "E" version of Windows 7 for European users, lacking both Internet Explorer and the option to upgrade directly from Vista, but this was scrapped. You may still see an "N" version, however, which omits Microsoft's Media Player.

One more edition of Windows 7 you may hear about is Enterprise. This is identical to Ultimate, but is only available to businesses that sign up to a licensing scheme.

As with Vista, then, that leaves three editions worthy of consideration if you're going to buy a boxed copy off the shelf: Home Premium, Professional and Ultimate. Since Windows 7 Starter edition will be shipped in the UK with some netbooks, we also cover what this has to offer.

**RETAIL OR UPGRADE?** If you already own a PC running Windows XP or Vista, you can buy an upgrade to Windows 7 for a lower price than the full retail version. At least, that's the theory: at the time of going to press, we actually found upgrade prices were higher than retail prices. We expect this to change in the coming months, so it's well worth checking before you buy. If you bought a machine with Vista during the summer of 2009, you may have received a voucher for a discounted upgrade to Windows 7. Depending on your PC maker, this should be valid until 31 January 2010.

Getting an upgrade pack doesn't mean you can't opt for a clean install of Windows 7 on your PC. You get the same options as anyone else, which we cover in chapter 2. The only difference in the installation routine is that you must prove your existing installation of Windows XP or Vista is genuine. All this means in practice is that you have

## FAQ

**Q:** If I choose the wrong version of Windows 7, can I change my mind?
**A:** Microsoft's Windows Anytime Upgrade system (see p12) lets you upgrade to a higher edition instantly via the internet. This option is available no matter which version you start out with. The only catch is that you may end up paying a little more overall.

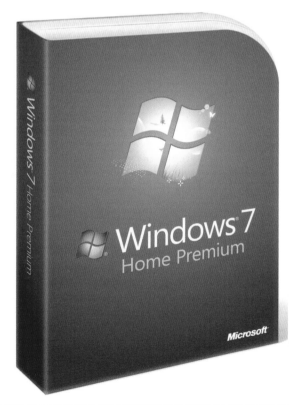

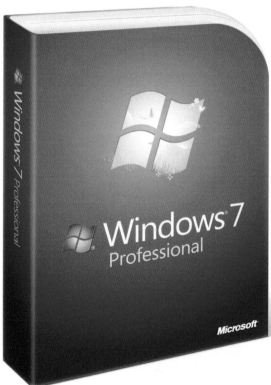

The Windows 7 Family Pack could save you a packet if you need to upgrade three different computers from earlier versions of Windows.

to start by booting up your PC in XP or Vista as usual, then insert the Windows 7 disc and follow the wizard to install the new operating system.

**FAMILY PACK** For the first time, Microsoft is issuing a Family Pack for Windows 7. This is designed to make it easier and cheaper for a whole household to upgrade its computers from previous Windows versions, which makes a lot of sense when so many of the new features (such as HomeGroup – see p86) are aimed at homes with multiple PCs all running Windows 7. The Family Pack costs around £150 and covers three computers. It's an upgrade rather than a full retail version, and will only be available for Home Premium, not Ultimate or the business editions.

Despite these restrictions, it makes a lot of sense for a family with three PCs, especially as you can still upgrade to a superior version of Windows 7 if you prefer through Anytime Upgrade (see p12). Our only concern is that Microsoft has said the Family Pack will be available in "limited quantities", so if demand is as high as we expect you may need to be fairly quick to take advantage. Then again, there's no saying how limited those quantities will really be.

**STARTER** The Starter edition is a stripped-down version of Windows 7 that will be cheaper for netbook manufacturers to buy, helping to keep down the price of these low-cost laptops while discouraging their makers from sticking with Windows XP, as so many have done up to now.

The biggest sacrifice comes in the multimedia features and cosmetic fripperies. For example, you can't stream music from a Starter edition system to other computers on your network, and Windows Media Center has also been removed. There are no see-through windows (Aero Glass themes) and no Taskbar preview feature, and you can't even change the desktop background.

Support for multiple monitors has also been dropped from Starter edition. The only good news is that, after initially announcing that Starter would only allow three applications to run at the same time, Microsoft has decided against this rather bizarre restriction.

Although Starter edition is a perfectly respectable operating system, we think most people will find it frustrating to use on a regular basis. If you have the choice, we recommend you opt for Home Premium instead. If you ▶

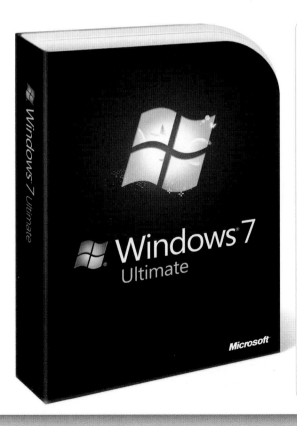

# Should you go OEM?

OEM stands for "original equipment manufacturer", and in this context represents the hundreds of PC makers who preinstall Windows on new machines. Microsoft sells them a special version with limited support and no manuals. Although it isn't officially sanctioned for sale to consumers, there's nothing to stop you buying an OEM copy, available from most online retailers, instead of a boxed retail copy of Windows 7.

While OEM prices will be cheaper, there are drawbacks. An OEM copy is restricted to the first PC it's installed on, so you won't be able to transfer it to another computer later (maybe one you build yourself or buy with a different Windows version). In fact, each OEM installation of Windows is tied to the individual PC's motherboard, so even attempting to upgrade your existing PC with a new motherboard, or replace one that suffers a fault, could cause Windows to stop working. Microsoft may be sympathetic if you phone up and explain the situation, but there's no guarantee of this.

You'll also need to decide whether you need the 32-bit or 64-bit version of Windows 7 at the time of purchase. Retail boxes of Windows 7 include both 32-bit and 64-bit installation DVDs, but OEM copies don't. Finally, as we've mentioned, OEM copies come without documentation and with less entitlement to technical support: beyond initial setup queries, Microsoft expects PC vendors to support their own users, and of course there will be no PC vendor responsible for your copy.

If you can put up with these restrictions, it may be worth going OEM. But if you like to heavily upgrade PCs, or may need support, it's probably a false economy.

don't have the luxury of this choice, and you do start to find Starter edition too annoying, you can use the Anytime Upgrade system (see box, below) to move up.

**HOME PREMIUM** As with Vista, Home Premium is the version that consumers – as opposed to business users – are most likely to encounter. As such, it contains new tools and options that will appeal to home users and anyone who uses their PC for entertainment. Prime among these is the revamped Windows Media Center (see p94). This can still be used as a full-screen entertainment system, and can even be controlled with a remote from the comfort of your sofa. It also works with Media Center Extenders, such as Logitech's Squeezebox Duet and Microsoft's own Xbox 360, so your PC can be your home's entertainment hub.

We've been impressed by the much-improved Media Player, now in version 12. See p92 for our in-depth coverage, but in brief it's a superb way to control a large music and video collection, thanks to an intuitive interface and media-streaming abilities.

The Windows Aero interface, which is only partially supported in Windows 7 Starter Edition, is fully installed in Premium, and it isn't just there to look pretty but to make using your computer more intuitive. It's the little touches – like easy ways to manage windows, and

some excellent desktop themes – that make it a superior environment to Vista. If you're fortunate enough to have a touchscreen PC, things go a step further thanks to a full roster of multitouch features.

More powerful options are still missing from Home Premium, though: there's no BitLocker disk encryption (see p134), no Remote Desktop (p152) and no Windows XP Mode (p52). The Backup and Restore Center is restricted to local hard disk or DVD backups, rather than offering the full versatility available with the Professional and Ultimate editions of Windows 7.

Most personal users will still be well served by Home Premium, but we certainly recommend that power users, professionals and tweakers should consider paying the extra for Windows 7 Ultimate – or Professional.

**PROFESSIONAL** As its name suggests, Windows 7 Professional is primarily targeted at businesses, but it may also appeal to home enthusiasts thanks to a range of new features that can be fully exploited by those looking for more power than Home Premium offers.

The full version of Backup and Restore Center allows you to back up both personal and system files and to schedule backups (Home Premium only allows for manual backup of personal files). Meanwhile, the Encrypting File

# Windows Anytime Upgrade

There's some good news for anyone who ends up with Windows 7 Starter but wants Home Premium, or who buys a Professional laptop but wants Windows 7 Ultimate. Microsoft has a scheme called Windows Anytime Upgrade that allows you to switch between versions easily by paying a suitable fee.

To start the process, type "anytime upgrade" into Windows' search box. Click Windows Anytime Upgrade and you'll be taken to the screen seen below. The advisor will guide you through the different features offered by each version of the operating system, and you'll then be offered the opportunity to buy a new product key that will essentially unlock all the features

of your chosen version – most of which may already be installed on your computer, but locked away.

The whole process could take as little as ten minutes, and all your existing programs, files and settings will be kept intact.

**HOW MUCH IS THAT UPGRADE IN THE WINDOW?***

| | |
|---|---|
| Starter to Home Premium | £70 |
| Starter to Professional | £120 |
| Starter to Ultimate | £140 |
| Home Premium to Professional | £120 |
| Home Premium to Ultimate | £125 |
| Professional to Ultimate | £85 |

*Prices in September 2009

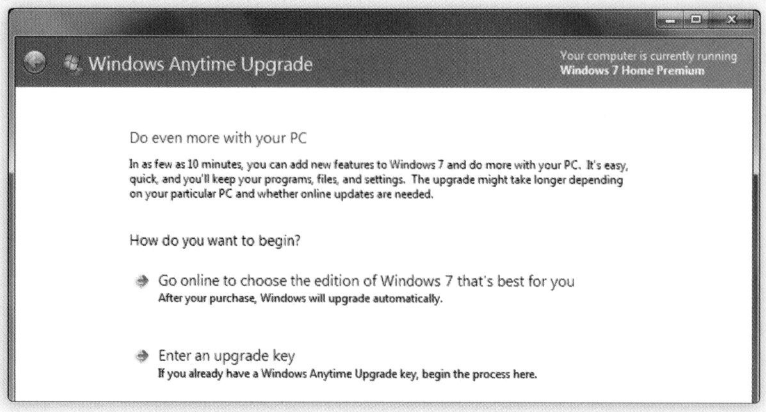

Microsoft's Anytime Upgrade system makes it remarkably easy to swap your edition of Windows 7 for a higher version, so if you outgrow the one you buy initially (or get preinstalled on a PC) it isn't the end of the world.

System, which adds another layer of protection, now offers more complex algorithms that are almost impossible to hack.

Windows XP Mode is an ingenious virtual machine that goes one step beyond running a copy of Windows XP alongside Windows 7. You can do that if you so wish, but it's also able to coexist more seamlessly, as we'll see on p52. Just bear in mind that, even if you're running Professional, you'll have to download Microsoft Virtual PC separately to use Windows XP Mode.

Corporate users will be pleased with several other Professional features, too, including Presentation Mode, which can reset your desktop wallpaper to a default image, specify a preset volume level and prevent your screensaver from appearing – an instant way to set up your PC for use in the boardroom. Unlike Windows 7 Starter and Home Premium systems, a Windows 7 Professional PC can also join a domain (a necessary feature if your computer is centrally managed by an IT department using a domain).

Every feature introduced in Windows 7 Home Premium is also included here, including Aero, multitouch functionality for touchscreen displays, Media Player 12 and (unlike with Vista Business) Windows Media Center. Couple this with a raft of technical, security and networking enhancements and it's clear that, if work is on your mind, Professional edition is probably the way to go.

Unless, that is, you need the additional features offered by the similarly priced Windows 7 Ultimate.

**ULTIMATE** As the name suggests, Windows 7 Ultimate contains every new enhancement from Home Premium and Professional along with extra features that appear only in this edition. In particular, the much-vaunted AppLocker and BitLocker are unique to this version of Windows 7 (along with the identical Windows 7 Enterprise). The former restricts which applications can run on a network, and the latter offers full-disk encryption to ensure no-one can get their hands on your sensitive data. BitLocker to Go (see p134) also allows encryption to be used on USB sticks and other portable devices, ensuring your data stays confidential if a drive is accidentally misplaced.

There are other technical improvements, too, including DirectAccess to enable seamless connections between mobile users and their office network. It's also possible to switch your operating system between 35 different languages, which isn't possible in either the Home Premium or Professional editions. Support for booting from Virtual Hard Disks, the benefits of which we describe in detail on p60, is reserved for Ultimate users.

While there's no sign of the Ultimate Extras that drew such ire when Vista was released, the Ultimate edition of Windows 7 excels in other areas, by including every new feature and enhancement from the other versions of Windows 7 alongside a host of technical improvements that will please enthusiasts, tweakers and IT managers. If you're looking for supreme power and every feature on the block, Windows 7 Ultimate will suit you perfectly, and it's hardly any more expensive than the Professional edition.

# EDITIONS COMPARED

| | Starter | Home Premium | Professional | Ultimate |
|---|---|---|---|---|
| Official price | — | £150 | £220 | £230 |
| Street price* | — | £65 | £148 | £160 |
| Official upgrade price | — | £80 | £190 | £200 |
| Upgrade street price* | — | £77 | £163 | £169 |
| Family Pack price | — | £150 | — | — |
| **USER INTERFACE** | | | | |
| Aero Glass | ○ | ● | ● | ● |
| Aero Peek | ○ | ● | ● | ● |
| Aero Shake | ○ | ● | ● | ● |
| Aero Snap | ● | ● | ● | ● |
| Instant Search | ● | ● | ● | ● |
| Live Preview | ○ | ● | ● | ● |
| Windows Flip 3D | ○ | ● | ● | ● |
| Multitouch | ○ | ● | ● | ● |
| **BUNDLED APPLICATIONS AND SERVICES** | | | | |
| Windows Live Essentials (free download) | ● | ● | ● | ● |
| Windows Fax and Scan | ● | ● | ● | ● |
| Gadgets | ● | ● | ● | ● |
| Paint, Calculator and WordPad | ● | ● | ● | ● |
| Windows Media Player | ● | ● | ● | ● |
| Remote Media Experience | ○ | ● | ● | ● |
| HomeGroup | ○† | ● | ● | ● |
| Device Stage | ● | ● | ● | ● |
| **ENTERTAINMENT** | | | | |
| Basic Games | ● | ● | ● | ● |
| Premium Games | ○ | ● | ● | ● |
| Media Center Extender support | ○ | ● | ● | ● |
| Windows Media Center | ○ | ● | ● | ● |
| **SECURITY AND BACKUP** | | | | |
| BitLocker | ○ | ○ | ○ | ● |
| AppLocker | ○ | ○ | ○ | ● |
| Backup scheduling | ● | ● | ● | ● |
| Backup to network | ○ | ○ | ● | ● |
| Encrypting File System | ○ | ○ | ● | ● |
| Windows Complete PC Backup and Restore | ○ | ○ | ● | ● |
| Windows Defender | ● | ● | ● | ● |
| Windows Firewall | ● | ● | ● | ● |
| Biometric support | ○ | ● | ● | ● |
| **ADVANCED FEATURES** | | | | |
| 64-bit processor support | ○ | ● | ● | ● |
| Maximum RAM supported (32-bit) | 4GB | 4GB | 4GB | 4GB |
| Maximum RAM supported (64-bit) | — | 16GB | 192GB | 192GB |
| DirectX 11 | ● | ● | ● | ● |
| Dual processor support | ○ | ● | ● | ● |
| Windows XP Mode | ○ | ○ | ● | ● |
| Mobility Center | ○ | ● | ● | ● |
| Presentation Mode | ○ | ○ | ● | ● |
| Virtual Hard Disk booting | ○ | ○ | ○ | ● |
| **NETWORKING** | | | | |
| Offline Files & Folders | ○ | ○ | ● | ● |
| Remote Desktop (ability to join) | ● | ● | ● | ● |
| Remote Desktop (ability to organise) | ○ | ○ | ● | ● |
| Windows Server Domain (join) | ○ | ○ | ● | ● |
| Multilingual User Interface language packs | ○ | ○ | ○ | ● |
| DirectAccess | ○ | ○ | ○ | ● |

*Street prices correct in September 2009  †Can join but not create a homegroup

IS NOW THE TIME TO UPGRADE TO A 64-BIT OPERATING SYSTEM? AS WE'LL EXPLAIN, THERE ARE SEVERAL GOOD REASONS TO MAKE THE LEAP.

# The 64-bit question

When you choose a new Windows 7 PC or decide to upgrade, it's an excellent time to think about what a 64-bit operating system could do for you. The choice between 32- and 64-bit is an important one to make, because – unlike the difference between, say, Home Premium and Professional – there's no easy way to change versions later. If you opt for 32-bit Windows 7 and later decide you need 64-bit, you'll have to start again with a fresh installation.

## FAQ

**Q:** Will adding more than 4GB of RAM make demanding applications run significantly faster?
**A:** For now, it's unlikely. In our tests, even when we pushed Photoshop to its limits, a system with 3GB of RAM performed at the same level as one with 8GB. Even a highly demanding HD video task in Adobe Premiere showed little to choose. We chopped up and re-ordered a 1080p video, spliced it back together with transition, motion and transparency effects, and rendered the resulting movie as a 720p H.264 file. With 3GB of RAM, this took 22 minutes and 20 seconds; with 8GB it was 43 seconds faster, an improvement of around 3%. You're more likely to benefit when running many apps simultaneously – and bear in mind that memory requirements always go up over time.

In a moment we'll discuss the advantages of 64-bit, but the first question is whether your PC can support it. If you're buying a new machine (other than a netbook), it's certainly going to be compatible. Most processors made by AMD and Intel over the past four years support 64-bit Windows, but if you're thinking of upgrading existing hardware it's worth double-checking. You can do this online: AMD and Intel use their own names for their respective x64 implementations, but if your CPU is described as supporting either "AMD64" or "Intel 64" it's compatible with 64-bit Windows.

You can also check from within Vista, if your PC is currently running it. In the Control Panel, go to the Performance Information and Tools and click View and print details. You'll see a technical breakdown that shows, among other things, whether your processor is 64-bit capable.

**PERIPHERAL COMPATIBILITY** A second factor to consider is compatibility with your other hardware devices. 32-bit device drivers (the pieces of software that allow Windows to communicate with hardware such as printers) won't work in

64-bit Windows, so you'll need to find 64-bit drivers. That shouldn't be a problem for devices manufactured in the past couple of years, but for older kit it's worth checking the manufacturer's website: you may have to take a decision to either upgrade your hardware or stick with 32-bit Windows.

The Windows 7 Upgrade Advisor (see p8) will also highlight any connected peripherals that aren't supported by the 64-bit version. Note that even if Windows 7 isn't explicitly mentioned by the manufacturer, drivers written for 64-bit Vista should work fine, so gadgets that lack specific support for the new OS may still be usable.

**SOFTWARE COMPATIBILITY** One bit of good news is that you don't need to worry much about application compatibility. Almost all modern 32-bit software should install and run flawlessly in 64-bit Windows, although if there's a 64-bit specific version it will probably be faster. The only exceptions you're likely to encounter are programs that try to hook into the system at a low level, such as 32-bit antivirus software, and the odd amateur program.

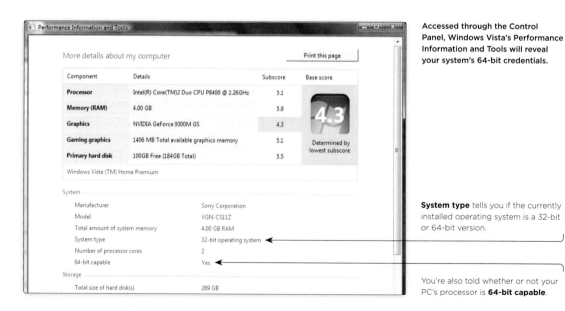

Accessed through the Control Panel, Windows Vista's Performance Information and Tools will reveal your system's 64-bit credentials.

**System type** tells you if the currently installed operating system is a 32-bit or 64-bit version.

You're also told whether or not your PC's processor is **64-bit capable**.

It's worth noting, however, that 16-bit apps such as old DOS games won't run in 64-bit Windows. If you can't live without your fix of Monkey Island, there are third-party tools, such as the free DOSBox x86 emulator, that may be able to help keep very old software running.

**THE BENEFITS OF 64-BIT** A 64-bit operating system offers three inherent advantages, but we'll happily admit you need to be quite technical to understand the first two. If you're not interested, feel free to skip to the next subheading.

The first benefit is that 64-bit applications can run more quickly than their 32-bit counterparts – after all, the CPU can process twice as many bits in a single operation. Don't expect everything to happen twice as quickly, though: in practice, only a small proportion of tasks will see a major speed boost. The application that typically gains most is cryptography, so if you regularly work with encrypted data, 64-bit could well yield worthwhile performance benefits.

64-bit processing also offers better native mathematical precision: a 64-bit binary value can represent a decimal value to around 14 significant digits, while 32 bits can only represent around seven. If a 32-bit application needs 64-bit accuracy, it must spread a "double precision" value across two CPU registers, which can be slower.

That's the theory. The reality is more complex, since modern, nominally 32-bit CPUs have various enhancements that allow them to extend their data precision. Chief among these is the SIMD registers, which are 128 bits wide, even in a 32-bit CPU. Apps that need high precision or fast maths tend to be written specially to use these rather than the general-purpose 32-bit registers.

The third difference between a 32-bit and a 64-bit system is the one that really makes the practical difference in a real-world context, and over the next few years it's going to be important to more or less everyone.

**THE RAM ADVANTAGE** In a 32-bit system, the CPU can address a total of 232 different memory locations. That means a 32-bit OS can work with up to 4,294,967,296 bytes – 4GB – of RAM. If you install more memory chips in your PC, Windows will simply ignore them.

4GB isn't a gigantic amount of RAM these days, and the 32-bit memory limit is even harsher than it may appear: some addresses are reserved for system resources such as video memory, so you can't even use a full 4GB of system RAM. We've found a 32-bit Windows PC can typically recognise a maximum of around 3.4GB.

With a 64-bit OS, such problems evaporate. A 64-bit address space can theoretically accommodate up to 16 million *terabytes* of RAM – which, for the next few years at least, ought to be enough for anyone. In practice, even 64-bit Windows isn't designed to work with such astronomical quantities. The Professional, Enterprise and Ultimate editions can use up to 192GB, while Home Premium is restricted to 16GB. The stripped-down Starter edition, only available bought with a low-end PC such as a netbook, is alone in omitting support for 64-bit.

**ADDITIONAL BENEFITS** A 64-bit operating system isn't necessarily any more robust than its 32-bit counterpart, but Microsoft has added extra technologies to 64-bit Windows 7 to improve security and stability. These include Kernel Patch Protection, which prevents third-party software from modifying key Windows files, and hardware-enforced Data Execution Prevention, which – if supported by the CPU – closes off potential vulnerabilities by making it impossible to execute code from an area of memory marked as data.

The most visible change is that 64-bit editions of Windows automatically reject device drivers that don't have a trusted electronic signature. That makes it harder for your system to be brought down by an untested driver, or by a virus masquerading as one – although it also makes it harder for technically minded users to tweak drivers themselves.

**IS IT TIME TO SWITCH?** Windows 7 fully supports both 32-bit and 64-bit, so there's nothing forcing you to switch in the immediate future. As we've discussed, however, the ability to use more than 4GB of RAM is going to be increasingly relevant, since memory requirements always go up over time, and RAM is one of the components users most often benefit from upgrading. The only reason to stick with 32-bit is if you need to use hardware or software that lacks 64-bit support, and that only applies if you already have these: new products now support 64-bit Windows.

If you elect to upgrade an existing system to 64-bit, this does involve the upheaval of wiping your system and doing a clean install of Windows 7. But this needn't be too painful, as we explain on p22, and it does mean you won't have to face the same hurdle next time you upgrade Windows. There's no doubt that the sun is setting on the 32-bit era; the only question is whether you make the move now or leave it until later.

**If you're unsure whether your printer – or any other piece of hardware you own – is supported by 64-bit Windows, just head to the manufacturer's website. While Windows 7 itself may not be listed, if there's a 64-bit driver for Windows Vista this should work fine with 64-bit Windows 7.**

## IN THIS CHAPTER

**2**

*Installing Windows 7*

# INSTALLING WIN

Windows 7's install process is a huge improvement on previous efforts. Gone are XP's ugly, intimidating textboxes and Vista's need for user input again and again throughout the process. Instead, Windows 7 asks you what you want up front, then goes away and takes care of everything itself. In this chapter, we guide you through the different install options available:

# DOWS 7

either upgrade directly from Vista, replace your existing system with a clean install of Windows 7, or create a dual-boot setup in which you can continue to use your old Windows as well. Whichever you choose, it's easy to move the important files from your existing PC. Later, we'll also investigate the new option of installing Windows on a virtual disk: see p60.

**HOW LONG?**

Anything from half-an-hour to several hours, depending on the amount of data.

**HOW HARD?**

Quite straightforward, but you'll meet a few obstacles on the way.

# HOW TO...
# MOVE FROM WINDOWS XP

*Windows XP's Files and Settings Transfer wizard is incompatible with Windows 7, but your Windows 7 installation disc provides an easy way to make the move.*

**START EASY TRANSFER** The file transfer process we describe here can be used whether you're moving from a PC running Windows XP to a new Windows 7 machine or installing Windows 7 on the same PC. If you're moving from Vista, see p20. In XP, insert your Windows 7 disc. Close the installation window if it opens. Open Windows Explorer by right-clicking the Start menu and clicking My Computer, then right-click on the DVD drive icon and select Explore. Browse to the Support folder, then open the Migwiz folder. You'll find a file called MIGSETUP or MIGSETUP.EXE: double-click it to run Windows 7's Easy Transfer Wizard in XP. The Welcome screen explains all the merits of Windows Easy Transfer; feel free to read it, then click Next.

**CHOOSE YOUR STORAGE LOCATION** You'll need some form of external storage to house your files during the transfer. If you only plan to copy a small quantity of data, you may be able to fit it onto a CD, a DVD or a USB flash drive, but it's more likely you've built up a large quantity of files over the years. The best option is a second hard disk, either inside your PC or an external drive connected via USB or FireWire. If your PC is on a network, you can use another computer or a network attached storage (NAS) device to store your data temporarily. Choose the method most appropriate to you from the choices given. The next screen asks if this is your old computer; it can tell it's running in XP, so it doesn't give you the option of selecting this as your new computer – that comes later, once you're in Windows 7.

**CHOOSE FILES OR SETTINGS** You'll have to wait briefly while the wizard scans your system to see what files and settings can be transferred – results will be presented in a ticklist. It divides the files into those kept by the main user ("asus" in our example) and Shared items, but if you want to see more details, click Customize. This will bring up a list of all the types of files it's currently set to back up, including Desktop items, Favorites and Program settings. If you don't want a particular element to make the move to your new system, just deselect it. If you need finer control, clicking the Advanced button at the bottom will take you to a full file tree, so you can specify files and folders to keep.

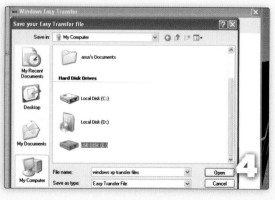

**④** **SAVE YOUR VITAL DATA** Having chosen the files to keep, click through and you'll be asked if you want to protect your backup with a password. Unless there are sensitive files, you can skip to the next step. You'll be asked to name your set of files; choose something you'll recognise easily later, such as "Windows XP transfer files" and browse to where you'll save your data, as discussed in step 2. In our case, it's a USB stick.

**⑤** **FINISH WITH XP** Once you've named the file and chosen the location, you can start the transfer. A window shows a progress indicator for each element. If you have a lot of data, now's the time to make a cup of tea. When the process is complete, you're told if any files didn't back up properly; if you need them, copy them manually onto a USB drive or other storage device so that you can transfer them yourself.

You've now completed the steps to get your data from your old PC to your shiny new Windows 7 system. If you're upgrading the same machine, or haven't already installed Windows 7 on your new PC, follow the steps on p22, then return to step 6 when you're ready to restore your saved files to your new system.

**⑥** **CONTINUE IN WINDOWS 7** In Windows 7, click the Start orb and go to All Programs | Accessories | System Tools. Click on Windows Easy Transfer to begin the second stage. Click through the Welcome

window and you'll be asked what method you'll be using. Select the storage you used earlier, and when asked whether this is your new or old PC click New to tell the wizard you already have your files backed up.

**⑦** **SELECT YOUR FILES** When asked if your files have already been saved to an external drive, plug in your chosen media and click Yes. (If you chose another method, such as transferring over a network, make the appropriate choice.) Select the relevant storage type and you'll be asked where your files are. Locate your storage device and navigate to the folder you selected earlier. You should see the file you named in step 4 ("Windows XP transfer files" in our case) with the label "Easy Transfer File". Select this and you'll be asked to enter the password you gave your backup in step 4.

**⑧** **RESTORE YOUR DATA** Windows 7 scans your backup and shows a window as in step 3. Choose what to restore, or leave everything selected. If necessary, click Advanced to select all sorts of fancy tasks, such as transferring a whole user account from the old system or mapping an entire drive from XP. Click the Transfer button to begin the final stage. At the end, you'll see exactly what was transferred; the wizard will also present a list of the software it detected on your old system, with links to product websites and information on Windows 7 compatibility, so you can start reinstalling.

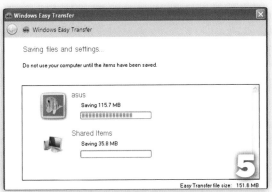

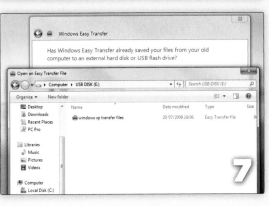

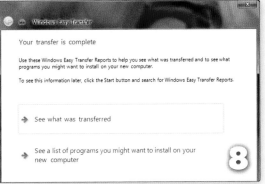

*Tip*

If you don't have a lot of files to transfer, and you don't need to transfer anything as complex as application settings or user accounts to your new PC, it can be just as simple to plug in a flash memory drive and manually copy across the files you need. You run the risk of missing files if your data is poorly organised, but being selective about what you keep is a great way of making a fresh start on your pristine new computer.

**HOW LONG?**

Half-an-hour to an hour.

**HOW HARD?**

Very easy: the Upgrade wizard takes you through the whole process.

# HOW TO...
# MOVE FROM WINDOWS VISTA

*If you're currently running Vista, it's incredibly simple to upgrade your PC to Windows 7 – in fact, your files and settings won't even be touched in the process.*

The best way to move to Windows 7 is always a clean install (see p22), as it ensures everything is precisely how Microsoft designed it to be from the start. However, that can be a real pain if you already have a Vista PC set up to your liking. Thankfully, Windows 7 can be upgraded very easily from Vista, but only when you match the version of Windows 7 you buy to your version of Vista.

It isn't hard to figure out which version you should buy: Vista Home Premium upgrades to Windows 7 Home Premium, for example, and you need to install 32-bit (as opposed to 64-bit) Windows 7 over 32-bit Vista. If you want to check for certain which version is right, use Microsoft's Upgrade Advisor tool (see p8), which scans your current PC and gives you the upgrade information you'll need.

In theory, the upgrade process should leave your existing files completely as they are, but there's always the slim chance of something going awry. If there are any files you can't afford to lose, just copy them onto an external hard disk or USB stick – or, if you have many, run a full backup. Once you're confident you have everything you need safe and sound, you can begin the upgrade process.

**(1) START THE UPGRADE** When you insert the Windows 7 disc, the upgrade process is similar to a full install. You can run a compatibility check online, which gives you a report similar to the Upgrade Advisor (see p8), but if you've reached this stage your PC should be ready for Windows 7.

**(2) GET THE LATEST INSTALL FILES** Click "Install now". You'll be asked if you want to go online to check for updates; if you have an internet connection it can't hurt to do so, although this often just consists of additional language packs for the early months after release. After reading Microsoft's terms and conditions, tick the box to agree and then click Next.

**(3) CHOOSE THE UPGRADE OPTION** Depending on your Windows 7 version, you may be offered the choice of a Custom (full) install or an upgrade. We cover the process for a full installation on p22, but if you want to move up to Windows 7 the easy way you'll click the Upgrade option to ensure Windows keeps all the important files from your Vista system in place.

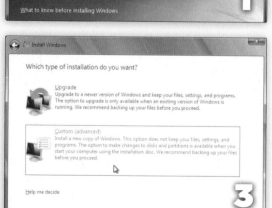

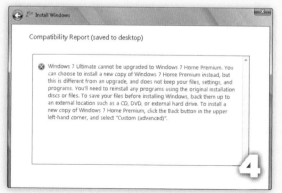

**4** **CHECK COMPATIBILITY** The wizard will then check the compatibility of your system. Provided you've followed the instructions and bought the correct version of Windows 7 to upgrade to, all you may get back here is a warning that certain currently installed programs might have problems running properly in Windows 7. These issues can often be circumvented later using Windows 7's Compatibility Mode, so don't worry too much. If there are any critical issues – such as an incompatible version of Windows 7 itself – the installer will inform you and the process will be terminated before you can go too far and mess up your system.

**5** **BEGIN THE UPGRADE** As long as no major compatibility issues are found, you'll be ready to begin the upgrade. Once it starts, it will proceed in a very similar fashion to a normal installation: you'll be given full details of what it's doing at all stages, and the system will restart several times. When it does, don't panic, just leave it to continue transferring its files until it asks you explicitly for some input. At that point, you're just a few steps from the Windows 7 desktop.

**6** **ENTER YOUR PRODUCT KEY** You don't strictly have to enter your Microsoft product key now – you have up to 30 days from installation to do so before you're locked out of your PC – but it makes sense to do it if you have it to hand. You'll find

the 25-character code somewhere on the packaging of your Windows 7 DVD, so just copy it out exactly into the dialog box and, provided you're made no mistakes, the wizard will check it for a few moments and confirm that your copy of Windows has been activated successfully. Make sure you keep the code somewhere safe, in case you decide to use it to move your Windows 7 licence to a new PC in the future.

**7** **FINALISE YOUR SETTINGS** You're almost there. Just choose your Automatic Update preferences: it's best to let Windows download and install its important updates automatically to keep your system secure and up to date. Then set the correct time and location, and you're done. The system may restart once more, and – a mere coffee break after you began – you'll see the new Windows logo, your desktop will appear, and you're up and running in Windows 7.

**8** **CHECK YOUR FILES** If all has gone to plan, all of your files should be right where you left them. In the rare instance that they're missing, get out the disk onto which you backed them up earlier and simply copy them across. Alternatively, if you ran Windows Backup, you should be able to run a restore to bring them back. Then you're free to explore your shiny new Windows 7 environment. At which point, we suggest you head straight to chapter 3.

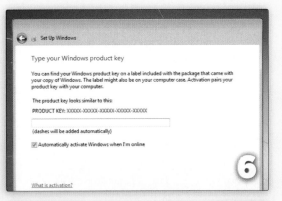

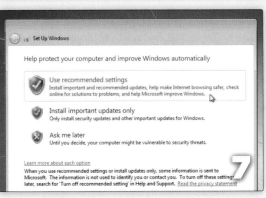

## Tip

Although upgrading is the simplest option, you can also do a clean install of Windows 7 without losing all your files and settings thanks to the Easy Transfer wizard (see p22). This can also be used to migrate between versions of Windows 7, so if you happened to install the early Windows 7 beta version that Microsoft put "into the wild" for testing purposes, you can still migrate your files to the final retail version of Windows 7 when you get round to installing it.

# 2

## Installing Windows 7

**HOW LONG?**

Should take less than an hour, and you can leave it alone to complete after the first few minutes.

**HOW HARD?**

The majority of the process is automatic, but read this guide first.

# HOW TO...
# CLEAN-INSTALL WINDOWS 7

*A clean installation of Windows 7 is the best way to give your PC a totally fresh start – and you can do it without losing all your files and settings.*

Windows Vista's installation was a leap forward from the text-based clunkiness of XP, and much the same process has been retained for Windows 7. Now, though, even less user interaction is required. Vista needed you to sit and watch as it asked for help throughout the job; now you can get everything done at the start and leave it running.

One choice you may need to make is which web browser to install, since Microsoft has agreed to include alternatives to Internet Explorer to comply with an EU competition ruling. Find out more about the options on p78 to 83.

**CHOOSE YOUR VERSION** Before you even start thinking about installing Windows 7 onto your machine, you need to be certain you've made the right choice when it comes to the version. We cover this in detail in chapter 1, and hopefully our four-page guide starting on p10 will make it obvious whether Home Premium, Professional or Ultimate are right for you.

However, while you can always perform an "Anytime Upgrade" to jump from Home Premium to Ultimate, this is your last chance to decide whether or not

you choose the 32-bit or 64-bit version of Windows. If you later decide you want to move to 64-bit – perhaps when you decide 4GB of memory is no longer enough – you'll have to perform a full reinstall. See p14 if you're in doubt.

**BACK UP YOUR STUFF** If losing all your Vista files and settings is a bit too "clean" for your liking, you can back them up using Windows 7's Easy Transfer wizard, then restore them to your new system after installation. In Vista, go to Start | All Programs | Accessories | System Tools and click on Windows Easy Transfer to kick it off. Opt to start a new transfer and tell the wizard that this is your old computer. You can choose where to store your files during the switch: an external hard disk is best, but you can also use a USB flash drive or a recordable DVD, or back up over your home network to another PC. Give your backup a name, then choose whether to transfer all your existing user accounts and their data, or just the currently active account. It's safest to click Advanced options and tick exactly which files and folders you need. This done, start the process and make a cup of tea while it completes.

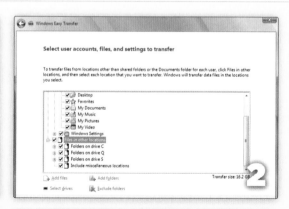

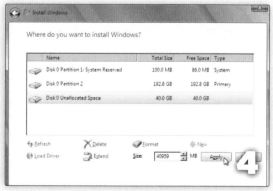

**3 BEGIN INSTALLATION** Insert the Windows 7 disc and restart the PC. If you get a message saying "Press any key to boot from CD or DVD", do so. If you don't see this and the installer doesn't appear, you'll need to access your BIOS and ensure it's set to boot from the DVD before any other drive, such as the hard disk. Check your PC's manual if you're not sure how to do this. You should soon see the initial Windows 7 setup screen, where you can alter the regional settings to the UK.

**4 CHOOSE YOUR DESTINATION** Next you'll be asked what type of installation you want: Upgrade or Custom. We want the latter. Now choose where to install Windows 7: you'll see a display of all your local hard disks and partitions. This may vary according to how many drives are in your PC and how they're set up, but for most Windows machines it will be more or less the same. Unless you want a dual-boot (see p24) or virtualised (see p60) system, pick the main partition containing your existing Windows system. You'll need at least 16GB free, although we'd recommend at least double that. Once you're sure you have the correct partition, click on it and click Next. You'll be warned you're about to lose the data on that disk, so be sure you've backed it up (whether using Easy Transfer or manually) before you continue.

**5 WAIT...** The install process is nowhere near as lengthy as with Windows XP or Vista, so you

can come back to your PC in as little as half-an-hour. Don't be alarmed if your system restarts itself several times.

**6 ENTER YOUR DETAILS** Windows 7 will now start for the first time, and you'll need to enter your details, beginning with a name for your PC (so you can recognise it on a network). You have the option of setting a password for your user account, sensible on a shared PC, before entering your 25-character product key, found on or in your Windows 7 packaging. As long as the "Automatically activate Windows when I'm online" box is ticked, Windows 7 will authenticate itself automatically.

**7 THE FINAL SETTINGS** Opt to let Windows check for updates automatically, so that your system is as secure and up-to-date as it can be. Then choose your location: selecting Home, Work or Public gives Windows different default security settings (see chapter 8). You may also be given the chance to create a HomeGroup, which links PCs on a network (see p86).

**8 ENJOY** And you're done. To restore your backed-up data, click Windows 7's Start orb and go to All Programs | Accessories | System Tools | Windows Easy Transfer. Navigate to where you stored your backup, choose what to restore and click Transfer. Finally, you should protect your system as soon as possible by adding antivirus software: see p114.

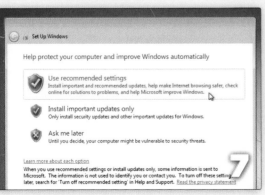

## Tip

Windows Easy Transfer does exactly what it says on the tin, and works both when replacing an existing Windows installation on the same PC and when moving to a new Windows 7 PC. However, note that it only works when moving up from Vista, not from Windows XP. If you want to preserve files and settings from an XP system, follow our guide on p18.

**HOW LONG?**

An hour or so; longer, if you take our advice and back up your data first.

**HOW HARD?**

Be sure you're confident with the concepts of hard disk partitioning.

# HOW TO...
# CREATE A DUAL-BOOT SYSTEM

*If you want to keep using older programs, a dual-boot system – retaining your previous version of Windows – might be the best option. Here's how to set it up.*

While we'd recommend that most people upgrade to Windows 7 sooner rather than later, there are reasons to stick with an older version. You might want to experiment before you commit to the change. Perhaps you have some vital applications that only Windows XP or Vista will run (although these should be few, as we explain on p52), or older devices whose drivers don't support Windows 7.

Fortunately, it's possible to have the best of both worlds by keeping your existing operating system and also installing Windows 7 on the same computer. You can then choose which to run each time you start up.

To create this "dual-boot" system, you'll need to make some fundamental changes to your hard disk, creating separate partitions to hold the two operating systems independently. This needn't be an excessively scary or complicated task, but it does carry a real risk of losing all the data that's currently on your hard disk, so you'll need to understand the process and prepare for it.

The Windows 7 installer will handle most of the changes, but there's one vital step to complete before starting this. To create a new hard disk partition, you must first clear an unpartitioned gap on the disk (usually C).

You need enough free space for a Windows 7 installation – a minimum of 16GB, and preferably at least twice that – and you need software that can resize the partition.

Before you begin altering the partitions on your disk, you really do need to back up everything. Altering partitions in itself won't erase your data, but it can't be undone or reversed, and if, for instance, there's a power failure at a critical moment, all your files will be gone. Use your usual backup process in your existing operating system to make sure everything is safely stored elsewhere.

To see if you have enough free space, go to Start | My Computer, right-click on your C drive and select Properties, which will show you a breakdown of your free space. Ideally, you'll need at least 30GB free on the drive, so that you can separate 25GB for your new partition, leaving 5GB breathing space for your old one.

Assuming you have enough free space to go ahead, you'll need software that can resize the existing C drive partition. Vista has a suitable utility built in, as we'll see below, but XP users will need third-party software such as Easeus Partition Master, which you can download for free from www.partition-tool.com

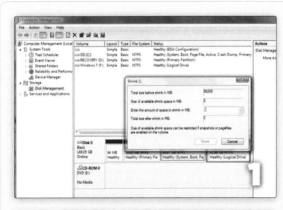

**①** **PARTITIONING IN VISTA** If you're using XP, go to step 3. In Vista, use the built-in partition tool. Right-click Computer, choose Manage and then Disk Management. Right-click on your main disk (Disk0) and opt to Shrink Volume. This reduces the space used by the current partition, freeing room for your new partition.

**②** **SHRINK TO FIT** Windows 7 needs at least 16GB, so make sure you shrink your main partition by at least this amount, bearing in mind you'll probably need lots more for new applications and files. A new volume will appear. Right-click this and choose New Simple Volume, then follow the default choices, naming your volume something obvious, such as "Windows 7" Unless you get an error message, head to step 4.

**③** **PARTITIONING IN XP** If you're using XP, or you get an error in step 2, download a third-party partitioning tool such as Partition Master (www. partition-tool.com). Follow its instructions to complete a similar process to steps 2 and 3. If your PC already has four active partitions (many new Dell PCs do, for example), you'll first have to delete one you don't need.

**④** **START THE WINDOWS 7 INSTALL** That's the hard part over with. Now you can simply insert your Windows 7 disc and proceed with installation in the same way as for a clean install (see p22). Insert the

disc, reboot the PC and hit a key to boot into the installer. Follow the clean install (Custom) steps until you get to the "Where do you want to install Windows?" screen. Click Drive options (Advanced) at the bottom right.

**⑤** **SELECT A PARTITION** Clicking this produces new buttons at the foot of the screen allowing you to delete selected partitions, format or create a new one. You want to create a new one, so make sure you click on the newly unallocated space and then click New.

**⑥** **PICK A SIZE** Choose a size for the new partition in the text area that appears. By default, the value is the whole of the available free space on the disk, which is what you're likely to want. If not, you can reduce it. The size is shown in megabytes, not gigabytes; 1,024MB is equal to 1GB. Remember, the recommended minimum free space for a Windows 7 installation is 16GB (16,384MB), but 30GB is a more practical amount.

**⑦** **INSTALL AS NORMAL** The installation should now proceed in the same way as a clean install of Windows 7 (see p22), with a few reboots.

**⑧** **CHOOSE ON STARTUP** Now, whenever you reboot your PC you'll get a Boot Manager screen that enables you to select either your old Windows XP or Vista installation, or the new Windows 7 system.

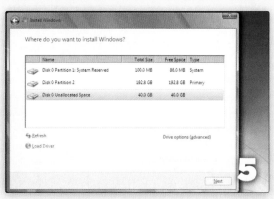

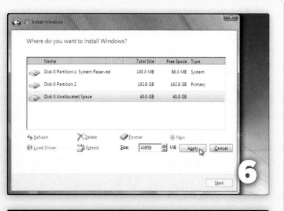

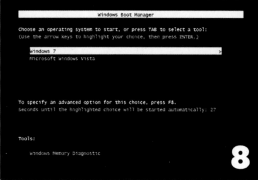

# IN THIS CHAPTER

# 3
## *Windows 7 The basics*

# WINDOWS 7: THE

In the past, Windows could be fairly accused of making the basics more complicated than necessary. Windows 7 sweeps away much of the confusion and clutter and delivers a clean, fast and attractive operating system. The most visible improvements have taken place on the desktop, the screen that you see when you first start your PC. From the revamped

# BASICS

Taskbar to the all-new Jump Lists that sprout from your favourite applications, Windows 7 delivers both speed and sophistication. In this chapter, we'll explain what these new features do and how to get the best out of them. We'll also take a look at the powerful new Libraries feature and explain how to keep your family safe with user accounts.

The only default icon on the desktop is the **Recycle Bin**. You can add shortcuts to files and programs as in previous versions (see p30), although the new Taskbar and Libraries make it less likely you'll want to.

Recycle Bin

**Gadgets** – small applications such as clocks, calendars and mini-photo galleries – can be placed anywhere on the Windows 7 desktop. Click and hold on your desired gadget and drag it to wherever you want it. Find out more about Gadgets on p34.

Go online t

• Discover new featu
• Find out everything

Go online to find out what's new in Windows 7

Choose when to be notified about changes to your computer

Change the size of the text on your screen

The **Start menu** gives a list of your most commonly used applications. It can be opened by clicking on the Start Orb or by pressing the Windows button on your keyboard. If you want to make an application a permanent fixture on your Start menu, right-click on the program's name and select Pin to Start menu. Alternatively, select the Remove From This List option if you don't want the software to show here. The little arrows next to the programs' names activate the Jump Lists (see p32).

The right-hand side of the Start menu provides one-click access to **common locations** such as your Documents, Pictures and Music folders. The **Control Panel** hosts a bunch of useful tools – such as the option to uninstall unwanted software – while Devices and Printers controls anything attached to your PC.

 Paint

Getting Started

Calculator

Windows Media Center

 Sticky Notes

Snipping Tool

Remote Desktop Connection

Magnifier

Solitaire

WordPad

 All Programs

Search programs and files

PC Pro

Documents

Pictures

Music

Games

Computer

Control Panel

Devices and Printers

Default Programs

Help and Support

Shut down

Click **All Programs** to see a list of every piece of software installed on your PC. Windows 7 has several applications pre-loaded to get you started.

The enhanced **Instant Search** is a fast way to find programs or files on your PC. Start typing and results for matching programs, documents, photos or other files will instantly appear.

As in Vista, the **Start Orb** is the equivalent of Windows XP's Start button. Click this to pop open the Start menu or, ironically, when you want to shut the PC down.

The **Taskbar** is completely revamped in Windows 7. The small text descriptions of open programs have been replaced with chunky square icons. Your favourite programs can now be 'pinned' to the Taskbar, so you don't have to go hunting around the Start menu to find the software you use every day. You can also change the order of icons on the Taskbar by dragging and dropping to your desired positions.

Windows 7's **Getting Started** screen can help you with most of the basic tasks you need to undertake after installing a new operating system, including customising settings and adding new user accounts. If the Getting Started screen doesn't appear on startup, find it by typing 'getting started' into the Start menu's Search box.

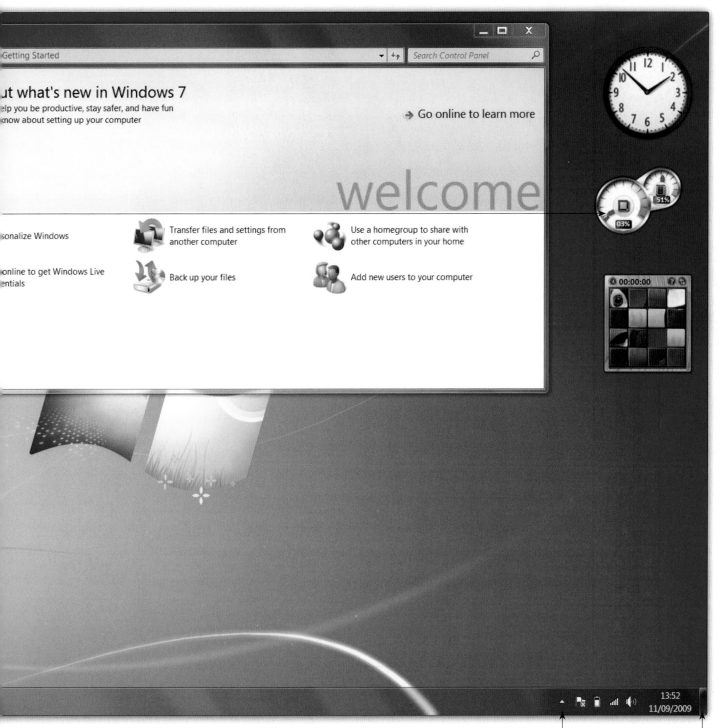

# The Windows 7 desktop

The desktop has undergone a thorough makeover since Vista, with a number of new or redesigned features. If you're running Windows 7 on a netbook or low-powered PC, don't be alarmed if you can't see the translucent window effects we show here – Windows turns them off automatically if your PC doesn't have the graphical grunt to cope.

The **notification area**, or System Tray, shows the status of programs that are running in the background, plus details of your network connection, volume level and other useful info. Click the up arrow to access hidden notifications and to customise notifications.

Hover over the handy new **Show Desktop** button and any open programs will temporarily disappear to reveal your desktop and Gadgets.

MAKE WINDOWS 7 LOOK JUST THE WAY YOU WANT IT TO WITH OUR GUIDE
TO TAILORING THE APPEARANCE OF YOUR BRAND-NEW DESKTOP.

# Personalise the desktop

Most people like to stamp their personality on their PC by adjusting the appearance of the desktop. Windows 7 makes it easier than ever to add a splash of character.

Many of these new features can be accessed by right-clicking on the desktop and selecting Personalize. You can also access these settings via the Control Panel, which is available from the Start menu. The simplest way to start tinkering is to use Windows 7's themes, as we explain on the opposite page. But there are a few basics you need to know first about controlling the appearance of the desktop.

**THE TASKBAR** The bar at the bottom of the screen has been completely revamped. The old text descriptions of programs that are currently open have been replaced by chunky icons. This can take a bit of getting used to, but if you really want to go back to the old way, you can: right-click on the Taskbar, click Properties, and select "Never combine" from the Taskbar buttons dropdown menu.

The best thing about the new Taskbar is that even programs that aren't currently in use can be shown here, giving you one-click access to your favourite software. To add a program to the Taskbar, open the program, then right-click on its icon and choose "Pin this program to Taskbar".

Unlike in previous versions of Windows, you can also shuffle the icons on the Taskbar into your preferred order. Left-click and hold on a Taskbar icon and drag into your desired position. It will stay there for good.

You don't have to keep your Taskbar at the bottom of the screen. Shift it the top or either side by right-clicking on the Taskbar, choosing Properties and taking your pick from the Taskbar location dropdown menu.

**DESKTOP ICONS** The first time you open Windows 7, you'll find only the Recycle Bin on the desktop, and perhaps a few other software icons installed by your PC manufacturer. If you want to add shortcuts to your favourite software here, find a program on the Start menu, right-click its name, select Send To and choose "Desktop (create shortcut)". You can do the same with your favourite files or folders.

**DISPLAY RESOLUTION** Windows 7 should select the correct resolution for your screen. If it looks fuzzy or you want to experiment, right-click an empty space on the desktop and select Screen Resolution. Adjust the sliding scale. If you pick an unusable option, don't worry: Windows gives you 15 seconds to revert back to your previous display setting.

## *Tip*

Today's widescreen monitors offer very high resolutions, which can make on-screen text so fine as to be almost unreadable. There's no need to artificially bump down the resolution – a new feature in Windows 7 allows you to simply make the text bigger.

**1.** Right-click on the desktop, choose Screen Resolution and then click on the link that says "Make text and other items larger or smaller".

**2.** Choose from the options to make the text and other items either 125% or 150% of their current size. You will need to restart your PC for the changes to take effect.

**3.** Now Windows text and desktop icons look bigger, without any loss of clarity or sharpness.

# HOW TO...
# CHOOSE OR CREATE A THEME

**① CHOOSE A THEME** Windows 7 comes with a series of default themes – ready-made packages of complementary desktop backgrounds, sounds and screensavers. These include an excellent UK pack with stunning photography of beauty spots including Stonehenge and the White Cliffs of Dover. Take your pick by right-clicking on the desktop, choosing Personalize and selecting one of the Aero Themes. Each theme contains a selection of photos, and your background will change periodically as it cycles through them. To move on to the next photo, right-click on the desktop and choose "Next desktop background".

**② DOWNLOAD NEW THEMES** Microsoft is making a series of alternative themes available for download. In the Personalize menu, click "Get more themes online" at the far right. Early examples include a serene Isle of Lewis pack. Click on themes to download them to your computer. Once downloaded, they'll be available from the My Themes section.

**③ BUILD YOUR OWN THEME** Beautiful as Microsoft's Windows 7 themes are, you might want to create your own. First, a little preparation: save all the photos you want in your new theme into a single Pictures folder. Now open that folder, right-click on one of those photos and choose "Set as desktop background". Close the folder, right-click on the desktop and choose Personalize, and you should see your photo appears as an unsaved theme.

To add more photos to the theme, click the Desktop Background link at the foot of the screen and browse to the folder containing your pictures. Select the pictures you want to add, holding down the Control button as you click them. Tweak the timing settings if you like, then click Save Changes (this can take a while to process). If you wish, you can also change the colour of the transparent "glass" on the desktop windows to match your photos, as well as the Windows sounds and the screensaver, using the options provided. When you've finished tweaking, click Save Theme and give it a name.

**④ SHARE YOUR CREATIONS** You can share your saved theme with friends and family, or upload it to a website for others to download (make sure you own the copyright to the photos before doing so). In the Themes menu, right-click your chosen theme and select "Save theme for sharing". Give it a name and save it. You can now email the file to other users or make it available for download. Beware: if you've used a lot of high-resolution photos, the file may be too large for some people's email.

**HOW LONG?**
About 15 minutes – a little more if you're planning to create your own theme.

**HOW HARD?**
It's blissfully simple to tweak the appearance of your PC and even share the results with others.

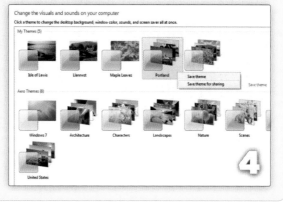

## 3
### Windows 7 The basics

# Introducing Jump Lists

One of the greatest strengths of Windows 7 is it makes it easier to find what you want on your computer, and one of the ways it does this is Jump Lists. This is a new feature closely associated with the new Taskbar. Right-click on a program's icon in the Taskbar at the foot of the screen, and a list sprouts upwards – hence the name Jump List. Alternatively, hold down the left mouse button on a program's icon and drag the mouse upwards. If you're using a touchscreen, hold your finger on the program's icon and swipe upwards to activate the Jump List.

Jump Lists aren't only accessible from the Taskbar. Click on the Start orb and hover over a program's name, and you'll see the Jump Lists emerge from this menu too. In the vast majority of cases, the Jump List will feature items that you've recently opened using that particular program. So, for example, in Microsoft Word it's a quick way of opening a document you were working on yesterday: hover over the document's title and left-click to open, instead of having to plough through your folders.

With applications such as Windows Media Player, Jump Lists can also be used to access basic controls, such as "Resume previous list" to continue playing your music from where you last left off. Alternatively, right-click on the Internet Explorer logo and its Jump List allows you to start surfing in the new InPrivate mode, which won't leave any trace of your web session lingering on your PC. As software makers get to grips with Jump Lists, we should see more features becoming accessible from these handy menus.

You also have some control over what appears in the Jump Lists. If you have a file or document that you open regularly – say, an expenses form or a welcome letter that you send out to new members of your club – you can "pin" this to the Jump List so that it's always ready.

There are two ways of doing this. If the document you want to keep is already in the application's Jump List, click the little pin icon next to its name. If it isn't, open the folder containing the relevant document and drag it down onto a blank space on the Taskbar.

It isn't only files and documents that can be pinned to Jump Lists. If there's a folder you want quick access to, you don't have to create a shortcut on your desktop any more: just drag the folder down into the Taskbar and onto the Windows Explorer Jump List (the icon that looks like a bunch of folders). You'll be offered the option to pin the folder there.

If you decide you don't want an item pinned to a Jump List any more, it's easy to remove: just hover over its name and click the little pin icon.

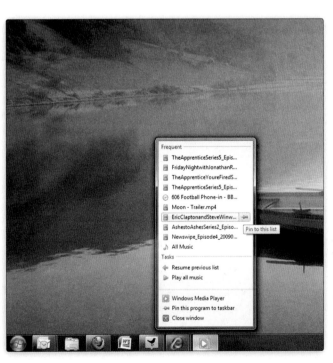

Jump Lists offer quick access to documents and tasks related to a particular program, such as playlists and playback controls in Windows Media Player.

Internet Explorer's new private browsing mode can be accessed this way, and programs from other makers should soon start to offer Jump Lists.

The ultimate Teufel complete set – for home cinema,
games and action – as we take your sound very seriously!

# Teufel

# The fun begins with the sound!

Bundle price only £**309**\*

## 7 good reasons for Teufel speakers

- Top-quality – best-in-test all across Europe
- Developed in our own sound lab in Berlin
- 30 years of experience
- Unbeatable value for money
- Excellent service plus an 8-week moneyback guarantee
- 12 years warranty on speakers, 2 years on electronic parts
- Only available from Teufel direct

e Teufel Concept E 200 Digital –
ltimedia sound
the highest order

complete system for Home Thea-
and Multimedia: Teufel Concept E
5.1 loudspeaker system + Teufel
coderstation 5 as control center.

- 300 watts maximum performance
- Five identical full range satellites
- Connector box with integrated
- Dolby Digital/dts Decoder
- Eight inputs
- (4 x Digital, 4 x Analogue)
- Remote control for all functions

rted price – Internet orders calculated in Euros incl. VAT

RDER NOW!
SAVE 10%

only £**171**\*

## CONCEPT C 200 USB

**Integrated sound card always provides good sound**

- Excellent 2.1 multimedia sound USB interface for sound improvement
- Subwoofer with 200 watts amp and 200 mm bass speaker
- Two-way satellites with table stand
- Cable remote control for microphone and headphones

only £**137**\*

## CONCEPT E 100

**Your entry-level system for surround sound at the PC**

- Entry to the Teufel 5.1 multimedia sound
- Subwoofer with 200 watts maximum performance
- 200 mm bass speaker in bass reflex casing
- Five identical satellites with high-performance drivers
- Recommended for rooms up to 15 m²

only £**369**\*

## MOTIV 5

**Uncompromisingly superb surround-sound for your PC**

- Fully active universal system with striking design
- Compact six channel subwoofer with 250 mm bass speaker
- 450 watt peak performance Five identical high-end micro satellites
- Suitable for rooms up to 30m2

CLICK: **TEUFEL.EU/UK**

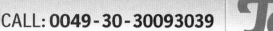
CALL: **0049-30-30093039**

# Teufel

FILL YOUR DESKTOP WITH LOTS OF HANDY LITTLE APPLICATIONS – FOLLOW OUR GUIDE TO FINDING AND INSTALLING THE BEST WINDOWS 7 GADGETS.

# Introducing Gadgets

First seen in Vista, Gadgets have become a key feature of the desktop. These tiny utility applications cover everything from the ridiculously trivial (virtual fortune cookie?) to the genuinely indispensible (see our top picks, below).

In Windows Vista, gadgets were docked in a sidebar at the right-hand edge of the screen. In Windows 7, Microsoft has dispensed with the dock and encourages you to place your Gadgets wherever you like. With other new features such as the revamped Taskbar and Jump Lists (see p32) reducing the need to clutter your desktop with shortcut icons, you should have plenty of space to play with.

**KEEPING TRACK OF YOUR GADGETS** Microsoft has made it easier than ever to keep an eye on your Gadgets, allowing you to quickly check the latest news headlines, for example. Previously you had to minimise your open windows before the Gadgets would be visible, then laboriously maximise them to carry on working. Windows 7 has a new Show Desktop button at the bottom right of the screen. Hover the cursor over this and all your windows fade away, allowing

you to take a glance at your Gadgets. Move away, and you're swiftly back to where you left off. The Gadgets menu is also far easier to find: right-click on a blank spot on the desktop and you'll see Gadgets listed among the options.

**WHERE DO GADGETS COME FROM?** Microsoft provides a dozen Gadgets to get you started in Windows 7, including a very handy headline reader and a picture slideshow that elegantly scrolls through the snaps in your Pictures folder. But the majority of Gadgets are supplied by third-party developers that have created hundreds of tiny tools to choose from. You can access this bountiful supply via Microsoft's website: see opposite for instructions on downloading new Gadgets. Many were created for Vista, but we've yet to find any that don't work in Windows 7 as well.

A word of warning: third-party Gadgets should be treated with caution, because, as with any software, there's a small chance they could pose a security threat. Make sure you have security set up (see chapter 8) before downloading more, and be wary of entering login details into Gadgets.

## *Tip*

Microsoft's Gadgets aren't the only type of desktop applet. Google offers a vast range with its Google Desktop service, which is free to download from http://desktop.google.com. Yahoo's similar Widgets are available free at http://widgets.yahoo.com. There's nothing to stop you running Google or Yahoo's applets alongside Microsoft's Gadgets, but it might start to impinge on performance for low-powered computers such as netbooks.

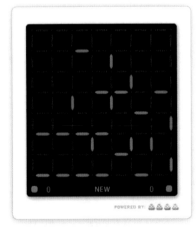

Bored of work? Waste five minutes by taking on the computer at the horribly addictive **Dots**.

**Network Meter** is one for the techies. All the information you'll ever need about your Wi-Fi connection, including signal strength, IP address and download data.

Provided with Windows 7, **CPU Meter** is a quick way to see how much demand is being placed on your PC's processor and memory. If the dials are swinging too far to the right, it's time to close some programs.

The **Currency Converter** is a must-have for anyone who deals with exchange rates at work, and handy for holiday money too.

The **Google** Gadget lets you do a quick web search straight from the desktop – no need to fire up your web browser first.

**Live Departure Boards** is a convenient way to keep an eye on your train times.

Listen while you work with the **BBC Radio** Gadget, which plays 11 BBC radio stations via the internet.

# HOW TO...
# DOWNLOAD MORE GADGETS

**① VISIT THE ONLINE GADGET GALLERY** The easiest way of getting to Microsoft's Gadget website is to click on the link from Windows 7's Gadgets menu. Right-click any blank space on the desktop, select Gadgets, then click "Get more Gadgets online". At the time of writing, the website was still linking to what was referred to as the Windows Vista Sidebar Gallery. Don't be put off: because the code base for Vista and Windows 7 is so similar, any of the Gadgets that worked on Vista's sidebar should work fine with Windows 7. Beware, though, that you might come across items called Web Gadgets: these are intended to work with the Windows Live website, not on the Windows desktop.

**② TAKE YOUR PICK** Gadgets are categorised into topics such as "Search tools" and "Music, movies and TV". To help sort the wheat from the chaff, find the topic you're interested in and click Sort by rating at the top of the list, which brings the Gadgets that are most highly rated by other users to the top of the pile. If you want to find one of the Gadgets we've recommended opposite, pop its name into the search box at the top and click the green Gallery button. The search engine is a bit erratic, so you might have to scroll through a couple of pages to get the desired Gadget. Although most Gadgets are free, some do cost money.

**③ DOWNLOAD MORE GADGETS** Once you've found a Gadget you like the look of, click the Download button. At this point you'll be presented with a warning message advising you to download Gadgets only from developers you trust. This is Microsoft's way of covering its back when pointing you to Gadgets developed by other companies. Check your security software is running, and click Install. You'll now see another pop-up asking whether you want to Open or Save the file; click Open, and in the next box click Install. The Gadget should now appear on your desktop.

**④ CUSTOMISE YOUR GADGETS** Once a Gadget is installed, you can move it to wherever you like on your desktop by clicking on the little grid of dots that appears when you hover over it and dragging it into place. If, when you hover over the Gadget, you see a little icon with an arrow pointing to the top-right corner, clicking this will show a larger version of the Gadget. You'll also notice a little spanner icon, which gives access to the settings for that particular Gadget. This is where, for example, you can set the radio station you want to listen to in the BBC Radio Gadget. If you don't want a Gadget on your desktop any more, click the "x" icon. It will still be available from the Gadgets menu, unless you choose to completely uninstall the item.

## HOW LONG?
Allow 20 minutes to wade through the list of Gadgets, but each only takes seconds to install.

## HOW HARD?
Except for the dodgy search tool, the process couldn't be much simpler.

MOST OF US NOW HAVE FILES, PHOTOS AND MUSIC ON A SECOND PC OR AN EXTERNAL HARD DISK. THAT'S WHERE WINDOWS 7'S LIBRARIES COME IN...

# Introducing Libraries

Libraries are quite simply one of the best things about Windows 7. They may seem a little counter-intuitive at first, but within a week or two you'll wonder how you ever put up with the old, fiddly way of working.

There are four categories of Library: Documents, Music, Pictures and Video. Each contains all the folders and files you'd previously have kept in My Documents (in Windows XP) or Documents (in Vista). What's different is that a Library isn't necessarily tied to what's contained on your PC's main hard disk. As you'll see later, you can choose to add folders from anywhere else – perhaps an external hard disk, or another computer on your network.

To use the Library metaphor, not only can you instantly grab any book from your own bookcase, you can also grab more from your local library. This means you don't need to duplicate files from other computers and drives; you can access them just as if they were sitting on your hard disk (so long as your computer is linked to that external device).

To see this in action, expand the Documents subfolder within Libraries by clicking the blue disclosure triangle that appears beside Documents when you hover over it. You'll see two entries by default: My Documents and Public Documents. These are the actual hard disk folders; right-click on My Documents and you'll see it lives in C:\Users\Name, where Name is your Windows username.

Note that if you left-click a folder on, say, your desktop and drag it into the Documents Library, the folder itself will be moved to the default save location. You'll get a tooltip-style message to let you know about this.

**CUSTOMISING LIBRARIES** As they stand, Libraries aren't terribly useful – you need to tailor them to your system. First, you can add folder locations to a Library. This is really the point of Libraries: to organise documents and files that may be on different physical media into one handy view.

Each Library view has an "Includes" label at the top right. By default, each Library location includes two folders: My Documents and Public Documents, My Video and Public Video, and so on. But click the "Library locations" link and you can add a folder to bring its contents into the Library view from anywhere. Remember, this isn't copying or moving folders, just allowing you to view them within a single window. Yet you can interact with them as normal here. Deleting or manipulating a file within a Library view affects the underlying physical file, wherever it may be.

The power of Libraries is that you can add folders from almost anywhere: different partitions, external hard disks, even network locations. The only limitation is the inability to add folders on "devices with removable storage", such as a USB flash drive or a DVD-R in your optical drive.

This is how your four Libraries will look by default, but there's an immense amount of opportunity to shape them to your needs.

# HOW TO...
# TWEAK AND SET UP LIBRARIES

Here's how to set up your own Libraries. Why bother? Well, the benefit of adding an external hard disk to a Library will be obvious to anyone who has a large media collection and has ever tried to upgrade their PC. With your media files on an external device, you can just unplug your drive from the old machine and attach it to the new, then add the location to the Library on the new machine.

It also means that as your data inevitably grows and fills up your drives, you can just plug in a new drive and add that to the Library. And by setting the default save location to the new disk, you have a super-easy way to get unlimited storage without having to copy files around or mess about with expanding partitions and suchlike. Bliss.

Just remember that the more disks you have, the more chance there is of one of them suffering a failure, so always back up your vital files.

**① ADD FOLDERS** By default, the only folders in each library are the standard Documents locations under C:\Users\. The power of Libraries lies in the ability to add folders. To do that, click the "Includes 2 locations" link at the top of any library view.

**② BEYOND YOUR PC** Click Add to start expanding the scope of the Library. You can add folders from almost any location, including network folders. Here we've browsed on the network to find a folder. The only ones you can't add are removable storage: flash memory drives and optical drives (CDs and DVDs).

**③ WHAT SAVES WHERE?** An initial difficulty with Libraries is what happens when you actually want to move a file into the library. Dragging the file will move it, but there may be several physical folders in that library. So where is it saved? The answer is simple: the default save location. In the Documents Library Locations dialog, one of the folders will be marked as the default save location. That's the physical folder that any files dragged into the library will be saved to. To change it, all you need to do is right-click on a library folder and select "Set as default save location".

**④ CUSTOM LIBRARY** You're not limited to the default Documents, Video, Music and Pictures libraries. To create a custom library, click on the top-level Libraries icon, right-click and select New | Library. Enter a name and you're away. New libraries don't include any folders – just add them as in step 2. Bear in mind that if you right-click on an already created Library and select New Folder, that's what you get – a new folder in the default save location.

**HOW LONG?**
15 minutes is a safe bet. You may want to set aside more time to get to grips wih custom Libraries.

**HOW HARD?**
It's a bit of a mind-bender at first, but once you understand how Libraries work you'll quickly get to grips with using them.

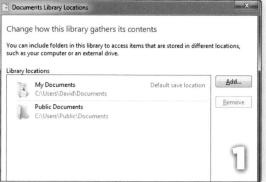

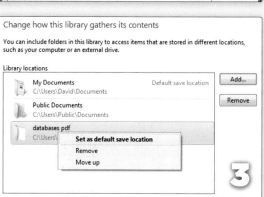

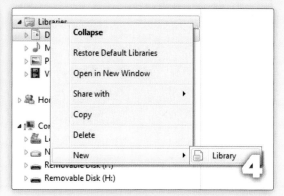

# 3

## Windows 7
## The basics

# Introducing user accounts

One of the most common security blunders people make with family PCs is to let everyone log in on the Administrator account, giving children the power to delete vital Windows files that could prevent the computer from working, and allowing them to rifle through your private documents.

Perhaps worst of all, it grants children permission to install their own software. This leaves your PC wide open to attack when they decide to load that tempting free game they found online, which turns out to be a piece of malware designed to steal your bank account details.

To help prevent younger (or even older) users running wild, Microsoft offers several security measures, one of which is individual user accounts. Each person can have their own account and password on the PC, which they enter when they sit down to use it, giving them access to all the files and documents they need, while limiting their access to features that could compromise security.

The other advantage of giving children their own accounts is that you can apply separate parental controls for each child, preventing them from using the computer late at night, for example. See p106 for more on setting up Windows 7's Parental Controls.

**TYPES OF ACCOUNT** There are three types of account in Windows 7. Administrator is the default that's set up for the first person on the PC. Administrator accounts have full control over the computer, with the ability to add new software and hardware, make changes to key Windows settings, and set up and delete accounts for other users.

On a family PC, it's sensible to have only one Administrator and everyone else on Standard user accounts. (As the administrator, you might even decide to set up your own Standard user account, as we discuss on the opposite page.) Standard users can make use of any of the software already on the PC, create and delete their own files, and personalise the desktop with their own themes, only displayed when they log in. They also have their own web browser bookmarks and toolbars, so Dad's setup isn't ruined by links to MySpace and Facebook.

Standard user accounts are banned from installing their own software, however. If a Standard user attempts to install a piece of software, they'll be prompted for the Administrator's password before being allowed to proceed.

**GUEST ACCOUNTS** Finally, there's the Guest account, which is designed to be used by visitors to the house who need access to a computer. They too are barred from installing software and making any changes to key files and settings. You can switch on the Guest account by going to Start | Control Panel | User Accounts and Family Safety | User Accounts. Then choose "Manage another account" and click on the Guest account icon.

## *Tip*

▲ It's best to secure your Administrator account with a strong password – a long phrase made up of both letters and numbers. Naturally, these are a little harder to remember, so it's a good idea to create a Password Recovery Disk just in case your memory fails. To do this, type "user accounts" into the Windows Start menu, then select the User Accounts option. Insert a USB flash drive into your PC, then click "Create a password reset disk" and follow the onscreen instructions. Store the flash drive in a secure place. If you ever forget your password, you can insert the flash drive into your computer and click on the Reset Password link that appears beneath the Windows password prompt to gain access to your PC.

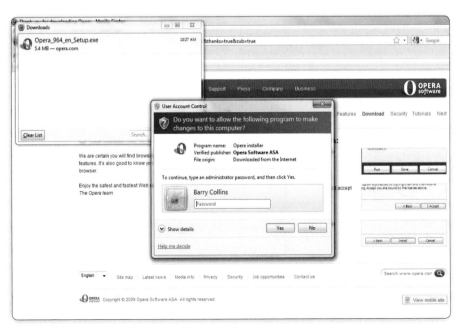

Only Administrator accounts are allowed to install software and make other potentially significant changes to the PC. Ensuring other users log in with Standard or Guest accounts will go a long way towards preventing accidental damage and security breaches.

# HOW TO...
# SET UP A STANDARD ACCOUNT

**①** **CREATE A NEW ACCOUNT** Type "user accounts" into the Start menu and click User Accounts. Now click "Manage another account" and "Create a new account". Type the name of the person whose account this will be into the Account name box, and make sure Standard user is selected. Then click Create Account.

**②** **PASSWORD-PROTECT THE ACCOUNT** Ideally, all user accounts should be protected by a password, so people can't log in as each other. If younger users forget theirs, the Administrator can reset it. To set a password on the account you've just created, return to "Manage another account", click the name of your new user and choose "Create a password". You'll be asked to type the password twice, plus a hint (such as "favourite footballer"), which will be shown on the login screen should the person forget their password. You can also change the user's picture and set Parental Controls (see p106) from this menu.

**③** **CHANGE ACCOUNT TYPES** For the ultimate in security, even the Administrator should do their day-to-day computing using a Standard account. That way, there's no chance of malware taking advantage of your Administrator privileges and installing itself on your PC.

If you've already spent time tailoring your Administrator account to your needs, you don't need to start from scratch. First create another Administrator account (you might call it something like Steve Admin) with a strong password, as in Step 2, but choosing Administrator rather than Standard. This account can be used every time you need to make sweeping changes to your system. Now go back to the User Account menu and select the "Change the account type" option. Choose Standard user, and all your settings and documents will remain in place under the new, safer Standard account.

It's worth noting that Microsoft has made vast improvements to the User Account Controls (see p112 for more on this) in Windows 7, and some advanced users may now regard running in Standard mode as overkill.

**④** **DELETING ACCOUNTS** Administrators can delete user accounts when necessary. In the User Accounts menu, select "Manage another account", click on the account you wish to erase and select "Delete the account". Be warned: deleting someone's account will delete their documents, music, photos and other files, unless you click the Keep Files option (which isn't the default choice). Either do this, or double-check there's nothing worth keeping in this user account before opting to Delete Files.

**HOW LONG?**
It takes only a few minutes to set up Standard user accounts for all the family.

**HOW HARD?**
It's simple to add this vital layer of protection – just beware of data loss when deleting accounts.

WITH WINDOWS 7'S ENHANCED SEARCH TOOLS, YOU CAN JUMP STRAIGHT TO WHAT YOU NEED – WHETHER IT'S ON YOUR PC OR EVEN ON THE INTERNET.

# Introducing Windows Search

We've seen how Windows 7's Libraries conveniently bring all your personal data together in a few virtual locations (see p36). But if you use your PC regularly, you'll quickly build up a large collection of data, and it can still be a pain to find the file you're looking for. Luckily, Windows 7's Search can scan all your files in a flash and show only the ones you want.

**FINDING A SPECIFIC FILE** Running a simple search in Windows 7 is easy. Imagine you're looking for a file called *Robyn's Plans for April.doc*, and you know it's somewhere in your Libraries. Start by going to Windows Explorer and clicking on Libraries in the left pane to see your Libraries. Look to the top-right of your Explorer window and you'll see a field labelled Search, like in a web browser. Type "Robyn's Plans for April" into this (you don't need to press Return). A dropdown menu will appear as you type, giving you some extra options, which we'll discuss – but ignore that for now. You should see a list of related files appear in the main view, and if you use Outlook or Windows Mail you'll also see any relevant messages and contacts found in your email archive.

What if the file you wanted isn't there? Perhaps you didn't save the file into a Library after all. If you didn't, Windows won't find it, as by default it only searches within your selected folder. In the main Explorer pane you'll see

options to broaden the search to your whole PC, specify other locations to search, or even search the internet.

Searching your whole computer can take a long time. Windows keeps an index of your personal folders, so it can locate their contents in moments; but when you start searching other folders, Windows has to inspect each file. You can choose which folders are indexed by opening the Control Panel and clicking "Change how Windows searches".

**FINDING MANY FILES** If you still can't find your file, perhaps you accidentally saved it under a different name. If you enter just the word "plans" into the Search field, Windows will show you all files within the current folder that include that word. Hopefully, this list will include the file you're looking for: if so, you can double-click to open it right away, or right-click it and select "Open file location" to view its folder.

If you'd find it useful to have all your plans at your fingertips, click the "Save search" button above the main display. Provide a name for this search when it asks, and you'll see that name appear under Favorites in the navigation pane of your Explorer window. In future, you can click this link and Windows will immediately re-run the search, showing all files with "plans" in their names – even new ones – in the folder you originally searched.

Windows Search makes it easy to find files, especially if you keep them in Libraries. Notice that it will find all files whose names contain the specified words; to match only the whole phrase, enter it within quote marks, such as "Robyn's Plans for".

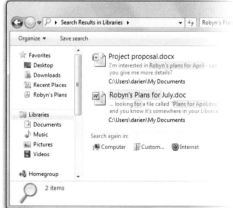

As well as searching for files by their names, you can even find phrases within files such as Word documents to track down the content you're looking for.

# HOW TO...
# CUSTOMISE YOUR SEARCHES

**(1) CUSTOMISE THE VIEW** You can view your search results in several ways. Click the "Change view" button towards the top-right of the Explorer window to cycle between various views. You can also click on the dropdown arrow next to the "Change view" button to choose your own display format. The Extra Large Icons view is handy if you're searching for pictures, since it shows thumbnails of all the images found without you needing to open them. The Content view shows excerpts from the text found inside each file, so it can be useful for identifying word processing files or pages you've saved from the web.

**(2) FILTER YOUR SEARCHES** As you type your terms into the Search box, you'll see a dropdown menu appear offering filters to narrow down your results. These filters change intelligently depending on the active folder: if you're in the Documents library, for example, you'll see an option to search by Author; move to the Music library and the filters include Artist name and Length. Click on a filter to see the options you can apply: Authors, for example, will let you pick authors from a list, while Length options range from "Very short (under 1 min)" to "Very long (over 60 mins)". You can apply as many filters as you like, enabling you to home in on the file you need even if you don't know its name.

**(3) ADVANCED FILTERS** Once you get adept at using filters, you can control them manually. For example, type "author:Robyn" as a search term and the results will be narrowed down to documents created by Robyn, even if that filter isn't normally offered for that folder. All the filters in Windows 7 can be used in this way, and you needn't worry if you don't know how to use each one: once you type the colon, Windows will pop up a list of options that you can choose from using the mouse. There's a huge range of filters available, and you can visit www.pcpro.co.uk/links/win7filter for a list.

**(4) FEDERATED SEARCH** Windows 7 also features a new Microsoft technology called Federated Search. Besides searching your own files, you can also use the Windows interface to search websites. To take advantage, you'll need to download a tiny piece of code called a Federated Search Connector for each site you want to search. These are available for sites including YouTube, Flickr, Amazon and Microsoft Bing. Advanced users can even create their own connectors, as we explain on p50. Once you've installed a Federated Search Connector, it will appear like a saved search in your Favorites. Click it and you can search websites and other online resources as easily as rummaging through your own computer.

**HOW LONG?**
It generally takes just a second or two to find files, but you might need ten minutes to get the hang of the features.

**HOW HARD?**
You could spend hours learning the filters and creating Connectors, but simple searches are easy.

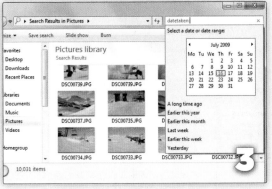

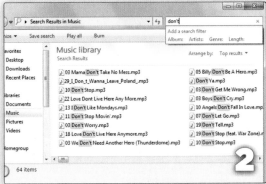

WINDOWS 7 INCLUDES A REVAMPED PAINT, WORDPAD AND CALCULATOR, EACH WITH A SNAZZY NEW INTERFACE AND PLENTY OF GREAT FEATURES.

# Windows 7's bundled applications

They might never match the power of full-blown third-party software, but the applications that come with Windows 7 do an admirable job for basic tasks – and they're free.

For basic document editing there's WordPad, while Paint handles simple image editing. Both now have Microsoft's easy-to-use Ribbon interface, first introduced in Office 2007. Plus there's the Calculator, now with modes for programming and statistics. You'll find them all in the Start menu, under All Programs | Accessories, along with the other free utilities Microsoft provides as part of Windows 7.

**WORDPAD** Windows' top text-editing app has had a redesign, and the toolbar now looks like a professional word processor. It's divided into two main subsets, Home and View, so you can make adjustments without having to dive into dropdown menus. As in Office, the Font and Paragraph tools take centre stage, along with Insert and Edit options. Click the View tab to adjust the zoom and turn word wrap on or off.

There's also a Quick Access bar in the top-left corner, which can be customised to hold whichever options you regularly use. WordPad can save documents in the XML-based format used by Office 2007, but you can also save to Text or Rich Text formats that any editor can open.

**PAINT** Windows Paint may not have the features of a proper photo-editing package such as Adobe Photoshop Elements, but for basic picture creation and manipulation it's a fun tool. (It's also handy for pasting screen captures made with the PrintScreen key.) Everything you need now sits in the accessible Ribbon, with rotating, cropping and resizing options beside Tools, Shapes and Colours.

There's a useful colour editor, and the main menu provides shortcuts to send the current picture in an email or set it as your desktop background. As in WordPad, a customisable Quick Access bar at the top-left carries your favourite tools. Images can be saved in all the most commonly used formats, including JPEG, PNG and TIF.

**CALCULATOR** You might not think there's much that could improve the humble Calculator, but it's worth a fresh look. Though it seems no different at first, if you open the View menu you'll find the Standard and Scientific modes have been joined by Programmer and Statistics options, which change the button panel to reflect appropriate functions.

This isn't all that's new. The Calculator now performs unit conversions and works out date differences, and even comes with quick tools for mortgage calculations, vehicle leasing and fuel economy.

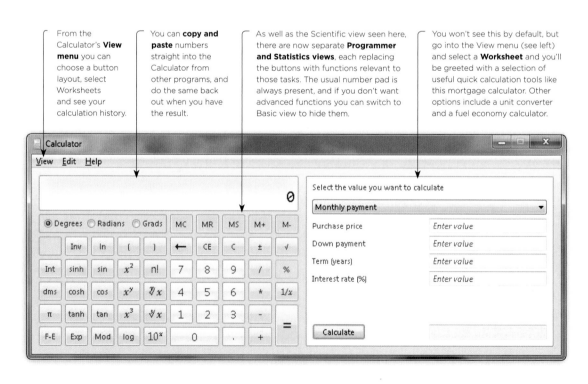

From the Calculator's **View menu** you can choose a button layout, select Worksheets and see your calculation history.

You can **copy and paste** numbers straight into the Calculator from other programs, and do the same back out when you have the result.

As well as the Scientific view seen here, there are now separate **Programmer and Statistics views**, each replacing the buttons with functions relevant to those tasks. The usual number pad is always present, and if you don't want advanced functions you can switch to Basic view to hide them.

You won't see this by default, but go into the View menu (see left) and select a **Worksheet** and you'll be greeted with a selection of useful quick calculation tools like this mortgage calculator. Other options include a unit converter and a fuel economy calculator.

# WHAT'S NEW IN...
# WORDPAD

The **Quick Access** bar holds the Undo and Redo buttons by default, but you can customise it to hold any of your favourite options.

You can **find and replace** words to save time in long documents. The only key tool that WordPad still sorely lacks is a word count.

The **File menu** lets you quickly attach a document to an email or open recently edited documents.

The new **Ribbon** interface divides the main tools into tabs instead of dropdown menus, so the tool you need is only ever one click away.

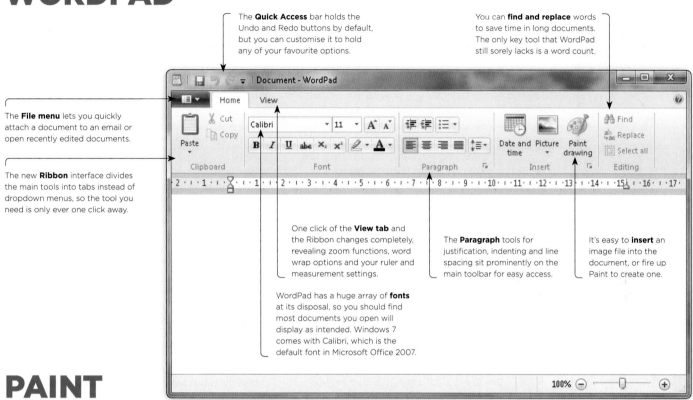

One click of the **View tab** and the Ribbon changes completely, revealing zoom functions, word wrap options and your ruler and measurement settings.

The **Paragraph** tools for justification, indenting and line spacing sit prominently on the main toolbar for easy access.

It's easy to **insert** an image file into the document, or fire up Paint to create one.

WordPad has a huge array of **fonts** at its disposal, so you should find most documents you open will display as intended. Windows 7 comes with Calibri, which is the default font in Microsoft Office 2007.

# PAINT

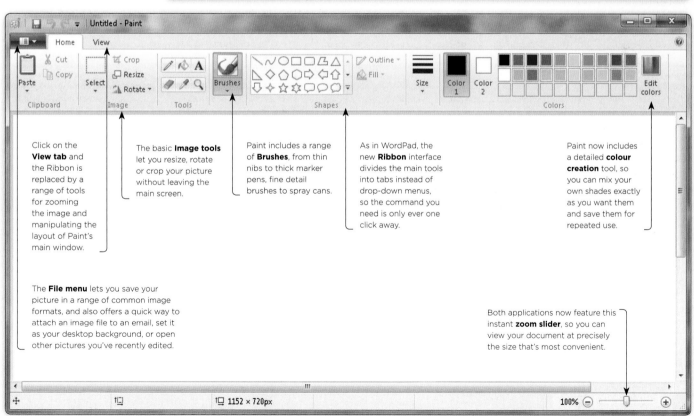

Click on the **View tab** and the Ribbon is replaced by a range of tools for zooming the image and manipulating the layout of Paint's main window.

The basic **Image tools** let you resize, rotate or crop your picture without leaving the main screen.

Paint includes a range of **Brushes**, from thin nibs to thick marker pens, fine detail brushes to spray cans.

As in WordPad, the new **Ribbon** interface divides the main tools into tabs instead of drop-down menus, so the command you need is only ever one click away.

Paint now includes a detailed **colour creation** tool, so you can mix your own shades exactly as you want them and save them for repeated use.

The **File menu** lets you save your picture in a range of common image formats, and also offers a quick way to attach an image file to an email, set it as your desktop background, or open other pictures you've recently edited.

Both applications now feature this instant **zoom slider**, so you can view your document at precisely the size that's most convenient.

Intel based PCs for all your tasks

**AFFORDABLE All-Rounder**

*Delivers excellent all-round performance with a generous storage capacity at a great price.*

## MESH Elite Inspire

- Intel® Pentium® **Dual Core E5200** Processor (2.50GHz, 2MB cache, Dual Core)
- Genuine Windows Vista® Home Premium 64-bit
- **4GB** DDR2 800MHz Memory
- **500GB** SATA Fast Hard Drive
- **256MB** NVIDIA GeForce Graphics Accelerator
- **20"** Widescreen LCD Display with internal Speakers
- 22x Multi-format Dual Layer DVD Writer
- New stylish mini tower with a black high-gloss finish
- Logitech Deluxe Corded Keyboard & Optical Mouse
- Plus many additional features - see below

**PRICE FROM £429 INC. VAT**
- GO ONLINE FOR UP-TO-DATE PRICING

---

*"BREAKTHROUGH SPECIFICATION: The first system we've seen with Core i7 at this price" Recommended - PC Advisor, Oct 09*

**AWARD Winner**

**PC ADVISOR RECOMMENDED**

**Now includes 2.1 Speakers & Wireless KB & Mouse for extra £50**

## MESH Elite Ice 7

- Intel® Core™ **i7 920** Processor (2.66GHz, 8MB cache, Quad Core)
- Genuine Windows Vista® Home Premium 64-bit
- **3GB** DDR3 Triple Channel 1333MHz Memory
- **500GB** SATA Ultra Fast Hard Drive
- **512MB** ATI Radeon **HD4850** Graphics
- **22"** IIYAMA **Full HD** LCD (1920x1080) - DVI, spkrs, 5ms
- 22x Multi-format Dual Layer DVD Writer
- Midi tower silver ATX Chassis with 550W PSU
- *Upgraded with* Hercules XPS 2.1 Speakers and Subwoofer
- *Upgraded with* Logitech Cordless Keyboard & Optical Mouse
- Plus many additional features - see below

**PRICE FROM £799 INC. VAT**
- GO ONLINE FOR UP-TO-DATE PRICING

---

**ULTIMATE Performance**

**FREE Double Memory FREE Double Hard Drive**

*Cutting edge performance with Intel Core i7 power and ATI Radeon HD4850 Graphics.*
*FREE Double Memory and Hard Drive*

## MESH XGS i7 920SL

- Intel® Core™ **i7 920** Processor (2.66GHz, 8MB cache, Quad Core)
- Genuine Windows Vista® Home Premium 64-bit
- ~~4GB~~ **8GB** DDR3 1333MHz Memory
- ~~500GB~~ **1TB** SATA Ultra Fast Hard Drive
- **1GB** ATI Radeon **HD4850** Graphics
- **22"** IIYAMA **Full HD** LCD (1920x1080) - DVI, spkrs, 5ms
- 22x Multi-format Dual Layer DVD Writer
- **NEW** XGS Xtreme Gaming Chassis
- Logitech Cordless Keyboard & Mouse
- Plus many additional features - see right

*Also available in red or silver*

**PRICE FROM £999 INC. VAT**
- GO ONLINE FOR UP-TO-DATE PRICING

---

**ADDITIONAL FEATURES ON ALL PCs (Unless otherwise stated)** ■ 7.1 HD Onboard Sound Card 8 Channel Cinema Sound ■ Free Microsoft® Works 8.5 + Free Limited Microsoft Office Trial ■ Free Cyberlink Video Editing Suite (includes 7 titles) ■ Free BullGuard Internet Security 8.5 (90 days trial) AntiVirus/Firewall/Backup/Spamfilter
**OPTIONAL EXTRAS** ■ 52-in-1 Multi-Format Card Reader - £11.50 inc. Vat

**MESH computers**
*Anything else is a compromise.*

# IN THIS CHAPTER

# 4

*Advanced features*

# ADVANCED FEAT

We've now covered the basics of Windows 7, but there's much more to it than a few tweaks. With just a little technical know-how, you can create virtual hard disks (and even install Windows 7 directly onto one), calibrate your monitor so that it displays colours more accurately, and speed up your day-to-day work in Windows with our pick of its keyboard shortcuts.

19°
London, GBR

19:26
27/07/2009

# URES

We'll also reveal what the enhanced Aero interface has to offer, and it goes way beyond glossy effects – from shaking a window so that the others fall away, to instantly tiling windows and moving them between screens. And you'll discover exactly why so many people are becoming excited about the new touchscreen technology built into Windows 7.

# Unleashing Windows Aero

Windows 7's Aero Glass interface doesn't only look good, it also provides a range of technologies that can make the operating system quicker and easier to use. Many of these are hidden away behind a desktop that may seem at first to have been only cosmetically enhanced. On these two pages, we reveal a series of secret interface tweaks that become apparent only when you drag windows in a certain direction or activate a keyboard shortcut. With these eight top Aero features, power users can get even more out of Windows 7.

1 **WINDOWS SHAKE** Often you can find yourself with a dozen application windows open. Not only does this make moving between programs more laborious, it can leave a distracting mess behind the document you're working on. You can now "shake away" the clutter by minimising all the open windows except one. Click and hold any blank space in the bar at the top of the window you're working on; drag it down slightly if the window is full-screen. Then shake the mouse gently from left to right. You should see all the other windows disappear. Don't worry if you have unsaved work in any of those windows – they haven't been closed, just minimised to the Taskbar at the bottom of the screen. Click on the program's icon there to re-open the window.

2 **GO FULL-SCREEN** If you're working in a window and want to make it full-screen, there's an alternative to clicking the fiddly little box icon at the top right. Drag the window's top bar to the very top of the screen; the window instantly fills the screen. To return it to its original size, drag it back down.

3 **SNAP TO THE EDGES** You'll often work in more than one window: reading information from a web page while writing a document, for example. Windows 7 makes it easy to show two windows side by side. Click on the bar at the top of the first window you want and drag it to the far left of the screen; you should find the window snaps into place, filling half the screen. Now do the same with the second window, but drag it to the right. The windows should be butted up. The only time this won't work is when you have more than one monitor on your PC. In this instance, use keyboard shortcuts instead: hold down the Windows key and press the left or right arrow key as appropriate.

4 **SHOW THE DESKTOP** Keeping an eye on the news headlines or your train times using a Gadget (see p34)? You don't have to minimise all your windows to take a peek at your desktop; just hover the mouse over the translucent vertical bar next to the clock in the bottom-right corner and all your open windows temporarily melt away, revealing your Windows desktop and all its Gadgets.

## Tip

 With a variety of windows and Gadgets open, it can sometimes be tricky to see where the mouse pointer is, especially if you're using more than one screen. Fortunately, Windows 7 can help locate a pointer that's gone missing in action. Type "mouse" into the Start menu's Search box and select the Mouse option that appears under Control Panel. Now go to the Pointer Options tab and click the checkbox that says "Show location of pointer when I press CTRL key". Now, whenever you lose the pointer, hit the Ctrl key and a sonar-like graphic will reveal where the little blighter is hiding.

Aero isn't just a pretty face – it adds convenience features that, once you know them, you'll use every day. Among the new options in Windows 7 are Shake (1), which fades out other windows to let you focus on what you're doing; the ability to make a window full-screen (2) just by dragging it to the top; snapping windows to the left and right for an instant side-by-side setup (3); quickly showing the desktop (4); and switching through application windows using Windows Peek (5). If none of this floats your boat, you can switch off Aero (8) and pretend your PC is stuck in the 1990s.

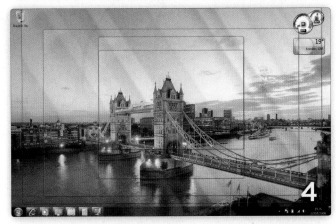

5 **WINDOWS PEEK** Without the little text descriptions of yesteryear, it's sometimes tricky to recognise the windows you have open from their Taskbar icons. A new feature called Windows Peek can help. Hover over any icon in the Taskbar and up pops a little thumbnail image, providing a visual reminder of what's in the window. Mouse over this for a full-screen preview. Peek really comes into its own when you have multiple web pages open in different tabs in Internet Explorer. Each tab is given its own thumbnail – just click on the one you want to open.

6 **TASK SWITCHER** If you don't want to scroll through thumbnails with Peek, there's an easier way to flip through your open apps. Hold the Alt key and press Tab to invoke the Task Switcher. You'll now be presented with the thumbnails slap-bang in the middle of the screen. With Alt still held down, keep pressing Tab to move to the window of your choice. Unlike Windows Peek, this won't reveal the tabs you have open in Internet Explorer, for instance.

7 **FLIP 3D** Task Switcher has a bigger, flashier brother called Flip 3D. Instead of seeing thumbnails of your open windows, you can flip through them in a full-screen three-dimensional carousel. Just hold down the Windows key and press Tab. Then keep on pressing Tab and watch the pseudo-3D windows you have open flit past you. It's the epitome of style over substance, and no more efficient than the Task Switcher, but we're all entitled to show off now and again, aren't we?

8 **SWITCH AERO OFF** Finally, if all the translucent glass windows, preview thumbnails and whooshing graphics leave you nonplussed (and your system slower than it needs to be), it's easy to switch off the Windows Aero effects and go back to the days of Windows XP. Right-click on a blank space on the desktop, choose Personalize, and select Windows 7 Basic or Windows Classic from the available themes. The picture of a koala bear is entirely optional.

 SEARCHING YOUR HARD DISK AND THE INTERNET USED TO BE SEPARATE TASKS, BUT WINDOWS 7 LETS YOU SEARCH EVERYWHERE FROM THE SAME WINDOW.

# Introducing Federated Search

Searching multiple websites has been a staple of internet browsers for some time; it's easy to take Internet Explorer 8's default Bing search and turn it into a Google or Wikipedia search. But, for the first time, Windows 7 makes it possible without using an internet browser at all. "Federated Search" may sound complicated, but it simply allows you to search the internet from an ordinary Windows Explorer window.

So why would you want to? Well, Windows 7 searches internet sites in the same way as it searches your hard disk: by sending information as you type it. This means you don't even have to finish a word before results appear in your search window. It's much faster than browsing to a search engine website and searching from there.

**SETTING IT UP** Windows 7 doesn't come with federated search set up by default, but it's well worth spending a few minutes getting it working. Adding an internet search requires you to download a very small file called a search connector. Lots of these are already available; entering "windows 7 search connector" into your favourite search engine (via your web browser, for one last time) should

find plenty. Windows search connectors are often only a thousandth of a megabyte, so they take virtually no time to download. At the time of writing, connectors exist for sites such as eBay, Google News, YouTube and Flickr.

Once you've found a connector from a site you trust, double-click it and you'll be prompted to install it; just click Add and you're done. We look at the process in more detail on the opposite page.

**USING IT** When you want to use your newly installed search connector for the first time, hold down the Windows key and press F for Find, or just type something into the Start menu and click the "See more results" link. The resulting window has a navigation bar on the right, giving options for all the places you can search, and your search connector will now be on that list. Select it and you'll be prompted to begin typing a search term in the standard box.

The result looks like a list of files; single-click on an item and a live preview of the web page will load in the right-hand pane. It makes finding the result you want quick, because you don't need to open a web browser or tell it to go back to your results every time you finish looking at a page.

*Tip*

If you want a search connector but can't find a suitable ready-made one online, you can make one yourself. It's relatively simple and takes only a few minutes for each website; instructions can be found at www.pcpro.co.uk/links/win7connector

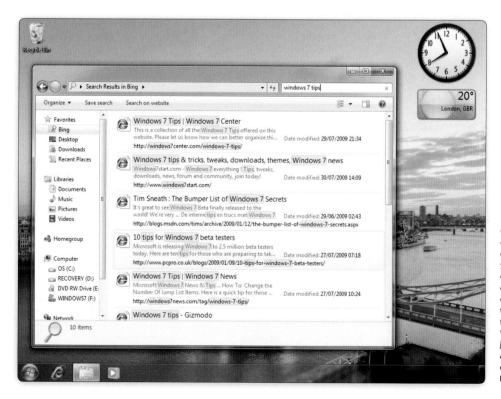

Once you add one or more connectors for your favourite online search engines, you can search the web from within Windows 7 just as easily as searching on your own hard disk.

# HOW TO...
# ADD A SEARCH PROVIDER

**①** **FIND A CONNECTOR** Finding a new search provider couldn't be easier, and the number available is growing all the time. Popular websites such as Flickr and YouTube already have search connectors. Enter "windows 7 search connector" and the name of a search provider into any search engine, via your web browser, and you'll get plenty of results. Connectors are available from a variety of sources, including expert users as well as internet companies, but be sure you trust the provider of any connector you download.

**②** **INSTALL YOUR CONNECTOR** We opted for a Flickr search connector from www.istartedsomething. com/flickrsearch, which not only provides a connector for the Flickr photo-sharing site, but also allows you to determine how that connector sorts your results: you can search by the date a picture was taken, or how interesting it's judged to be by Flickr's servers. Once you've downloaded it, just double-click on the resulting file and you'll be prompted to add it to Windows 7.

**③** **SEARCH** This is where the fun starts. Hold down the Windows key on your PC's keyboard and press F. By default you'll be taken to a screen that wants to search your PC, but pay attention to the list of locations under the Favorites banner (only visible after you type something into the search box). This normally holds default locations such as your desktop and places you've added manually, but now there's a new icon called Flickr Search. The Windows 7 Ultimate Guide team is planning a trip to Cuba, so we click the Flickr Search icon and type "cuba".

The results appear after just a few seconds, sorted by whatever criterion you selected when you downloaded the connector. If you click on any of the preview images, the far right-hand pane will show the Flickr page that hosts the image. It's a live preview, which means it appears on your PC as it is currently on Flickr's server. If you click any of the links, your default internet browser will launch and the page will be loaded in that.

**④** **CUSTOMISE YOUR VIEW** The results page is very flexible. Not only can you grab the edge of any of the panes and drag it around to fit on the screen, but you can also view more or less about your results, either by clicking the thumbnail button near the top right or by holding down Ctrl and moving your mouse wheel (up to make the thumbnails bigger, down to make them smaller). The smaller they are, the more you can see on one page. At the smallest size you also get information about the page on which the item appears, plus a few of the tags applied to it and the name of the author.

**HOW LONG?**
A matter of moments to find and install the search connector of your choice.

**HOW HARD?**
Dead-easy; just think twice before installing search connectors from unknown sources.

# 4

## Advanced features

## Tip

⊿ You may not need Windows XP Mode to run older applications. First, try the Compatibility mode by right-clicking on a program in the Start menu and then selecting the self-explanatory Compatibility tab.

## Tip

⊿ By default, Windows XP Mode runs at a reduced screen resolution in the relatively primitive 16-bit colour depth. This is unsuitable for any photo-editing tasks and many other applications. You can fix it by going to Tools | Disable Integration Features, then changing the settings in the Desktop Properties of your XP desktop.

 WINDOWS 7 WILL RUN MOST WINDOWS XP APPLICATIONS, BUT FOR BUSINESS USERS WITH PROBLEM SOFTWARE, WINDOWS XP MODE IS HERE TO HELP.

# Introducing Windows XP Mode

One of the biggest challenges Microsoft faced with Vista was dragging people to a new operating system when they were quite happy with the ageing but stable Windows XP. While most software designed for XP worked fine in Vista, some didn't, and this proved a particular problem for companies that had invested in software for specific business needs.

With Windows 7, Microsoft has ensured there's no excuse for XP users not to upgrade. Windows XP Mode is based on Microsoft's Virtual PC 7 software, and creates a full virtualised Windows XP system on your Windows 7 PC. It's like a program window with a Windows XP PC inside. You can even access all your hard disks, optical drives and USB devices straight away from within XP, without any of the additional configuration this would usually require.

Windows XP Mode isn't supplied and installed with Windows 7 as standard, but it's free to download – along with the version of Virtual PC 7 it needs to run – from www.microsoft.com/windows/virtual-pc/default.aspx

**THE BAD NEWS** It's worth noting straight away that not all Windows 7 systems will be able to run XP Mode. Your computer needs to have a processor that supports either Intel's VT technology or AMD-V. In Intel's case, that includes most recent Intel Core 2 and Core i7 chips. With AMD, most

recent Athlon, Opteron and Phenom processors are covered. You may need to Google your processor name to find out.

What's more, you also need to ensure that you have virtualisation enabled in the PC's BIOS. Check your manuals or the website above for details if you don't know how to do this. The final and perhaps most significant limitation is that, as XP Mode is primarily aimed at businesses, it's only installable on the Professional, Enterprise and Ultimate editions of Windows 7. That's bad news for anyone hoping to use their hoariest old programs on an installation of Windows 7 Home Premium.

**RESURRECTING THE DEAD** Once you have XP Mode up and running, you'll be faced with a window containing the old-fashioned XP desktop and not much else. If you want to maximise screen space, or hide Windows 7 from users, just select View Full Screen from the Action menu at the top.

You'll be able to browse the web using Internet Explorer within your XP virtual machine, so as a safety measure you should first install XP antivirus software. You may be able to install the same security suite you're using on your Windows 7 system, if its licence permits, or download the latest free XP version of Avast (www.avast.com) or AVG (www.avg.com) using a web browser in Windows 7. Back in

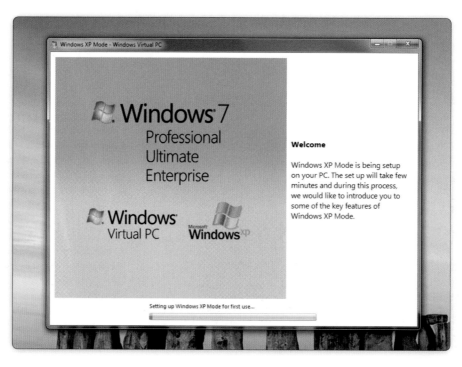

Installing Windows XP Mode gives you two PCs for the price of one – you can run even the oldest and fussiest XP programs within Windows 7 without them knowing they're not on an ordinary Windows XP system. Unfortunately, it's only available with the Professional, Enterprise and Ultimate editions of Windows 7, so Home Premium users will have to rely on Windows 7's inherent ability to run most XP (and Vista) software without any extra help.

the XP Mode window, go to Start | My Computer and locate the setup program for your security software on the host system's hard disk. Note that the C drive you normally see in the XP window will be a virtual hard disk, so instead look for C within <Your PC>. Run the installer and you're safe.

Next, add your XP-loving, Windows 7-hating applications, installing them on your virtual XP desktop in exactly the same way as you'd have done on a standard Windows XP machine. Again, you can use My Computer to access your PC's optical drives or any files stored on the host system's hard disks. Once installed, you'll be able to use your applications just like you could in the good old days.

Here's where XP Mode gets clever. Once an application has been installed to your XP Mode virtual desktop, you can launch it from your standard Windows 7 desktop too. Go to Start | All Programs | Windows Virtual PC | Windows XP Mode Applications, and you'll find a list of any programs you've installed on your virtual XP machine. Select one, and it will load straight onto your Windows 7 desktop; the only way you'll know it's not running locally in Windows 7 is that it will appear in the classic Windows XP-style window frame. In other words, you can use apps in XP Mode without having to remember that you need XP Mode to use them. It's pretty seamless.

XP Mode gives you two ways of running applications: from inside a virtual XP desktop (top right), which you can either run in a window or full screen, or virtualised within the Windows 7 desktop (below right). Here, the application window can be used just like any Windows 7 program, without explicitly treating it as a virtualised XP application.

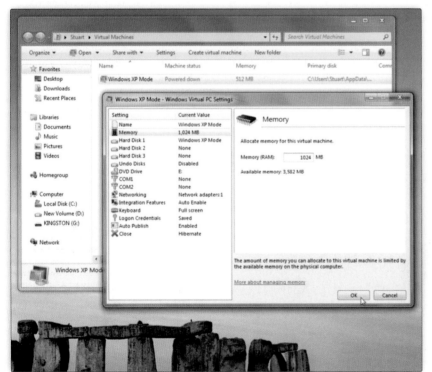

Running virtualisation software such as Virtual PC 7, on which Windows XP Mode is based, often means some fiddling around to get your peripherals and storage working from the virtual operating system as well as your main one. Fortunately, XP Mode simplifies this.

Only half a gigabyte of RAM is allocated to Windows XP Mode by default – after all, 512MB was a lot of memory in those days. If you need more, and there's plenty available in your PC (bearing in mind you also have Windows 7 running), you can adjust this.

**USING EXTERNAL DEVICES**  Normally, getting a virtual system to interact with external hard disks, USB drives and other peripherals can be tricky, but the technology behind XP Mode does the work for you.

When you start XP Mode as a desktop, not an application, you'll see a USB menu at the top. Click it to list any USB devices connected to your PC. Printers and scanners may first need to be "attached": this option forces XP Mode to install drivers for new hardware.

Normally, USB storage devices, like memory sticks and hard disks, are shared between your Windows 7 system and the Windows XP virtual system. You'll find them listed with your host system hard drives as <Drive X> on <Your PC>. Alternatively, you can attach them to the virtual PC only, making it simpler to access them from Windows XP.

**A LITTLE MORE POWER**  XP Mode is brilliant at what it's designed for, but it isn't really built for speed. The desktop and any 3D or video acceleration required are powered by a generic S3 graphics adapter driver, rather than any drivers for your PC's specific graphics chipset, so you can forget about games, and graphics-intensive apps may be slow.

Memory is also limited by default to 512MB. This should be enough for the kind of business applications XP Mode is designed to run, but you can allocate more. First, shut down the Virtual PC by selecting <Ctrl-Alt-Del> from the menu bar and choosing "Shut down". Now (in Windows 7) go to Start | All Programs | Windows Virtual PC | Windows Virtual PC. Right-click on Windows XP Mode and choose Settings. You can now click on Memory and allocate more in the Memory (RAM) box provided.

# 4

## Advanced features

# Introducing Device Stage

Windows 7 debuts a new feature called Device Stage that could either be unbelievably handy, a great idea doomed to failure, or a licence for manufacturers to trap consumers into expensive purchases. The idea is that when you plug in a supported media player, digital camera, mobile phone or printer, you're presented with the Device Stage screen. This shows a picture of your device alongside a range of tasks and options specifically tailored to that very model.

Notably, Microsoft is handing control of the Device Stage screen to the hardware manufacturers. They can embed links to their online services, manuals and software, so a printer maker, for example, might include a direct link to buy new ink cartridges for your particular printer from their website, or a link to the latest driver. Mobile phone manufacturers could include a facility to record your own ringtone, synchronise contacts, or perform specific tasks using your model's dedicated PC software.

**MIXED BLESSING** On one hand, it's a perfect opportunity to make life easier for consumers by opening their eyes to features and services available for their particular devices. On the other, it could end up being used as little more than a rather intrusive form of advertising, with manufacturers taking the opportunity to entice consumers to their

proprietary software and services. Still, while we remain unconvinced it will match Microsoft's promise, it's certainly an advance over previous versions of Windows. Double-click on your printer's icon in Vista, for example, and all you saw was a list of queued jobs and a vague status message.

Do the same in Windows 7 and you get something more like the screen below. We know our printer is ready and the default setting is A4 portrait, and we can even play around with the scan settings on this multifunction model.

**REALITY BITES** However, Microsoft's dream of providing a simple way to order replacement ink cartridges, for example, is still some way from reality. As you can see, there are no links at all for our HP C4200, a popular mainstream unit. When we tried a rival Epson all-in-one, there was no Device Stage page for it at all. What hope for less common devices?

These are early days, of course, and it's quite possible that support for Device Stage will improve dramatically as Windows 7 becomes the dominant operating system. Until this has been proven, though, Device Stage looks set to be of limited use, and its main benefit may simply be as a graphical guide to all the devices whose drivers you've loaded onto your PC: to see this, simply click Devices and Printers on the Start menu.

## Tip

 To remove a device from Windows 7, all you have to do is head to Devices and Printers from the Start menu, right-click on the device you no longer use and choose Remove device.

This is what Microsoft describes as a **photorealistic image** of your device – although HP's C4200 series printers don't actually look anything like this.

**Customize your printer** shows the kind of options you'd get by clicking Advanced in a Print dialog, such as ports and sharing.

If your device contains removable storage, such as the memory card readers in this printer, you can click **Browse files** to view the contents.

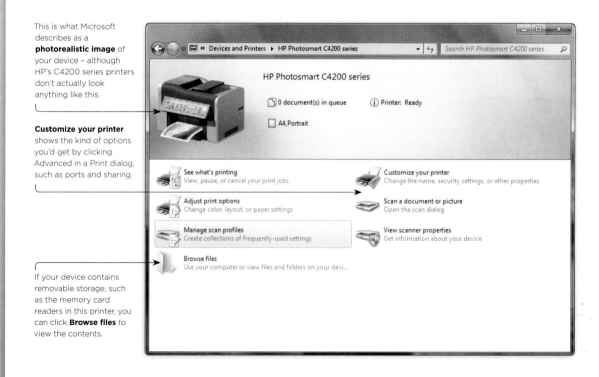

# Fine-tune your display

*It's astonishing how many people put up with a display stuck at the wrong resolution or a monitor left at its default settings since it was bought. Windows 7 makes it easy to take control of how your screen handles colour and text.*

Despite its usefulness, Microsoft hasn't made much effort to promote the Display Color Calibration tool, perhaps because it wants to preserve the impression that Windows "just works" out of the box rather than requiring any fiddly setup. It certainly isn't essential to go through this process, but it's well worth seeking out the tool. The simplest route is to type "calibrate" into the Start menu's search box; this should bring up "Calibrate display color" as the first result. Press Return (or click on the item) to launch it, and a large grey window will appear with the title Display Color Calibration. If you have more than one screen and this window isn't sitting on the appropriate one, the first thing you need to do is move it over.

You'll then be taken through a string of steps to adjust your system's gamma setting (which determines the curve from dark to light tones) and your display's brightness and contrast. Note that not all screens allow you to adjust contrast, especially laptop displays and screens attached over a digital connection such as DVI or HDMI. The final step is to adjust the colour balance.

**GETTING IT RIGHT** When setting the gamma, you may find it useful to use the highly unscientific method of scrunching up your eyes to blur your vision: this actually makes it easier to see that the area you're examining

is at the right gamma level, as the whole square you're squinting at should become the same shade of grey.

Note that a display's apparent brightness and contrast will almost certainly vary depending on the angle from which you're looking at it. So make sure you make your calibration judgements from your normal sitting position. Apparent brightness will also vary depending on the lighting wherever you're working, which is why it makes sense to use your monitor's ability to store custom settings if you can: save one for daylight, for example, and another for fluorescent light.

**TUNING TYPE** When the Display Calibration wizard has finished, you'll be invited to adjust your ClearType settings. ClearType is Windows' built-in technology that intelligently smoothes the edges of text to make it appear sharper onscreen. However, some people find it actually has the effect of making text look fuzzy, and results will vary on different monitors, which is why it makes sense to run through the four steps provided by the ClearType wizard to see if this improves the perceived sharpness.

To launch the wizard at any other time, just enter "cleartype" into the Start menu's search box and "Adjust ClearType text" should be the first option you'll see.

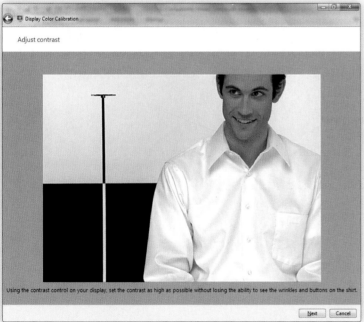

Using the contrast control on your display, set the contrast as high as possible without losing the ability to see the wrinkles and buttons on the shirt.

It's worth running Display Color Calibration three or four times: after each, you can either apply the changes or revert to the previous setup, so you can fine-tune your fine-tuning.

ClearType is a technology built into Windows that uses advanced anti-aliasing methods to make text look smoother on screen. In practice, the effect depends on the particular screen you're using, and different users have their own personal preferences, so take the opportunity to pick your favourite setting here.

**HOW LONG?**
Two minutes to pick some new backgrounds, but you can easily waste a lot more time...

**HOW HARD?**
Very easy, and messing about won't do your PC or pictures any harm.

## Tip
Desktop slideshows are only available in the Home Premium, Professional and Ultimate editions of Windows 7.

# HOW TO...
# CREATE A DESKTOP SLIDESHOW

*Desktop slideshows let you select multiple wallpapers, so instead of looking at a static desktop background you can watch it change through the day.*

 **GET PERSONAL** You can create a desktop slideshow from any selection of images – JPG, PNG, GIF or BMP – stored on your PC. Windows 7 comes with several ready to go, including those in the supplied themes. To choose pictures, go to Control Panel | Appearance and Personalization | Personalization | Desktop Background. Or right-click on the desktop, select Personalize from the dropdown menu, then click the Desktop Background link at the bottom of the window.

 **CHOOSE DEFAULT IMAGES** There are several ways of choosing which images to include in your slideshow. By default, you choose from the Windows Desktop Backgrounds that Windows 7 installs on your hard disk. Clicking on the name of a theme or folder (for example, Landscapes) will select every background image included in each theme. You can also lasso a selection of images, or simply click on whichever images you like, one by one, while holding down the Ctrl key. Using the Select All and Clear All buttons, you can either pick all the images in the current Picture Location or remove them all from your selection.

 **CHOOSE YOUR OWN IMAGES** Alternatively, use the Picture Location menu to select photos from your own Pictures Library or other Libraries and locations on your PC. Alternatively, use the Browse button and navigate to your favourite shots using the standard Windows Explorer file browser interface.

It's also possible to create a desktop slideshow from any group of images. Open a folder in Windows Explorer, click to select some photos, then right-click and choose "Set as desktop background" from the menu.

 **TWEAK YOUR SLIDESHOW SETTINGS** Do you want your desktop background to change every minute, every hour, or just once a day? The dropdown menu below the label "Change picture every:" allows you to set how long each background image will stay on your desktop before neatly transitioning to the next. By default, the desktop background rolls on from one selected image to the next, from folder to folder or theme to theme, until it gets to the end and cycles back to the beginning, but check the Shuffle box if you'd rather see your pictures in random order.

## 4

### Advanced features

MICROSOFT HAS TRIED AND FAILED WITH TOUCHSCREEN INTERFACES BEFORE, BUT WINDOWS 7 FINALLY GETS IT RIGHT – IN SPECTACULAR FASHION.

# Working with a touchscreen

Touchscreen PCs have been on the horizon for as long as we can remember, but they're now heading for the mainstream, and Windows 7 is the first desktop operating system with finger-based touch capabilities built in. Vista allowed Tablet PC users to make "flicks" with the stylus – the electronic pen required to interact with their touchscreens – but this hardly compares to the amazingly user-friendly multitouch screens on portable devices such as Apple's iPhone, which respond intuitively to direct contact with your fingers.

As the first desktop operating system to have full multitouch capabilities throughout, Windows 7 knows when you put more than one finger on the screen at a time and responds accordingly. If you have a touchscreen PC, an instant way to test this is with Microsoft's supplied Paint program: load it up and drag four fingers across the page, and four lines of virtual ink will trail behind. It's an experience as life-changing as the first time you moved a pointer with a mouse instead of the cursor keys.

**MAKING GESTURES** Of course, you probably *don't* have a touchscreen PC – but in the next few years, Microsoft reckons they'll become more common. The real power of a multitouch system lies in gestures. If you put two fingers on the screen while an image file is open and push them apart, you'll zoom in. Pinch your fingers together and the image becomes smaller. You can also rotate images by moving your fingers around your thumb.

This works both in Windows Explorer – you can also move windows around by pulling them about by their title bars – and in applications. Drag your finger up a list of files, as if you were sliding a piece of paper away from you, and you'll scroll smoothly down the list. Within applications, if you're reading a document you can scroll through it by touching the screen. If you try to scroll beyond the end of a list of files or the end of a document, the window will give a little joggle to show that you can't go any further. Zooming works well in Internet Explorer and with

## Tip

Using Windows 7's touchscreen features is easy, but you'll find it hard going if you try to use your fingers on systems with smaller screens, such as Tablet PCs. You can make onscreen text easier to read and give your fingers larger icons to tap by changing the way Windows displays these elements. Go to the Control Panel, then click Appearance and Personalization. Under Display, click "Make text and other items larger or smaller". Choose one of the options to make text and dialog boxes bigger. Note that to activate this you'll need to log out from your user account and then log back in again.

Windows 7's **virtual keyboard** now responds to multitouch on compatible screens, so key combinations, such as holding Shift while pressing a letter key to get a capital, work just like on a physical keyboard.

While you type, Windows **predicts** words you might be aiming for, based on its own dictionary and also on what you've entered previously – so it won't keep offering words you never use.

documents, and it's great in Windows Live Photo Gallery too (see p67). Meanwhile, placing a finger on the screen and tapping with another is equivalent to a right-click.

**FLICKING OFF** The "flick" concept, which seemed to have died out with the Tablet PC, is back in Windows 7 and makes a lot more sense. To flick, you place a finger on the screen, then lift it off as you move it. Flicking right or left will skip to the next or previous image in a gallery. Place a finger on an application shortcut on the Taskbar and flick upwards, and the Jump List for that application will open (see p32). Flicks also work in Internet Explorer to take you forwards and backwards through your browsing history.

**WRITTEN EXAMINATION** One thing fingers aren't good for is writing, but there's now even better support for users who want to create and edit documents using a stylus. Windows' handwriting recognition has always been pretty good, and Windows 7 continues the tradition. When activated, the Tablet PC Input Panel peeks onto the screen from the left-hand side, and Microsoft claims its accuracy has improved since Vista. We're inclined to agree: despite our messy handwriting, Windows 7 did a good job of turning even cursive (joined-up) script into correct editable text.

When you wrote this way in Vista, you were given Windows' interpretation of your scrawls in little boxes underneath the handwriting area. Now, Windows 7 converts your characters as you write them. The way you make corrections has also improved. If you need to break a word into two, for example, just draw a vertical line where you want the break; or to join up two words, draw a curved line beneath them. If you need to correct a word after Windows has misinterpreted it, you can simply tap it with the stylus, tap the incorrect letter, and write the correct one over the top of it.

**KEY CONCEPTS** If handwriting isn't your thing, the onscreen keyboard in Windows 7 has also undergone massive surgery, and it's now incredibly capable. (Note that the keyboard within the Tablet PC Input Panel, which we're describing here, is subtly different from the onscreen keyboard; find both of these by typing their names into the Start menu's search box.) With a multitouch screen, you can hold down the onscreen Shift key while tapping a letter to get a capital, for example. With practice, it's possible to get up a terrific head of speed in your "virtual typing", even if the lack of tactile feedback means you may never quite manage to touch-type. Windows also makes suggestions, so if you get part of the way through a word and pause, you'll be given a few likely ways to complete it along the top of the keyboard.

This works via the wonders of predictive text. Windows 7 includes a comprehensive list of words by default, and will also modify its suggestions as you use the touchscreen features, either by writing with a stylus or tapping at the onscreen keyboard. The upshot is that eventually Windows will suggest words that aren't only a logical fit with the letters you've just entered, but are also likely guesses based on what you've typed in the past.

# DELIVERED BY HAND

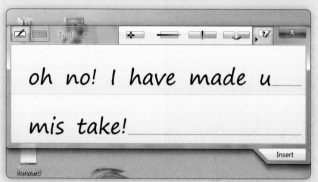

Windows 7's handwriting recognition is even better than before, managing to convert quite scruffy efforts into accurate text. It can be used anywhere you'd normally type.

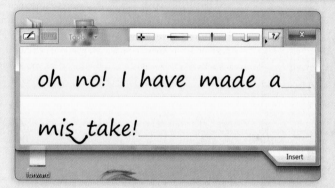

Any mistakes in the resulting text – whether your fault or Windows' – can easily be corrected. Instead of appearing in separate boxes, the letters instantly replace your writing. To change any word, just tap it, tap the incorrect letter within it, then write over the top.

Further gestures split or combine words. Here we're drawing a curved line to join two word fragments together. Similarly, drawing a vertical line through a word splits it at that point. A horizontal line through a word deletes it. Animated examples are given to show you how.

On a touchscreen PC, you can control many things in Windows 7 with your fingers. For example, in Internet Explorer you can scroll around web pages and move forwards and back simply by dragging and flicking.

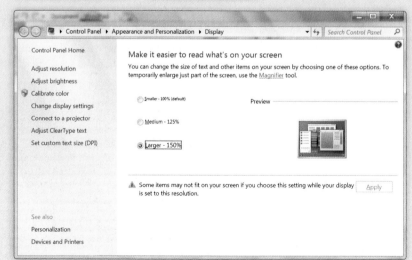

If text and icons are too small to interact with easily, use the options in Appearance and Personalization to make them bigger onscreen while leaving the overall display resolution unchanged.

**HOW LONG?**

Allow at least an hour to complete the setup.

**HOW HARD?**

If you don't consider yourself an advanced Windows user, don't mess with this feature.

# HOW TO...
# USE VIRTUAL HARD DISKS

*You can install Windows 7 independently of your existing system by using one of its best new features: virtual hard disks. They have lots of other uses, too.*

Windows 7 is the first operating system that really lets personal users exploit virtualisation: the idea of separating the system you're using from the underlying resources. One example is Windows XP Mode (see p52), which makes programs think they're running in XP. Another, which we explore here, is the ability to create virtual hard disk images that behave like physical disks, even though they're really just files on an existing hard disk. All versions of Windows 7 allow you to create virtual hard disks, but only Ultimate allows you to boot from them.

We've looked at achieving something similar with a dual-boot system (see p24), but virtual disks offer advantages. Creating a virtual disk is much quicker than the lengthy process of resizing and moving disk partitions, and if you decide you don't want the new partition, you can just unmount the disk with a quick command and delete its associated virtual disk file. Finally, backing up the contents of your "disk" is as simple as copying a single file – which is essentially what it is.

**1 DISKPART** The key to creating virtual disks is a command-line tool called DiskPart. It's included with Windows 7, and you can start it by entering **diskpart** at the command prompt. We'd stress that if you don't know how to get to the command prompt in Windows, you shouldn't be playing around with this kind of tool.

A new command line window will open (after you've clicked Yes at the UAC alert), with the usual C:\> command prompt replaced by DISKPART >.

**2 LIST DISKS** You can now start issuing commands. To start with, type **list disk**. When you hit Return, you'll see a list of disks on your system, along with their status, size and free space.

**3 CREATE THE IMAGE** The first step in creating a virtual disk is issuing a "create" command, with a few parameters to set the size and the type of disk. The command goes like this: **create vdisk file=filename maximum=xxx type=[fixed/expandable]**. Filename is simply a path; maximum is the size of the disk in KB. If you select type=fixed, a virtual disk file is immediately created that fills the entire maximum size and won't change. With type=expandable, the file starts at just

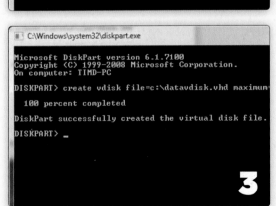

a few KB and grows as required up to the maximum. Note that its size is always reported to the OS as the maximum, for instance when you right-click on the disk and choose Properties to see the free-space pie chart.

So to create a disk that starts tiny but could go up to 30GB, you'd enter **create vdisk file=c:\datavdisk. vhd maximum=30000 type=expandable**. When you do this for the first time, Windows 7 will automatically install a driver called Microsoft VHD HBA. Look in the location you've set for the disk (in our example, the root of C) and you'll find a virtual disk file with the name you specified.

 **SELECT THE DISK** The disk won't pop up in Windows Explorer just yet, however; there are still a few more steps. You first need to select that disk so it has focus in DiskPart, and to do this you use the "sel" tool: **sel vdisk file=c:\datavdisk.vhd**. Now attach the disk file to the system by typing **attach vdisk**.

 **CREATE A PARTITION** So far, the virtual disk is like a blank, unpartitioned and unformatted drive. Create a primary partition, select it, make it active and format it using the following commands:
**create part primary**
**sel part 1**
**active**
**format fs=ntfs quick**

 **ASSIGN THE DISK** Now a single magic word will make the disk visible to Windows: **assign**. A new disk immediately pops up in Windows Explorer and you can use it just like any other drive.

 **CLEVER INSTALLATION** At this point, Ultimate owners could do a clean install of Windows 7 (see p22). Alternatively, use DiskPart with your existing Windows installation. To start installation, put the Windows 7 DVD in the drive, reboot, and hit a key to run Setup when you're prompted. Once you get to the welcome screen, the clever part begins. Your virtual disk needs creating, so hit <Shift+F10> to pop up a command prompt. Type **diskpart** to start the DiskPart tool.

**INSTALL WINDOWS 7** Now to create your virtual disk. Type **create vdisk file=c:\win7disk.vhd type=fixed maximum=30000**. Give the disk the focus by typing **sel vdisk file=c:\win7disk.vhd**. Now attach it to the system with **attach vdisk**. Enter **exit** twice to exit both DiskPart and the command prompt.

Proceed with the installation as normal, opting for Clean install and selecting the virtual hard disk as the installation drive. As far as the system is concerned, the virtual drive acts as a fixed disk. After installation, you effectively have a dual-boot system, but if you select Windows 7 as the OS it boots from the virtual disk image. To back up the whole system any time, just copy the file!

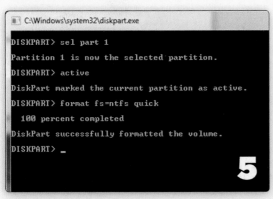

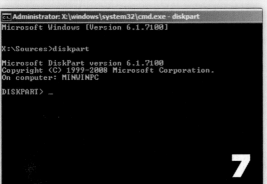

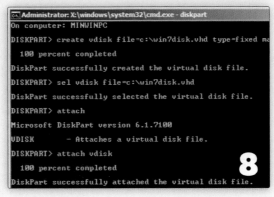

*Tip*

As you might expect, you can't just delete a virtual hard disk file once it's mounted in Windows. That's just as well, since it prevents nasty accidents. To remove a virtual disk, fire up DiskPart and make sure you have the correct disk selected. Use the **list disk** command to check: the currently selected disk is marked with an asterisk. Then enter the **remove** command by itself. The disk will disappear from the Computer view and you'll then be able to delete or move the file.

YOU CAN OFTEN COMPLETE TASKS MORE QUICKLY IF YOU AVOID USING THE MOUSE. HERE ARE THE HANDIEST KEY SHORTCUTS TO BE FOUND IN WINDOWS 7.

# Windows 7 keyboard shortcuts

Press the Windows key to open the Start menu. Begin typing when you let go, and Windows will search for whatever you enter. Try the first few letters of the name of a program, for example. Once the correct item appears, press Return.

To jump to an advanced search, including any search connectors you've installed (see p50), hold down the Windows key while pressing F.

To minimise all the currently open windows, giving a clear view of the desktop and your Gadgets, press <Windows+D>. Hit it again and your windows will reappear as before.

Press <Windows+E> and Windows Explorer shows your Computer window.

## Tip

You can carry on adding your own keyboard shortcuts until you run out of keys, and you're not limited to assigning them to applications – you can also launch specific files or folders by creating shortcuts to them and assigning key combinations to the shortcuts, as explained on the opposite page.

Pressing <Windows+L> locks your PC – ideal if you're going out and don't want others to access it. You can also switch users.

A favourite of Windows pros, <Windows+R> brings up the Run dialog box. Enter an application name or folder to open it.

Holding down the Windows key, keep pressing T and Windows will cycle through all the programs sitting in your Taskbar.

If you know you want to launch, say, the third program in the Taskbar, press that number with the Windows key and it will instantly activate.

If you want to start a new instance of a program – say, you already have Internet Explorer open, but you want to open a separate browser window – press Shift and the number of the program in the Taskbar to launch it afresh.

Similarly, press Alt with a number and the Windows key to open the Jump List for that program. Could be handy.

Windows' Aero Flip 3D effect always looks great in computer showrooms. Impress your friends by activating it using the <Windows+Tab> keyboard shortcut.

This one requires nimble fingers, but if you have a huge desktop spanned across multiple monitors it's a godsend: use this triple combination to move a selected window from one screen to another in an instant.

The Windows key plus the up arrow maximises the window you're working on. Yes, the down arrow minimises it.

Even better, the Windows key plus the left cursor arrow will move a program to the left of the screen; the right arrow moves it to the right.

# HOW TO...
# CREATE YOUR OWN SHORTCUTS

*If you're not satisfied with the ability to pin a program to the Taskbar or find it with a quick search, use this method to assign a keyboard shortcut to it.*

Probably the shortcut we use most, this quickly selects which monitor is active. You can duplicate your display, extend it, or switch to an external monitor or projector alone. Great when setting up a PC for a presentation.

Opens the Ease of Access Center, ready for you to start up tools such as the Narrator, Magnifier and On-Screen Keyboard.

One for laptop users only: <Windows+X> launches Windows Mobility Center.

And finally, here's another way to minimise all your windows at once. Unlike with <Windows+D>, you can't repeat it to restore them: instead, use the same combination with the addition of the Shift key.

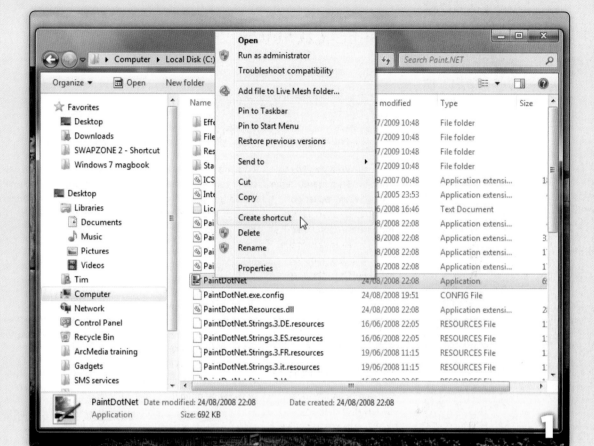

**FIND YOUR APPLICATION** First, navigate your way to your chosen program. You'll probably find it hiding away in C:\Program Files. Our example is the excellent free utility Paint.NET, installed by default to C:\Program Files\Paint.NET. Having found the application file, right-click it and select Create Shortcut.

**ADD A KEY COMBINATION** You may be prompted to save the shortcut to the desktop; click Yes. Right-click on the newly created shortcut icon and select Properties. You should see this dialog (left), which controls everything from the compatibility level of the file – for example, telling Windows 7 that it must be run in Windows XP compatibility mode – to its displayed name. Here, click on the Shortcut tab. We're interested in the "Shortcut key" box, so click on this. Whichever key you next hit will be the nominated shortcut key to work in combination with Ctrl and Alt.

Click OK. You may be prompted to enter the Administrator password before your shortcut takes effect. This done, you can press <Ctrl+Alt+1> (or whichever key you chose) and your program will instantly launch. Note that certain keys aren't valid – Esc, Enter and the spacebar – and that if the program already has a shortcut associated with it, your new key combo may not work.

# IN THIS CHAPTER

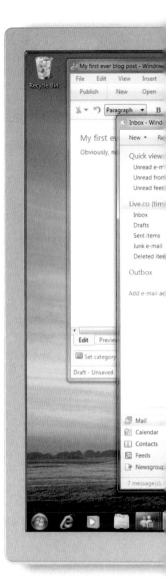

**5**

*Enhance Windows 7*

# ENHANCE WINDO

Windows 7 is the most streamlined version yet. By that we mean it's efficient, but also stripped-down: there's no email client like Outlook Express, no photo manager and no MSN Messenger. Instead, updated versions of these applications (and more) have been rolled into Windows Live Essentials, which you need to download. These useful apps integrate tightly with

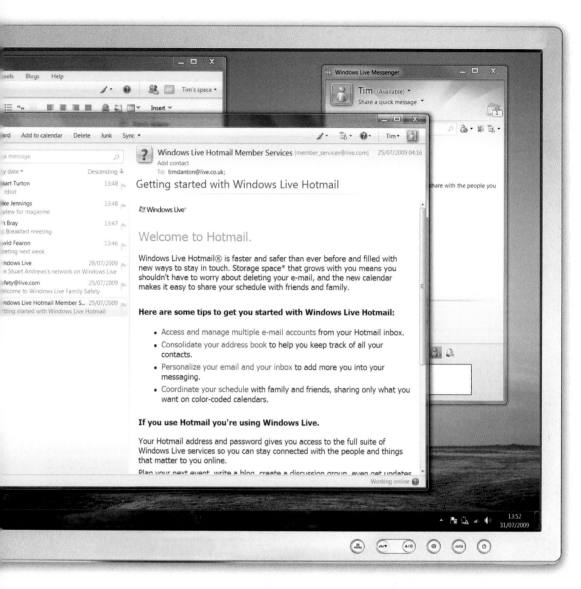

# NS 7 FOR FREE

Microsoft's online Live service, so albums created in Photo Gallery can be dropped into emails or posted on your Windows Live Spaces blog. It's all easy to use and, most importantly, free. Here we examine what each Live Essentials app offers, and round things off with our pick of the excellent non-Microsoft additions to Windows 7 that you can also get for free.

WINDOWS LIVE MAIL IS A SURPRISINGLY POWERFUL OFFLINE MAIL APPLICATION, WITH BUILT-IN ANTI-PHISHING AND A HANDY CALENDAR TOO.

# Introducing Windows Live Mail

If you currently use a webmail service such as Microsoft's Hotmail or Yahoo! Mail, then Windows Live Mail (not to be confused with the Windows Live Mail webmail service) is your ticket to freedom. Instead of relying on a constant internet connection, Windows Live Mail downloads email to your hard disk, so you can refer to it whenever you want, and indexes it, making it easy to find messages. Alternatively, if you prefer to use the email supplied by your internet service provider (such as BT or TalkTalk), you can receive and reply to email in Windows Live Mail rather than using a web browser. It's much easier and more integrated.

**PHISHING TRIP** There are numerous websites out there that are designed to look like a trusted site – such as an online bank – and encourage you to enter your details, which they record and then use to hijack your account. To hook you, they send emails purporting to be from, say, Barclays, telling you to check your balance or update your information.

This is "phishing", and Windows Live Mail has extra features to beat it. Messages from suspicious sources are partially blocked, allowing you to see plain text but not links or images. This helps to protect you from objectionable content, as well as reducing the chances of you clicking on a fraudulent link without thinking. Viewing an image could confirm back to the scammers that your email address is working, encouraging them to target you again.

**ADDING PICTURES** If you email a lot of pictures, you'll also appreciate Live Mail's close ties to Windows Live. When you add pictures to a message, they aren't simply attached, as in Outlook, but are sent to a Microsoft Live server, while the body of your message and the image thumbnails go to the email recipient. The resulting email is smaller and faster for the recipient to download. To see your full set of pictures, they simply click on one of the image thumbnails and are taken to an online slideshow.

**DATING GAME** There's no longer a separate calendar application supplied with Windows 7 or the Windows Live suite. Instead, Live Mail now includes a full-blown calendar. You can invite people to events on your calendar via email. If you want other people to be able to see your appointments, you can set up an online calendar at http://calendar.live.com and then edit it with the Windows Live Mail application.

## Tip

Live Mail has a surprising number of features for a free application. For instance, click "Add to calendar" at the top to copy the contents of an email into a new calendar entry, avoiding the need to flick between the Calendar and Mail sections of the applications. To set up a service that sends upcoming calendar appointments to your mobile phone as text messages, click on the Menu button, then on Deliver my reminders.

This is the main Windows Live Mail interface. If you look down at the bottom of the left-hand navigation bar, you'll see extra options for features such as the Calendar, Contacts, RSS feeds (from news sites and blogs) and – a relic of the 1990s, surely – internet newsgroups.

# Introducing Windows Live Photo Gallery

*No matter how large your photo collection, Windows Live's Photo Gallery will keep it organised. It may be the only photo management tool you need.*

With the advanced handling of image thumbnails within Windows 7, you could be excused for thinking you don't need a standalone photo gallery application at all, but there's a lot to be said for having all your photo folders accessible through the same interface. Windows Live Photo Gallery offers exactly that, with plenty of options for sorting your pictures. You can add tags to your images en masse, for example, or view every photo taken on a particular day. There are plenty of applications out there that offer similar features, such as Google's terrific Picasa (see p74), but Photo Gallery is well worth trying first.

**GET TAGGING** Photo Gallery's logical approach to displaying images makes it easy to use, but to get the most out of it you need tags. In the left-hand navigation bar, browse down to Descriptive Tags, then click "Add a new tag". You might name it something like Holidays – a category that will apply to a number of images across multiple folders. You can then drag individual photos to your tag, or select images by clicking the tickbox that appears when you hover over one, then drag any of those selected files to the tag to apply it to all the images at once.

In future, whenever you want to see all the photos with a particular tag, you need only click on the tag in the left-hand column and they'll instantly appear in the main window. Another nice feature is that Live Photo Gallery automatically detects the names of your friends from other Live services (such as Messenger), and auto-fills the People tags with their names.

**MAKE IT BETTER** Live Photo Gallery also includes a number of photo-editing tools. None of them will trouble photo software giants such as Adobe, but if you have an image that's too dark or needs rotating a little, clicking Fix is the first step. Here you can make colours punchier, or make the image brighter or darker using Adjust exposure. The all-important red-eye tool will exorcise satanic mates.

**SHARE YOUR SHOTS** Besides the option to turn a selection of shots into a video slideshow – as simple as pressing the "Slide show" button – Windows Live Photo Gallery offers many ways to get your shots online. The simplest approach is to select a batch of photos, then click Publish | Online album. Using your Windows Live account details, your images are automatically resized and sent. Once they're online, you can determine who else can see them – if anyone – and view a slideshow. Alternatively, you can use Live Photo Gallery to send images to www.flickr.com.

## Tip

Even if you already use a more advanced image editor than Windows Live Photo Gallery, don't write off the application before you try it. For example, it has a very easy-to-use Print feature, which lets you see exactly how your images will print on your choice of photo paper. Much better than an expensive course of trial and error.

## Tip

Photo Gallery now supports face recognition. Click on a photo and if there's a face, you can choose who from your contacts it is via the dropdown menu.

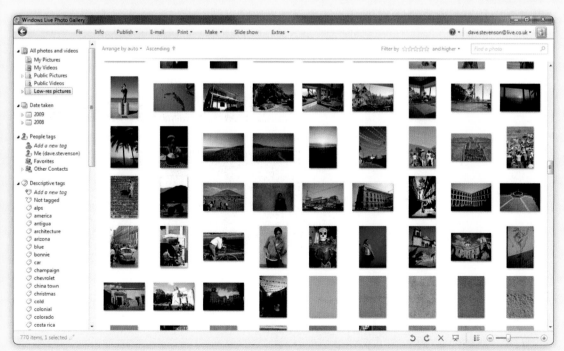

What makes Live Photo Gallery such a clever tool is that it's easy to use – anyone will quickly understand it. But it has a number of extra tools if you want to tap into its power. Just beware that its editing skills are basic; it's there to organise photos, not manipulate them.

WINDOWS LIVE WRITER MAKES IT EASY TO CREATE YOUR OWN BLOG, FROM SETTING IT UP TO POSTING TEXT, PHOTOS, VIDEO CLIPS AND MORE.

# Introducing Windows Live Writer

Starting a blog is almost obligatory these days, but it can be hard work. Signing up, managing the design and keeping it updated all takes time. Windows Live Writer ties in closely with Windows Live Spaces and, with minimum fuss, allows you to edit a blog from a user-friendly text editor. If you've used WordPad or Microsoft Word, it will feel familiar.

**MAKE A DEBUT** When you first start Live Writer, you'll be asked which blogging service you currently use. If you're already signed up to WordPress, for instance, this is the place to give Writer your details. Alternatively, if you click the option labelled "I don't have a blog; create one on Windows Live for me", you'll be prompted to enter your Windows Live details. Once that's done, you'll be greeted by a standard-looking text editor. Tap in a few lines, hit the Publish button at the top left and your first post will appear.

**MAKE IT SHINE** It isn't just words, though. The right-hand toolbar has a number of options to spice up your new blog. This starts with Pictures, which embeds single images and can produce spectacular results. Hit Photo Album, for instance, and a selection of your images will be transformed into a single image, with a link that takes your readers to your Live photo albums. Alternatively, clicking Video lets you select a video from MSN's Soapbox or YouTube to embed in your post. Writer is also smart enough to look at any videos you've created using Windows Movie Maker.

Finally, clicking Maps brings up Microsoft Virtual Earth. Drag the map around until it looks how you want – centre it on the location you're blogging about, for example – then click Insert and the map will appear. The only limitation is that your readers can't drag the map around within your page; instead, clicking it will take them to Virtual Earth.

**MAKE IT COMPLICATED** Writer also conceals some surprisingly complex and powerful tools. Click "Add a plug-in", on the Insert menu, and you're taken to a website where you can get free add-ons for services such as Flickr, or a tool that lets you add files for your readers to download.

Finally, take note of the three tabs at the bottom of the screen. Clicking on Preview will allow you to see what your post will look like in a web browser, while Source, for the more ambitious blogger, lets you edit the source code of your post to get it looking exactly the way you want.

These days, blogging is about far more than just text, which is why Windows Live Writer – despite its name – offers numerous ways to add pictures, video and other extra titbits to your posts. It's easy to create a blog, or you can work with a blogging service you already use.

*Tip*

The key to a widely read blog is frequency, so try to make sure you write a few new posts every week. Keep things interesting by including plenty of pictures and responding to other users' comments, and the hits will stack up. The easier it is to do, the more likely you are to keep doing it regularly, which is one reason why a tool such as Windows Live Writer is such a boon.

# Introducing
# Windows Live Movie Maker

*These days we're all shooting video, but the free-to-download Movie Maker means you don't need to spend money on software to edit and enhance it.*

Removed from the standard Windows installation in Windows 7, Movie Maker is now part of the Windows Live Essentials pack and has undergone a massive overhaul. It's well worth trying before you invest in third-party video editing software, which could set you back about £100.

In fact, Movie Maker includes most of the tools you're likely to need to create impressively polished home movies. It might not turn you into Steven Spielberg, but it will let you get the most out of your footage, whether shot on the latest HD kit or a point-and-shoot pocket camera.

**EDITING SUITE** Movie Maker's innovative storyboard/timeline editing view occupies the right half of its window, providing the main overview of your project. Here, all the clips that will go to make up your movie are displayed in a "film reel" thumbnail view. Adding clips – and audio or photos, for that matter – is simply a matter of dragging them onto this pane. Rearranging them in time is a simple matter of dragging clips from A to B, and navigation is incredibly easy: just use the cursor to skip to whatever point in your project you want.

**CLIP SHOW** Movie Maker has adopted the Ribbon interface seen in WordPad and Paint (see p42). This tabbed toolbar makes it simple and quick to access a wide range of tools. Just click any clip, and anything not applicable to the movie in question disappears from the bar.

There's also a neat Ribbon enhancement, specific to the new version of Movie Maker, where coloured flags appear above "active" toolbars. Move the cursor to a segment of movie featuring audio and text, and labels appear above the appropriate toolbar tab.

**CUT TO THE CHASE** It's no match for Adobe Premiere Elements, but the editing tools in Movie Maker are both surprisingly powerful and easy to use. You can trim and split clips quickly to get rid of unwanted bloopers; boost or reduce volume levels; and even lift dull footage with the Brightness tool. Animations and fades can be added to text elements, and there's a gallery of transitions to add fades or wipes between scenes.

You can spend hours perfecting your productions, but you don't have to: a number of automatic tools can speed up the whole process. AutoMovie takes your choice of movie clips, photographs and music, and adds titles and credits, crossfade transitions between each clip, and even zoom and pan effects to make your still photos more interesting to look at.

see p42

## Tip

Once you've created your movie, you need to render it to a video file. Movie Maker includes a number of formats, including an option to upload straight to YouTube, so friends and family across the globe can see the results of your handywork.

There's a library of transitions (the bits that go between your clips) on the **Animations** ribbon, including fades, wipes and reveals.

**AutoMovie** takes the hassle out of home movies, adding title, credits and transitions for you, and even automatically fitting the movie to a music track.

Once you're happy with your movie, you can use the **Sharing options** to upload it straight to YouTube, burn a DVD, or produce a plain video file for viewing on a computer.

Movie Maker's hybrid storyboard/timeline **Editing pane** gives you an at-a-glance view of the length and content of your clips. Drag the **cursor** through clips to view from a specific point or position edits.

You can add **titles, captions and credits** with a single click, then edit the text in the Preview pane below.

See how your movie is taking shape in the **Preview pane**; the controls below allow you to go forward or back frame by frame for more precise editing.

The simple **zoom slider** makes it a doddle to get a full overview of your project or move in to see parts in detail.

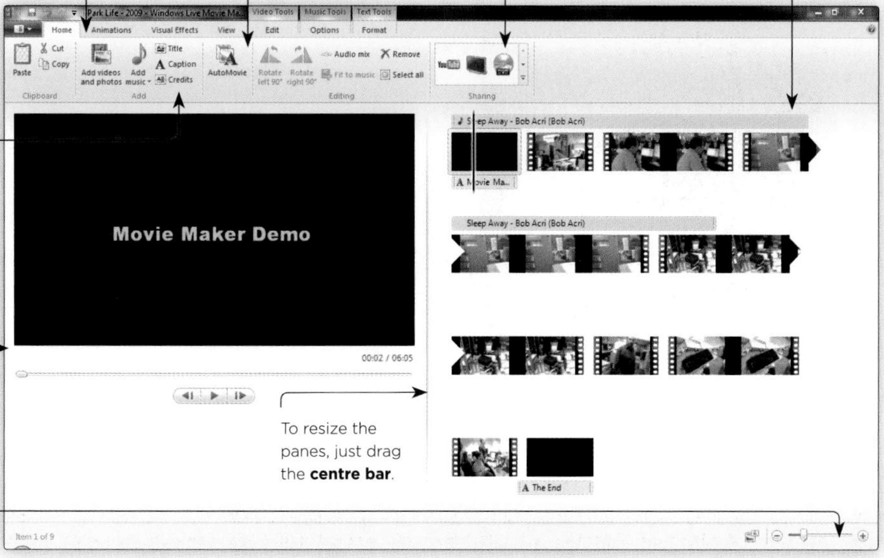

Movie Maker Demo

To resize the panes, just drag the **centre bar**.

MICROSOFT'S NEW ONLINE STORAGE SERVICE OFFERS AS MUCH SPACE AS
YOU'RE LIKELY TO NEED, FOR FREE. AT HEART, IT'S ALL ABOUT SHARING.

# Introducing SkyDrive

SkyDrive from Microsoft gives you an enormous 25GB of online space, dwarfing the 1 or 2GB you get free with rival services such as Dropbox ([www.getdropbox.com](www.getdropbox.com)). All you need is a browser and a Windows Live ID, and you can access this space from any PC with an internet connection.

Uploading files is easy. Sign into Windows Live using your Windows Live ID (you already have one if you use Hotmail, for example), click the More link at the top of the homepage, then select SkyDrive from the menu. There are four folders – Documents, Favorites, Shared Favorites and Public – and you can add your own via the Create Folder link. Choose a folder, then click "Add files". You can upload five at a time by clicking Browse and navigating to your file(s). To download files, sign in, access your SkyDrive, find the relevant folder, click on a file, then click Download.

It's possible to use SkyDrive as a safe online store for vital files and documents, or as a space to transfer files between PCs. However, since SkyDrive can't actively schedule backups or synchronise updated files, a service such as Live Mesh or Mozy ([www.mozy.com](www.mozy.com)) might be a better option. SkyDrive scores highly on two other counts, though. First, that 25GB capacity makes it better suited

to today's large media files than more restrictive services. Second, SkyDrive is more than just a dumb online space: it's designed to let you share files, photos and documents.

**GROUP THERAPY** SkyDrive integrates with the sharing and collaboration features of Windows Live, so you can make files available to the world at large or to your contacts. These can be divided into categories, so family members don't get confidential business reports and colleagues don't get baby photos, and members are alerted when you add or change files. SkyDrive is especially well suited to photo sharing. You can upload individual images, or even create galleries and upload them to your online space. Share your holiday snaps with friends or contacts in your network and they'll get a message announcing your new uploads. They can view your images singly or in a slideshow, and add comments to tell you exactly how silly you look in your favourite beach shirt.

If you want informal comments on a speech, sales pitch, letter or report, this is a quick-and-dirty way of getting a document out there and feedback back in. Why not use the Description field to give your contacts an idea of what you're doing and what you're expecting from them?

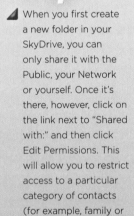

*Tip*

When you first create a new folder in your SkyDrive, you can only share it with the Public, your Network or yourself. Once it's there, however, click on the link next to "Shared with:" and then click Edit Permissions. This will allow you to restrict access to a particular category of contacts (for example, family or co-workers) or even to specific individuals.

With its more-than-generous 25GB of free storage space, SkyDrive lends itself well to photo sharing, but there's no reason why you can't use it for more businesslike purposes, such as sharing notes on a big project between a number of colleagues.

# Introducing
# Windows Live Messenger

*Formerly known as MSN Messenger, what started off as a simple, instant messaging application is now a great all-round communication tool.*

When it launched ten years ago, MSN Messenger was a simple program that allowed you to contact friends or associates and text chat to them in real-time. Since then, it's grown to become the Windows Live Messenger we know today: a real-time chat client that's just as much at home with voice and video calls as text-based chat.

Messenger works with your existing Windows Live identity and can share contacts with Windows Live Mail and SkyDrive. The main window makes it easy to set your current status (Available, Busy, Away, or the sneaky Appear Offline) and check the status of your contacts. To start a conversation, just double-click on a name; to initiate a PC-to-PC voice or video call, click the Show menu button to the right of the Search bar, then Actions | Call A Contact's Computer Or Video | Start A Video Call.

Even text chat is as rich as it gets. Static emoticons are supported by animated "winks". During chat, you can switch to video or voice, and even play a selection of simple games with your contact. You can send files to other users during a conversation, or publish them to your SkyDrive from within Messenger.

Over the last few years, Microsoft has tried to make Messenger a sort of hub for your social networking, both in Windows Live and outside. As well as a Search bar and links to MSN services, you'll find What's New updates on changes within your Windows Live networks, plus a Facebook button that lets you make and check updates to the social networking service without leaving Messenger.

**TEAM EFFORT** The program's real sharing power lies in its group features. You can create groups with the same ease as adding contacts: click the button next to the Search bar, then select Create a Group and follow the simple instructions. Once you have a group, you can invite contacts to join it, then use the group as a place to have online and offline discussions and share photos and files.

It's easy to set up text chats with multiple users, and each group gets its own Windows Live web page and shared calendar. This can be a great way of sharing interests or keeping in touch with family or friends, but it also turns Messenger into a business tool for simple collaborative projects or maintaining communications between colleagues with a shared agenda.

Finally, don't forget Live Messenger isn't tied in to desktop Windows. A browser-based client works on most mobile phones, and a more fully featured version is available for Windows Mobile, BlackBerry and Symbian S60. It's becoming a very handy service indeed.

## *Tip*

Messenger allows you to set a different background for the window that displays each of your conversations. If this seems like needless cosmetic frippery, think again: when you're moaning about your useless boss to your friend in one window, and discussing a crucial project with that same boss in another, it really helps to have a clear visual reminder of which window is which as you casually type your next reply. Take it from us.

It's easy to set up chats between **multiple users** for a family confab or virtual meeting.

Extras like **animated smileys** make chat more fun – although you're not forced to use them, of course.

You can send messages to friends even when they're **offline**.

**5**

*Enhance Windows 7*

MICROSOFT'S PIONEERING CLOUD STORAGE SERVICE IS A GREAT WAY TO SHARE DOCUMENTS AND DATA BETWEEN COMPUTERS AND BETWEEN PEOPLE.

# Introducing Windows Live Mesh

When its own SkyDrive (see p70) provides 25GB of free online storage, offering another 5GB service might seem a redundant move for Microsoft. Live Mesh, however, is something different – and potentially more powerful.

On one level, it's a means of ensuring that every Windows PC, notebook and netbook that you use (and, eventually, every Linux system, Apple Mac and smartphone) will have access to the files and media you need to do your work and live your life. It's also a remote access service, so you can use your own PC from another via the internet.

On yet another level, it's a system for sharing and collaborating. Sure, you can share photos or documents with SkyDrive or Dropbox, but Live Mesh goes further.

Think of it as a connected "mesh" of devices, each hosting a number of identical folders, marked for synchronisation. Whenever a file is added or modified in one of these folders on one device, the others update too. And the same files are synchronised to a folder in a 5GB online storage space, your Live Desktop. Files on the Live Desktop are available to you from any device with a web browser, protected by your Windows Live ID and password.

**SIGN ON** All this might sound complicated, but working with Live Mesh is surprisingly easy. First you need to sign on to Live Mesh from your main PC. Then, from the main

Devices page, you click the Add Device button to download and install the Live Mesh software. Then you repeat those steps for every Windows XP, Vista or Windows 7 PC you use.

To choose what to synchronise, right-click any folder on your PC and select "Add folder to Live Mesh". Or upload or create a new folder on your Live Desktop, and any file you add will appear in a new folder of the same name on every PC. All you need to do is double-click the new shortcut that appears on each machine's desktop and click OK when the "Synchronize folder with this computer" dialog appears.

That covers *your* systems, but what happens if you need to access a file from someone else's? Well, like most online storage services, Live Mesh also allows you to connect using a standard web browser. In fact, you can even download files onto many internet-capable mobile phones by pointing the built-in browser to https://m.mesh.com. If your smartphone uses Windows Mobile 6, a specific Live Mesh mobile client allows you to add it to the mesh and keep it in sync with your desktop and laptop systems.

**HIT THE BAR** Live Mesh likes to keep you informed. When you open a synced folder on any PC, you'll find a slimline info bar, the Mesh Bar, attached to it. Click on the double arrows to expand it, or one of the three icons underneath, and you'll get a tabbed window with news on any files that

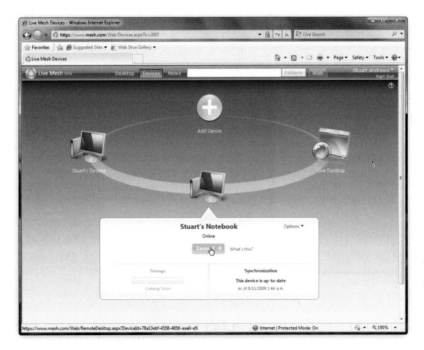

Live Mesh keeps your documents and media synchronised between all your PCs and also makes it easy to share data with other users. This ensures everyone is always looking at the latest version and can get access to it from wherever they may be.

*Tip*

Live Mesh will synchronise across a local network if two synced systems are connected to it, making it a remarkably speedy solution if you want to sync media libraries between several home PCs. Just ensure your media folders aren't set to sync with the Live Desktop too. You must also be very wary of what you delete: once a synced file is gone, it's gone from all your PCs.

have recently been added or modified, details of the devices where the folder is synchronised, and the names of all Live Mesh users who are listed as "members" of the folder.

This is where Live Mesh becomes interesting. It's a great tool if you want to synchronise important documents, a music library or a collection of photos between several PCs that you own, but even better if you're collaborating on a project with family, friends, colleagues or associates. Click the Members tab in the Mesh Bar that's glued to any synced folder, and you'll see an option to invite other Live Mesh users to share it. Do that, and each prospective member will receive an email asking them to accept your invitation (and sign up for Live Mesh if they haven't already). Once they've done so, any file you add or change in the shared folder will be updated across all its members' folders. To keep things under control, there are three levels of access: Owner (with full administrative rights), Contributor (who can read/write files but not administer) and Reader (who can only read files, and whose changes won't be synced back).

The News section of the Mesh Bar and the smaller Live Mesh pop-up that appears above the taskbar keep everyone up to date on any changes, and members can also post messages for each other using the New Post link in the News section.

**GRAB THE REMOTE** We're not done yet, however: Live Mesh has one more trick up its sleeve. Provided you allow it, you can use Live Mesh as a remote access tool, controlling any Windows PC in the mesh from any other. Hook up your work system and your PC at home, for example, and you can find and open documents, send and receive emails and run most applications on your home machine from the comfort of your office desk – or vice versa, if you don't have a particularly security-conscious IT department.

To connect, click on the Live Mesh icon in the taskbar, click on the Devices icon in the middle of the bottom bar, then click on the "Connect to Device" link under the system of your choice. Remote access also works even if you can't use a PC that's already linked in to the Mesh. In Internet Explorer, go to www.mesh.com, sign in, click on your home PC and then click the yellow Connect link. You'll need to have enabled the synchronisation and Live Mesh Remote Desktop enhancements on your home PC when you set it up on the Mesh; annoyingly, there's no easy way of doing this after installation.

It's a great technology, but there are a few caveats. First, the system you're trying to control must be on and signed in to Live Mesh for it to work; you can put a system to sleep by remote control, but not wake it up. This isn't good news if you're going away for a week and you want to access your home PC from your laptop while away.

Second, you need to be realistic about which applications you can use. With everything limited by the speed of the connection between your home PC and your away system, intensive apps such as BBC iPlayer or Call of Duty: Modern Warfare are, unfortunately, unlikely to work.

Your Live Desktop is accessible both from your own PCs, via Windows 7, and from other systems using a web browser interface. Files can be shared with other members as well as synced between your own devices.

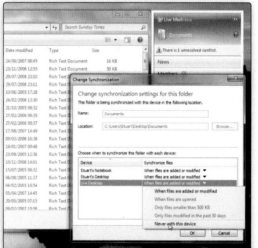

You can control which folders synchronise with which devices, or with the Live Desktop. Right-click a folder on your Live Desktop and select Change Sync Settings, and you can choose which devices will sync and when. This is a useful way of keeping, say, a large music library up to date across multiple PCs, without copying every track to your 5GB Live Desktop or your netbook.

By installing the Live Mesh Remote Desktop software on your own PC, you can control it from elsewhere via Live Mesh, using your files and applications just as if you were sitting at your computer.

GET EVEN MORE OUT OF YOUR WINDOWS 7 PC WITHOUT SPENDING A PENNY: WORK, PLAY AND COMMUNICATE BETTER WITH THESE TEN FREE PROGRAMS.

# Top ten free apps for Windows 7

## *Tip*

There are lots of places online to find more free apps, including reputable listings of freeware, shareware and demo programs such as www.tucows.com, and open-source software repositories such as www.sourceforge. net. Even advanced tasks can be catered for without shelling out: for example, Google's SketchUp (sketchup.google.com) is a comprehensive 3D drawing system, while Audacity (audacity. sourceforge.net) offers excellent sound-recording and editing tools. Just remember to double-check that you trust the source before downloading any software, since the risk of unwittingly installing malware is very real – see chapter 8, Staying safe in Windows.

## 7-Zip

As long as anyone has to package large files – or groups of small files – for transfer across the internet, there will always be a need for a good file compression/decompression utility. Windows 7 has its own built-in options, but 7-Zip is speedier and more efficient, and you can make your own compressed archives just by right-clicking on a folder, then selecting 7-Zip and "Add to archive". 7-Zip will compress to the common ZIP and TAR file formats, plus 7-Zip's own, ultra-efficient 7z, and will also read RAR and LZH formats. www.7-zip.org

## Google Picasa

Windows Live Photo Gallery (see p67) can organise your photos, but Picasa does a more comprehensive job, scouring your hard disks for images and filing them in reverse chronological order. From there you can organise them into albums, with handy searchable descriptions. Its built-in editing tools provide a range of basic corrections and adjustments to your images, and even add special effects. Other options allow you to create slideshows and screensavers, order prints from UK services, and upload pictures to Picasa web albums. http://picasa.google.com

## Pidgin

Windows Live Messenger is great for communicating via Windows Live or Yahoo, but what if you have friends on AIM, Google Talk, ICQ or Apple iChat? Pity the fool who uses separate chat apps, when Pidgin allows you to access all of these from one. Just add your own account details for each of the various chat services, and Pidgin presents you with a unified "buddy list" for them all. You can even hold several conversations on different services at the same time. You'll love it when a plan comes together. www.pidgin.im

## Paint.NET

This much-loved image editor has more than enough tools for most amateur photographers. It's also blessed with a user-friendly interface, and will run on any modern PC. Features include serious adjustment and retouch tools, plus the ability to build up and manipulate parts of an image in Photoshop-style layers. Paint.NET also boasts a range of special effects, and a strong community of users is constantly adding features in the form of free plugins. http://paint.net

# Mozilla Thunderbird

Windows Live Mail (see p66) is a fine email program, but there are a number of free alternatives, and if you use Mozilla's Firefox web browser its natural complement is Thunderbird. It's always been adept at handling multiple accounts, and now Firefox-style tabs make it even easier to keep track of incoming and outgoing email, as well as your favourite blogs and RSS feeds. Accounts are easy to set up, and efficient search contributes to a fast, responsive feel. www.mozillamessaging.com

# FileZilla

If you ever have to transfer files using FTP via Internet Explorer, you'll know how slow and painful the process can be. FileZilla makes it easy. You can add frequently used FTP sites to the Site Manager, or just enter the details into the Quickconnect bar at the top. After that, it's just a question of selecting a folder on your computer on the left, navigating through the FTP site on the right, then dragging the files you want from one to the other. If you have lots of files to transfer at once, FileZilla saves a huge amount of time and bother. http://filezilla-project.org

# Google Earth

Google's majestic virtual globe was a breakthrough Web 2.0 app, and it keeps getting better. Enjoy the satellite imagery, zoom in to Street View to nose around, or take a trip through the 3D skyscrapers of New York. It's also a rich source of information, whether you want to find local hotels or take a tour of WWF conservation projects. Then there's the built-in flight simulator and the cosmological Sky layer... http://earth.google.co.uk

# HandBrake

Video files are the fiddliest to convert between formats. With built-in support for the widely used H.264, XviD and DivX codecs, Windows 7 is the most video-friendly version yet, but there are still formats it doesn't support, and getting video onto mobile devices remains tricky. HandBrake can no longer copy commercial DVDs without major tweaking (it's illegal, you see), but if you have unencrypted material that you want to play on your PC, iPod, media player or handheld games console, it's a great tool. There are presets for iPods, but it isn't difficult to create custom settings for other players. And if you do obtain files in formats that Windows 7 can't manage, HandBrake will convert them. http://handbrake.fr

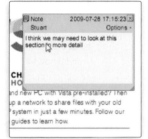

# Foxit Reader

Adobe Reader, the standard tool for viewing PDFs, is a bloated 25.5MB download and notorious for its update nags. At 3.5MB, Foxit is much faster to launch and use, yet it supports advanced features such as interactive forms and annotations (above). It may lack the 3D and multimedia feature support of the official Adobe package, but few PDFs use these. For everyday purposes, it's the aggro-free way to read PDFs.
www.foxitsoftware.com/pdf/reader/

# OpenOffice.Org

Microsoft Office remains the standard business suite, but this free alternative will suit many individuals and small firms just fine. OpenOffice.Org may not quite be able to match Office 2007's easy-to-use Ribbon interface or the incredible depth and breadth of features in programs like Word, but if you've used Office it's easy to get started with this suite, and the core word processing, spreadsheet, database and presentation apps offer most of the everyday features of their Microsoft equivalents. These aren't cut-down tools but highly capable applications, and strong online documentation along with an enthusiastic user base provide the reassurance of comprehensive support should you get stuck. www.openoffice.org

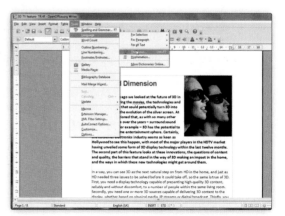

# IN THIS CHAPTER

**6**

*Internet & networking*

# INTERNET AND

Windows 7 is designed for a networked world, and in this chapter we'll show you how to get up and running online – both on the internet and on your home network. However you use Windows, you're certain to want a web browser, so we start with an overview of the major options: there are more choices than many people realise, each with its own strengths and

# NETWORKING

weaknesses. We'll also explain how to set up a wireless network and connect your Windows 7 PC to it with maximum speed and security. Finally, we'll show you how Windows 7's new HomeGroup feature makes it a breeze to share files and even printers between multiple PCs, and walk you through the steps involved if you need the flexibility to share individual items.

MICROSOFT'S WEB BROWSER ISN'T YOUR ONLY CHOICE, BUT ITS LATEST
INCARNATION IS FAST, FRIENDLY AND FULL OF FEATURES TO MAKE LIFE EASIER.

# Introducing Internet Explorer 8

Microsoft's web browser has been around since the mid 1990s. But the latest version, designed alongside Windows 7, is the fastest yet – albeit that others, including Mozilla Firefox, are faster still. But what makes Internet Explorer 8 more interesting is a host of exciting new features.

**BROWSER BALLOT** Previous editions of Windows came with Internet Explorer as their one and only web browser. Although details are still under wraps at the time of writing, if you buy a Windows 7 PC in Europe it's likely to come with a "browser ballot": the option to choose your preferred web browser on installation. The five major choices on the market are Internet Explorer 8, Mozilla Firefox, Google Chrome, Opera and Apple's Safari. As we'll see on the following pages, these are all perfectly good alternatives – but there are also reasons to stick with Microsoft's browser.

Internet Explorer 8 (IE8) is a powerful application. For everyday web surfing, though, it works much like previous versions and other browsers, and its new features are mostly straightforward. One such feature is the address bar along the top. As you'd expect, you can type or paste a web address into this; but you can also type a word, and IE8 will list pages you've visited whose titles or addresses contain that word.

Another way to find pages is via the search box in the top right. Type in a phrase and you'll get results from Microsoft's Bing search engine. If you prefer to use Google or another search service, click the dropdown arrow next to the magnifying glass and follow the instructions.

**TABBED BROWSING** The idea behind tabs is simple. Rather than open a new window for every site you visit, press <Ctrl+T> to open a new tab within the same window, and explore without losing the original page. You can also open a tab by clicking the mini-tab to the right of the tab titles.

You can open any link in a new tab by holding down Ctrl while you click it, or by clicking with the wheel or third button of your mouse. Internet Explorer groups and colour-codes your tabs, so you can see at a glance which tabs are part of the same session. And if you still manage to lose track of them, you can click on the Quick Tabs button, to the left of the tab titles, to see thumbnails of all your tabs. Then just click on one to jump to it.

These are IE8's most useful features for everyday browsing; we look at some of the more advanced additions on the opposite page. There's plenty more to discover, and if you want to know more about any feature there's a help menu just to the right of the Tools menu.

## Tip

Some free software – and indeed some paid-for packages – will "helpfully" add extra toolbars to Internet Explorer (and other browsers). You can easily hide unwanted toolbars by going to the Tools menu, selecting Toolbars and unticking the item in question – although you may prefer simply to uninstall the software altogether.

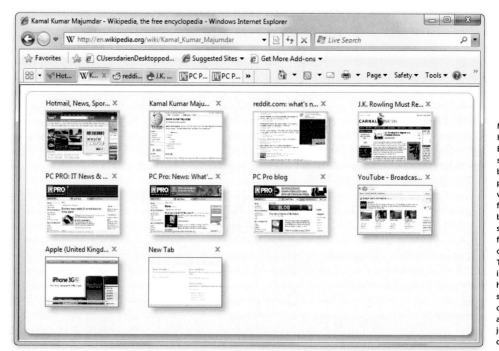

Microsoft's Internet Explorer 8 sticks to the basic browsing principles we're all familiar with, but mixes in some novel features of its own. Quick Tabs is an incredibly handy way to see all your open tabs at a glance and jump to the one you want.

# HOW TO...
# USE IE8'S ADVANCED FEATURES

**① COMPATIBILITY VIEW** Internet Explorer 8 is designed to comply with web standards, so that it displays pages the same way as other browsers. It isn't perfect (as we note overleaf), but in everyday use you shouldn't see any major problems. Unfortunately, this means it doesn't work exactly like IE6 or 7, so pages designed for those versions may not render correctly. To work around this, IE8 provides a "broken page" icon in the address bar. Click it and the browser will switch to Compatibility View, showing the page as it would appear in IE7. You'll find more settings on the Tools menu, including the option to have IE8 automatically enable Compatibility View for sites known to have issues.

**② INPRIVATE BROWSING** While you surf the web, your browser records where you've been and even keeps copies of the pages and graphics you've viewed. It's just to make it easier for you to retrace your steps, and quicker to redraw pages as you navigate back and forth. However, these saved files could leak your personal information to a thief, or reveal to your partner where you've been shopping for a surprise gift. So Internet Explorer 8 introduces a browsing mode called InPrivate, which lets you go about your business without anything being recorded in your browser history or on your hard disk. Turn it on and off from the Safety menu.

**③ WEB ACCELERATORS** Web Accelerators are handy plugins that let you select text from a website and feed it directly into another. For example, if you were reading a technical document and came across an unfamiliar phrase, you could drag the mouse over it, click on the Wikipedia accelerator, and see the definition pop up instantly in a new tab. Another possibility is to send a postcode to Google Maps in just a few clicks. There are dozens of useful accelerators available from the Microsoft website, and more are constantly appearing.

**④ WEB SLICES** At first glance, Web Slices look like ordinary entries on the Favorites bar. But when you click on one, you won't be taken immediately to its originating site; instead, you'll see a small preview window showing the latest content from that site. You can then visit the full-size site, follow a link within the preview, or just go back to what you're doing. The especially clever bit is that slices turn bold to notify you when there's new content available, so you can stay informed without constantly reloading multiple websites. As yet there aren't many sites that work with slices, but hopefully the system will take off, as it's perfect for tracking a news story, following a blog or – as one plugin already allows – keeping on top of an eBay auction.

**HOW LONG?**
Compatibility View and InPrivate browsing can be enabled with a click, but allow 20 minutes to set up accelerators and slices.

**HOW HARD?**
You don't need to be a genius, but configuring online services isn't easy for the novice.

# Introducing Firefox

Firefox, published by the Mozilla Foundation, is a powerful, free web browser that you can use as an alternative to Internet Explorer. If you're running Windows 7 on a new PC, you might find you already have it installed; otherwise, you can download the installer from www.getfirefox.com

Firefox is the world's second most popular browser, after Internet Explorer. It's built up a following by proving faster and less vulnerable to malware attacks than Microsoft's browser. Today, Internet Explorer 8 has stronger security than its predecessors, so malware is less of an issue. But if you use rich, interactive websites – such as Google's Gmail or Google Docs – Firefox feels more responsive than its rival. On our test system, we found the latest version completed the SunSpider web applications benchmark in 1.3 seconds, while IE8 took 5.9 seconds for the same test.

Firefox also uses a more standards-compliant rendering engine, which in English means it's more likely to display pages correctly. It isn't perfect: in the strict Acid3 test it scores 92/100. But that's streets ahead of IE8, which, despite Microsoft's best intentions, manages just 20/100.

**FIREFOX FEATURES** There are other reasons to like Firefox, too. Its default layout is simpler than IE8's, with more space for tabs and a standard menu bar along the top, and if you want something a little more adventurous you can choose from hundreds of downloadable Themes. Firefox also offers a handy Download Manager, so you can see at a glance when files have arrived and launch them from within the program, without having to find the folder you saved them in.

By default, the search box in the upper-right corner uses Google, but as with Internet Explorer you can add other searches. Indeed, it's more versatile than IE: click the dropdown arrow and you can pick from a range of searches, including Wikipedia and Amazon. Go online and you'll find hundreds more to choose from.

There's an equivalent to Internet Explorer's InPrivate mode, too: turn on Private Browsing and you can surf without your steps being recorded on your computer.

**WELCOME ADDITIONS** The jewel in Firefox's crown is its support for add-ons. These can provide almost any feature, from simple things such as multi-language spellchecking to radical enhancements such as changing the way websites display. Those that add major new features are known as "extensions", and since Firefox is fully open source, anyone can write and publish their own. On the opposite page you'll see some of our favourites, but there are thousands more to choose from: visit http://addons.mozilla.org to see them all.

## Tip

As you use Firefox, it will learn the sites you frequently visit. Click the "Most Visited" button to the left of the Bookmarks Toolbar and you can instantly hop to any of your regular sites, or open them all at the same time, each in its own tab.

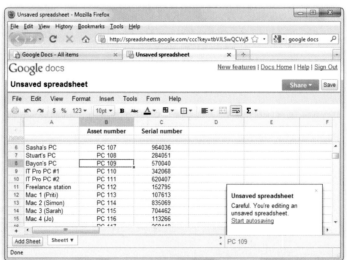

The most popular rival to Microsoft's Internet Explorer, Firefox is a free application that's faster and – in many ways – better, with a neat layout that makes it easy to work with modern online services such as Google Docs.

Firefox's Downloads pane helps keep track of files retrieved from the internet, while add-ons, developed by numerous third parties, taking advantage of the program's open-source nature, provide even more features.

# HOW TO...
# USE FIREFOX EXTENSIONS

There's an extension for everything: some are frivolous or highly specialised, while others can benefit almost everybody. Here's a selection of the most useful.

**(1) FLASHBLOCK** You've seen web pages that present graphics and sound using Adobe's Flash plugin. It's become an integral part of the web. But there's no denying that some sites get carried away, obscuring the content you want to read. Flashblock puts you back in control: with this extension installed, Flash animations load up "frozen", and won't display until you click the Play button. It's a simple but excellent tweak.

**(2) FIREGESTURES** The standard browser controls are easy to master, but once you start using multiple tabs, and paging back and forth in your browsing history, things can get fiddly. FireGestures lets you ignore Firefox's buttons and menus, and navigate with mouse gestures. For example, to go back to the previous page you hold down the right mouse button and drag to the left, no matter where on the screen your pointer happens to be. You can switch between tabs by dragging up and to the side, or using a rocker motion on the mouse buttons. The controls can be customised, and you can download scripts for more actions. Before long you'll wonder how you ever got by without mouse gestures.

**(3) FOXLINGO** One of the great things about the web is that it's truly global, and since you're lucky enough to understand English you can access a huge proportion of international information. All the same, there's a lot more out there in foreign languages – and FoxLingo's translation toolbar can help you read it. The extension uses free online resources to translate selected text or an entire web page between 53 languages, and also offers quick links to many other language resources, including dictionaries, text-to-speech translators and proofreading services. You can even enter search terms in English and find pages in other languages.

**(4) GREASEMONKEY** Greasemonkey is an amazing extension that can dramatically improve the way websites look and function. It works by downloading a page from the web, then adding in its own custom scripts to provide new features. Anyone can write a script (although it takes a little programming expertise), and there are already hundreds available for free. The features they add are as diverse as showing larger pictures in Facebook; adding features to Twitter; finding song lyrics on YouTube; and changing Google from white to black. Greasemonkey can even save you money, as there are numerous scripts designed to alert you automatically when better deals are available online.

**HOW LONG?**
Adding a Firefox extension is a two-minute job, although you can happily spend hours downloading scripts and configuring gestures.

**HOW HARD?**
Installing extensions is just a matter of a couple of mouse clicks.

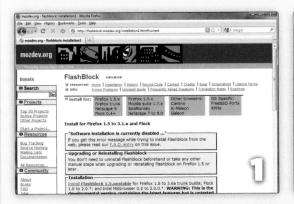

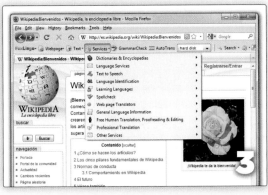

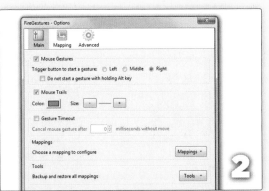

# Alternative web browsers

How many web browsers do we need? Most people would say just one, but the question is which. On the previous pages we've looked at Internet Explorer and Firefox, currently the most popular choices. Here are several other free browsers that might suit you better. They all work in fundamentally the same way, but each one has its own distinctive user interface and unique features.

**SPEED TESTS** We've already referred to the SunSpider benchmark, which compares the speeds of different web browsers. But don't take our word for it: you can run the test on your own browser by visiting http://webkit.org/perf/sunspider-0.9/sunspider.html. Your results won't match ours precisely, because your PC's processing speed affects how quickly any browser can run. But if you compare two or more browsers on the same computer, you'll see a clear difference in performance. Remember SunSpider only checks how quickly a browser can run the JavaScript instructions that are used in web applications such as Google Docs. It can't analyse more touchy-feely issues, such as how quickly a browser responds when you click a button; that's something you'll have to gauge for yourself.

**WEB STANDARDS** You've probably noticed that websites look different in different browsers. That's often an unintentional result of the nature of the web. Although pages are written in specific programming languages, browsers can interpret their code in various – and not always very smart – ways.

The Acid3 benchmark is designed to catch out web browsers with 100 samples of obscure and tricky code. You can run it for yourself in any browser: visit http://acid3.acidtests.org and you'll see a brief animation that builds up to a final score out of 100, showing how many tests were completed correctly. Note that "correctly" relates only to web standards: it doesn't tell you how many real web pages will work as intended. As Internet Explorer's Compatibility View shows, some pages are designed to take into account the foibles of a popular but non-standard browser, so they look right only when the browser does the *wrong* thing.

However, most modern websites will work fine in all of these browsers, and they all support extras such as Flash and Java too. One thing to watch out for is that some third-party security software suites will offer to add malware protection features to your browser. Typically, this only works for Internet Explorer and Firefox.

## Tip

Browser benchmarks such as the Acid3 test (see above right) are a useful comparison tool but a rather blunt instrument. What really matters is that your browser works well for the pages you visit, offers the features you want, and feels responsive. The best test is your own experience, so it makes sense to try a few browsers before settling on the one you'll use every day. Some people keep two or more regular browsers, using each for different purposes, such as general surfing and managing a website.

Apple's Safari is just one of several excellent browsers now available for Windows. One unique feature is its Top Sites view, new to version 4, which shows a multiscreen view of all the pages you access the most. You can rearrange or change these, and a star shows when any site has been updated since your last visit.

# Opera

The independently developed Opera browser has been around for years, and is now up to version 9. Originally, its selling points were its unrivalled speed and simplicity, but now other browsers have caught up. In fact, the latest version of Opera (at the time of writing) took more than twice as long as Firefox to complete the SunSpider speed test.

All the same, the Opera interface still feels extremely responsive, and its distinctive Speed Dial page lets you configure nine of your favourite websites and jump straight to them from an attractive graphical interface. If you don't like its appearance, you can download more "skins" to customise it, and the program includes built-in support for mouse gestures.

While Opera doesn't support extensions in the same way as Firefox (see p81), you can download Widgets – small programs that add interesting information displays or functions to your Opera desktop. Popular Widgets include a live weather report, a simulated aquarium and an analogue clock.

Opera also includes some features that will be of interest to more advanced users. If you use the software on more than one computer, the Opera Link system can automatically keep your personal bookmarks and other configuration settings synchronised on multiple PCs. There's also a complete email client built into the browser. www.opera.com

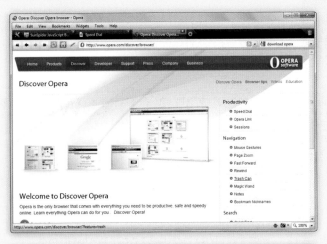

Opera has lost its lead over other browsers in areas such as speed, but still has many fans and can be extended and customised with Widgets and skins. It may also appeal to people who use Opera Mini or Opera Mobile on phones and other portable devices.

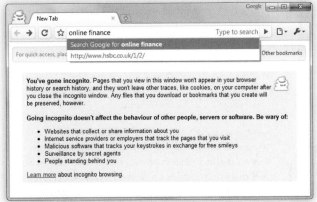

Google Chrome is a stripped-down, high-speed browser that's extremely compact yet incorporates plenty of useful features, such as "Incognito" browsing to preserve your privacy.

# Apple Safari

The Safari web browser (pictured opposite) is included with Apple Macintosh computers, and although a relative newcomer it's good enough that most Mac users weren't bothered when Microsoft discontinued its version of Internet Explorer. Safari has become a decent choice for Windows PCs as well, the most obvious attraction being its ultra-compact design: the buttons and window frame have been made as small as possible, and the tabs are combined with the title bar so as not to waste space.

Safari isn't only small, it's also fast, completing the SunSpider speed test nearly 20% faster than Firefox. But it's less versatile browser, with only limited extension support: there aren't as many available, and those that do exist are often only for Mac OS X, not Windows.

Still, Safari does have great features. One is Top Sites, which lets you jump straight to the pages you visit often – and with characteristic style, Apple hasn't settled for a list of sites: instead it shows a 3D wall of thumbnails arranged over a shiny black floor.

It's a similar story with the History view. All browsers let you look back at the pages you've visited, but Safari 4 uses Apple's Cover Flow, as seen in iTunes, to let you scroll back and forth graphically between pages. It's a highly intuitive way to find a site that you only dimly remember. www.apple.com/safari

Online benchmarks such as SunSpider and Acid3 can tell you how fast a browser works, and how accurately it renders web pages according to the current industry standards – but they don't tell the whole usability story.

# Google Chrome

From the same people as the search engine, Gmail and many other online services, Chrome is designed to make the best of such sites, so performance is a priority. Chrome is the fastest browser we've seen, completing the SunSpider test in 0.76 seconds – almost twice as fast as Firefox, and nearly eight times as fast as IE8.

Like Safari, Chrome is designed to be compact, hence its slightly unusual design, with tabs poking up into the title bar area. There's no separate search box: instead, the main input bar (dubbed the Omnibar by Google) will accept either web addresses or search terms.

Chrome shares Safari's limited support for extensions, and since it's the newest browser – the first version was launched in September 2008 – there are almost no add-ons available so far. But it does have a few useful features: its Most Visited page works like Safari's Top Sites, minus the sparkle, and Incognito Browsing – indicated by a spy icon – is similar to the private browsing modes in Internet Explorer and Firefox, preventing details of your surfing being kept on your PC.

It's designed to be stable, too. In Windows 7, every tab you open in Chrome is a completely separate program. That means if something goes wrong, only the tab you're using will be affected; your other Chrome windows can sail on as normal. Overall, it's probably the simplest, fastest browser. www.google.co.uk/chrome

**6**

*Internet & networking*

 WINDOWS 7 IS DESIGNED TO WORK SEAMLESSLY WITH WIRELESS NETWORKS, SO IT ISN'T A DIFFICULT JOB TO SET UP A HOME ROUTER AND CONNECT YOUR PC.

# Setting up a wireless network

If you're a broadband internet subscriber, there's a good chance you already have a Wi-Fi router in your home. If you don't, this could be a good time to acquire one, so you can enjoy wireless internet access anywhere in your house. Even if you do already own a router, it's worth making sure it's configured to give you the best performance and security.

The specifics of setting up a router vary from model to model: you'll need to check the manufacturer's instructions for precise details on how to connect to the router from your PC and change its settings. In general, you can log in by visiting http://192.168.0.1 or http://192.168.1.1 in your browser.

**CHOOSE A PASSWORD** Your router will have an administration password – by default a preset password that's given in the manual (either "admin" or nothing at all are two favourites). Change it as soon as possible. Standard passwords are common knowledge among hackers, and you don't want strangers to be able to change your settings.

**CHOOSE AN SSID** The SSID (Service Set Identifier) is the name that your wireless network shows to the world. It will probably start off as something like "Default Network", or the name of the router's manufacturer. Change this

to something more distinctive to minimise the risk of confusion with your neighbours' Wi-Fi routers, but don't use your name or address in your network name: this just makes life easier for tech-savvy thieves.

**SET UP SECURITY** To avoid any passer-by connecting, your router will offer various security systems. Your best bet is WPA2-PSK, which stands for Wi-Fi Protected Access 2 with a Pre-Shared Key (your router may call it WPA2 Personal, or just WPA2). It's very secure and works with smartphones, Wi-Fi printers, games consoles and other wireless devices. If some of your kit doesn't support WPA2, standard WPA should still deter casual hackers, but WEP, the least secure option, is much less effective protection.

Once you enable WPA2, you'll be asked to choose a password. It should be more than eight characters long; it should be memorable to you, but impossible to guess.

**PICK A PROTOCOL** Ensure your router is set to use the fastest Wi-Fi protocol your PC supports (see Tip, left). This may not speed up web browsing, as even a fast connection is slower than your network. But a higher protocol can make a big difference when transferring files within your home, and may improve Wi-Fi reception too.

## Tip

 Wireless networking uses four standard protocols, all within the 802.11 specification. 802.11a was designed for business use, but after this they're arranged by speed: 802.11b is the slowest, followed by 802.11g and, fastest of all, 802.11n (known as "draft n" because it's still officially under development). Catchy names, aren't they? Most hardware supports multiple protocols: modern laptops, for example, can connect to 802.11b, 802.11g and 802.11n networks, and most routers can work with several protocols at once. They can even act as a go-between, so computers using different protocols can talk to one another, although always at the speed of the slowest.

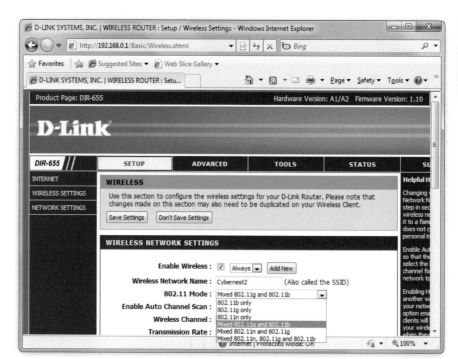

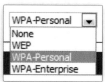

Today's wireless routers generally come with easy setup wizards. There shouldn't be many tasks to complete, but among the most important are setting an admin password, to prevent other users changing your settings, and applying encryption-based security, such as WPA2 (aka WPA-Personal), to ensure unauthorised users can't access your network or intercept your data traffic.

# HOW TO...
# CONNECT TO A WI-FI NETWORK

**① ENABLE WI-FI** Obvious, but easy to overlook. Many laptops have a Wi-Fi switch (so that you can turn off wireless networking in a public place or simply to increase battery life), while some use a key combination – typically the Fn key plus the key marked with an antenna. There's usually an indicator light.

**② PICK YOUR NETWORK** Left-click on the wireless icon in the Windows System Tray and you'll see a list of networks in range. At home, look for the name you gave your router. At a public hotspot, there should be a network with the name of the advertised Wi-Fi provider; if in doubt, ask. A yellow warning symbol next to a network means it's unprotected, so you can connect but your data won't be encrypted as it travels over the airwaves, so it could be intercepted by snoopers. This is common with public Wi-Fi hotspots.

**③ MAKE THE CONNECTION** When you click on a network name, you'll see an option to connect to that network automatically. Enable this and, in future, Windows will connect to that network whenever it's in range. You can enable this for any number of different networks; if more than one is in range at a given time, Windows will choose the most recently used, or you can go to "Open Network and Sharing Center" at the bottom of the network list and select "Manage wireless networks" to choose which networks take precedence.

When you click "Connect to join a protected network", you'll be asked to enter a security key. If you're attempting to connect to your own router, this will be the passphrase you chose during the setup process (see "Set up security", left). If it's someone else's network, you'll need to ask for the password before you can connect.

Note that when you tell Windows to automatically connect to a network, it will also remember that network's passphrase, and provide it whenever it needs to connect. That's a convenience, but it could also be a security risk: if you let someone else use your network temporarily, in theory they could reconnect to it later without your knowledge. If you think your passphrase could be abused, change it.

**④ CHOOSE A NETWORK LOCATION** Once connected, you'll be asked whether this is a Home, Work or Public network. If you tell Windows you're at home or work, you'll be able to share files and printers with other computers on the same network. If it's a public network, those types of connection will be automatically blocked to prevent strangers from accessing your files. As Windows suggests, don't choose Home or Work for "public places such as coffee shops or airports".

**HOW LONG?**
If your PC and the router are working normally, it's quick to get them talking.

**HOW HARD?**
A few clicks and it's done. If you can't see a network, first check your Wi-Fi on/off switch, then try moving closer to the router.

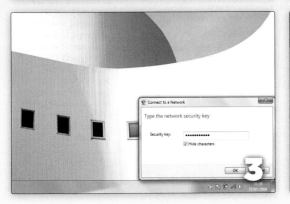

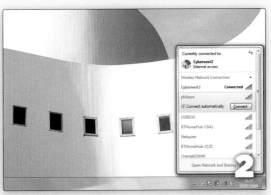

# Introducing HomeGroup

If you have more than one computer, it's very useful to be able to share files and resources between them. Windows 7's brand-new HomeGroup feature makes it effortless to set this up. Perhaps you have a desktop and a laptop, or several members of your family each have their own PC. No matter how your computers are distributed, it's likely they're all connected to the same router (see p84). This means not only can they all access the internet, but they can also share files with each other. So you don't need to keep multiple copies of your data on multiple PCs, and everyone can get at files on your main PC without interrupting you. If one of your computers is connected to a printer, you can share that, too, so other users can print to it from their own PCs. You can even play music and videos from one PC on another.

If you're an experienced Windows user, you might be thinking this all sounds rather familiar. And you're right: these abilities aren't new to Windows 7. File and printer sharing is a well-established technology, although it's only really become commonplace in the past few years as home networks with multiple PCs have become the norm.

But setting up file sharing has always been a tricky business, requiring you to understand user accounts, permissions and workgroups. Windows 7 makes it much easier with a new system called HomeGroup.

**GROUP THERAPY** Simply put, a homegroup is a collection of computers that can access the files in one another's Libraries (we discussed Libraries in chapter 3). You can set up a homegroup with a few clicks from any computer in your home running Windows 7. Once it's created, other PCs connected to the same network can join by entering a password. You can set this yourself, or you can have a secure code automatically generated by Windows.

The beauty of HomeGroup is that, unlike previous Windows file-sharing systems, at no point do you need to know the name or network address of any of the computers. Nor do you have to worry about the various user accounts and permissions of different members of your family. You can see just how straightforward the process is in our tutorial on p88.

Once your homegroup is up and running, you'll see it appear in the Windows Explorer navigation pane, with a list of all the other computers in your homegroup that are online. Simply click into one and you'll be able to access its Libraries as if they were your own. You can even incorporate files from your homegroup into your own Library.

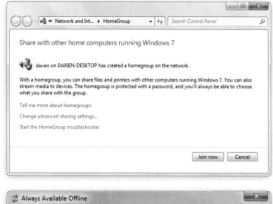

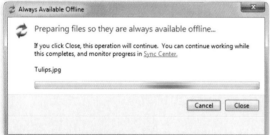

Windows 7's HomeGroup makes it easy to get all your computers sharing files. By making files "always available offline", you can even access files on a PC that isn't currently switched on. Spooky.

Of course, this could raise some concerns about the security of your personal files, so there are a few points we should make clear. You don't have to share all your Libraries: on each computer, you can choose which of your Pictures, Videos, Music or Documents Libraries to share. By default, Documents is disabled, so you can let other family members listen to Dire Straits' "Private Investigations" without giving them the ability to snoop on your financial records. You can also manually mark specific files or folders as private to prevent anyone else accessing them.

And as an extra level of security, when you first set up a homegroup, all the folders you share will be read-only to other users in the group – so you don't need to worry about anyone accidentally deleting or corrupting your files. Nor will the kids be able to fill your hard disk with temporary files and unwanted downloads. But if you do want to enable other users to edit a particular file, or let them add files to one of your folders, that's easy to set up, as we'll show you over the page.

**KNOW YOUR LIMITS** HomeGroup is designed to be as simple as possible. That's its strength, but it means it isn't very versatile. When you share files and folders using the HomeGroup system, your sharing settings affect everybody in the group. If you want to create a more complex sharing system – for example, you want to give your partner access to your Documents Library without extending it to your kids – you'll need to go back to the old, slightly more complicated way of sharing folders.

Another important limitation of HomeGroup is that it works only with PCs running Windows 7. If some of the computers in your household are still using Windows XP or Vista, they won't be able to join your homegroup. Nor

**STREAM MUSIC AND MOVIES** It's very convenient to be able to use HomeGroup to give others access to your Music and Video Libraries. But there may be hundreds or even thousands of files in these folders, so it can be a pain for users to find what they're looking for in Windows Explorer. Happily, there's a better way: when you set up a homegroup, you'll be given the option to enable media streaming. If you do so, other members of your homegroup will be able to use Windows Media Player to browse your music, video and photo collections, just as if they were sitting at your PC. They can even listen to songs and watch videos without having to copy the files onto their own PC first. For more information on media streaming, see p100.

can you use HomeGroup to share files with anyone using an Apple Macintosh or a Linux-based computer. In all these cases, you'll need to use traditional file sharing to let other computers access your files and folders. We'll show you how at the end of this chapter.

**GO OFFLINE** The bane of any file-sharing arrangement is finding that the PC containing the files you want to access is switched off. Even Windows 7 can't talk to a system that's powered down. The good news is that there's a workaround: while browsing files or folders that reside on a different PC, you can tell Windows to make them available "offline". After you do this, you'll find that, magically, you can access them even when the other computer isn't available.

Of course, there's a trick to it. When you make a file from another machine available offline, Windows creates a hidden copy of it on your own hard disk. Later, if it can't access the file over the network, it shows you this local copy instead. It all happens transparently. The other user might change the file, of course, but Windows synchronises its copy with the original whenever it can – and files won't get changed on the other PC while it's turned off. So for most purposes it's just like working with the actual file. For more on offline files, see our guide to Sync Center on p124.

# HOW TO...
# SET UP A HOMEGROUP

*There are just four simple steps to HomeGroup heaven, making it easy to share files and resources among all the Windows 7 PCs and laptops in your house.*

**(1) HEAD HOME** As we've explained on the previous page, HomeGroup makes the painfully difficult task of sharing files over a home network more bearable. However, there's one complication: Windows 7 won't let you create or join a homegroup unless the network you're connected to is designated as a Home network, as opposed to Work or Public. To change that, go to the Network and Sharing Center. Under "View your active networks", click to change the location to Home.

**(2) GROUP PRESSURE** Once you're on a Home network, a dialog box will appear extolling the virtues of HomeGroup and prompting you to start setting one up. You can choose what type of files you want to share, and whether or not to stream music and video to all the other PCs in your homegroup.

**(3) INVITE ONLY** After a short pause, a window will appear in which a password will fade elegantly into view. You'll notice the password is long and random. You can write it down or, preferably, copy and paste it into a new text document. On the positive side, it's

very secure. The annoying part is that there's no facility for transferring the key to a USB flash drive that you can simply plug into other computers; you have to type it in.

**(4) TIME SHARE** With the homegroup set up, you can join it from any other Windows 7 PC on the network by clicking the HomeGroup entry in the left-hand pane of any Windows Explorer window. When the Join HomeGroup box opens, enter the password you wrote down, select which of the documents you want to share on this computer, and that's all there is to it. (You can leave the group at any time from the HomeGroup settings window.) This PC can now also share devices plugged into your main computer; most obviously, an external hard disk or a printer. Handy if you need to print something from your laptop.

By default, a homegroup shares everything under the banner of Documents, Music, Pictures or Video, depending on which options you select when you create or join it. To exclude a folder or file, go to the top menu bar (known as the Command bar) and click "Share with"; then, to make this item private, select Nobody.

**HOW LONG?**
The great thing about HomeGroup is that you can set it up in seconds.

**HOW HARD?**
This has deliberately been kept simple – the most difficult step is entering the password.

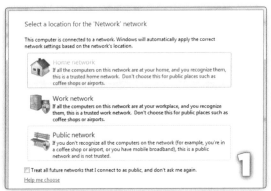

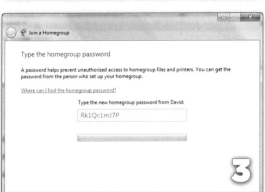

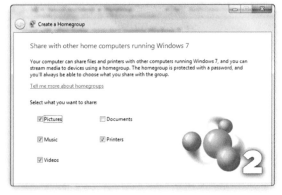

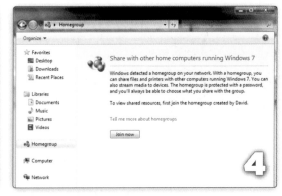

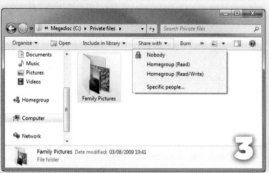

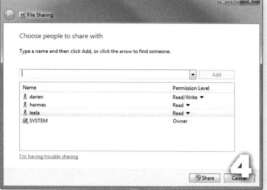

**HOW LONG?**
Five minutes should be enough to create the necessary user accounts and set up sharing.

**HOW HARD?**
It can be a little fiddly, but the principles are simple once you understand them.

# HOW TO...
# SHARE FILES MANUALLY

*HomeGroup makes it simple to share, but if you want more security or flexibility, you can share any file or folder on your system with specific users. Here's how.*

**(1)** **CHECK SHARING SETTINGS** Open the Network and Sharing Center, click "Change advanced sharing settings", and, in the window that opens, scroll down and ensure password-protected sharing is on. Also check that the top two items, "Network discovery" and "File and printer sharing", are on: if not, other computers may not be able to find or access your shared items. Then, click "Save changes".

**(2)** **CREATE USER ACCOUNTS** Password-protected sharing requires users to log in to your PC before they can access shared items. So you need to create a Windows user account (see chapter 3) on your PC for each person. You can simplify things by having, say, one account called Kids and giving the password to all your children. But if you want to let your eldest child access more shared items than the others, he or she will need their own account.

**(3)** **SELECT WHAT TO SHARE** To share a folder, select it in a Windows Explorer window and, in the bar at the top, click "Share with". If you're in a homegroup, you'll see options to share with either the group or specific people. Select the latter for password-protected access. If there's no homegroup, choose Advanced sharing settings.

**(4)** **SELECT WHO TO SHARE WITH** A panel will appear showing who has access to this item. Your name will already be there; if you click OK now, the file or folder can be accessed from other PCs on your network by entering your personal username and password. To give access to another user, click the dropdown arrow next to the Add button, select their username and click Add. You can click below Permission Level to choose whether each user has full read/write access or read-only.

Anyone on your network should now be able to see your PC under Network in Windows Explorer. To access it, they'll be asked to log in, and when they do so they'll see the folders you chose to share with them.

For security, Windows 7 won't let people log on to your PC over the network if their user account has no password. Make sure you create a password when you set up each account, and that it isn't blank.

# IN THIS CHAPTER

# 7

*Windows 7 entertains*

# ENTERTAINMENT

All work and no play would make Windows a very dull place, but Microsoft's latest is also designed to please. In the Home Premium, Professional and Ultimate editions, you'll discover the new and vastly improved Windows Media Center. Together with a TV tuner, this is the key to turning any PC or laptop into a fully featured cutting-edge home entertainment system.

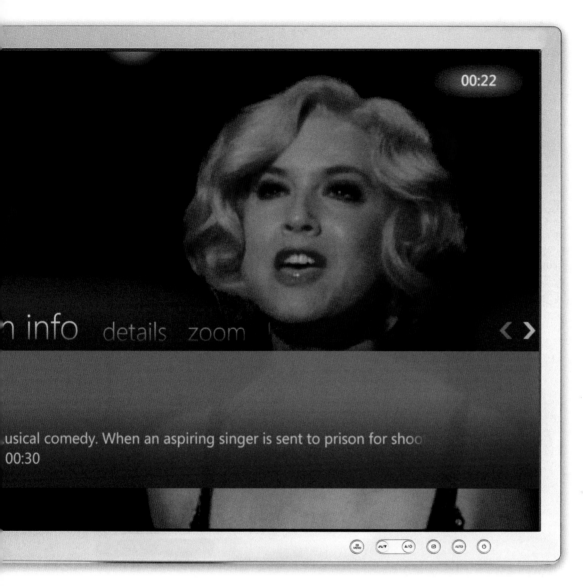

# IN WINDOWS 7

Whether watching and recording TV, enjoying DVD movies or listening to your favourite music, it's the place to come for playing and managing all your digital media. In this chapter, we delve into Media Center and show how to get it up and running with minimum hassle. We also sing the praises of Media Player 12 and explain how to stream your music.

IT'S YOUR DIGITAL GATEWAY TO MUSIC AND VIDEO. WINDOWS 7 BRINGS YOU THE MOST CAPABLE VERSION OF WINDOWS MEDIA PLAYER YET.

# Introducing Media Player 12

Following on from Windows Media Player 11, as bundled with Vista, Media Player 12 might not seem very exciting. Again, the interface has been tweaked to little benefit; the large buttons for Now Playing, Rip, Sync and so on are gone, and a new line-up of tabs occupies the right-hand side. Hoped-for features like Blu-ray playback are still missing.

Given time, however, you'll find it smarter and more streamlined, better focused on playing media and moving it between devices. The main window acts as a permanent Library view, no longer segregating content into music, video, pictures and TV, and you can use the left pane to flick between media types. Click Music to select by Artist, Album or Genre; if you'd rather go by Year or Composer, just right-click on Music, then pick Customize Navigation Pane.

The views, heavy on cover art, make it easy to find what you're looking for, and covers are stacked in Artist, Genre and Year views; double-click a stack to show a list. The Search bar, near the top, works as brilliantly as it did in Media Player 11, narrowing down results as you type.

Those tabs on the right let you make drag-and-drop playlists for listening, burning to disc, or syncing with a portable media device. You can still hide the panel if you want, but the tabs help avoid losing it altogether.

**IN SYNC** Synchronising content to an MP3 or media player is even easier: just connect it, open the Sync tab and click Start Sync. For more control, click the Menu button below the Sync tab, select "Set up sync", and choose which playlists to synchronise. Alternatively, clear them all and just drag songs, albums or videos manually onto the list.

You can switch from the Library view to Now Playing using the button to the far right of the playback controls. If you want visualisations (graphics that follow the music), right-click in the window, choose Visualizations and browse the extensive list. Right-clicking also enables you to alter EQ, add enhancements or view the current playlist. To return to the Library view, click the button at the top right.

**VIDEO STAR** When it comes to video, Windows Media Player is now a lot less fussy about formats. DivX, XviD and H.264 are finally supported, as is the AVCHD format used by most HD camcorders. Even Apple's MOV format is supported, although this and M4V may still refuse to play.

Media Player 12 really comes into its own when you want to share your media around a home network. If you keep a library on your laptop but want to play tracks on a media PC hooked up to your TV, first enable an option on the PC: go to the new Stream dropdown, between Organize and Create Playlist, and choose "Allow remote control of my Player", then "Allow remote control on this network".

The Stream menu contains one more gem. Select "Allow Internet access to home media", and you can stream audio, video and images from your home system to another Windows 7 PC. Both PCs and your user accounts must be linked to a Windows Live ID, and you'll need to download a small applet to create the link. See p100 for more.

See p100 for more.

## Tip

Want a quick preview of the track you're about to play? Hover over it with the mouse pointer, then click on the Preview button in the box that appears. The Skip link handily skips 15 seconds further into the track, making light work of browsing longer pieces.

**Windows Media Player 12** may not look like a giant leap forward, but under the hood are new features including enhanced network support. If you have Media Extenders – whether music-streaming devices, an Xbox 360 games console or a networked media player – you can now highlight an item in your Library within Media Center, right-click on it and select Play To. Choose a device and the file plays on it. See p102.

# HOW TO...
# RIP A CD TO YOUR HARD DISK

**①  INSERT A DISC**  When you insert a music CD, two new buttons, Rip CD and Rip settings, appear to the right of Media Player's "Create playlist" button. To copy and encode all the tracks at the default settings, just click Rip CD. To select or deselect tracks, click the checkboxes to the left of the track names.

**②  CHOOSE YOUR TRACKS**  If the album art or track information is incorrect, right-click on the cover art and select Find Album Info. Media Player 12 goes online, compares the CD data against Microsoft's database, and comes back with a list of possible matches. Run through the results, flicking through the pages using the links at the foot of the scrolling list, until you find the correct details. Click Next, then Finish.

**③  SELECT A FORMAT**  To see more options before going ahead and ripping the tracks, click the Rip settings button. The key options are Format and Audio Quality. For Format, MP3 (as you probably know) is the most widely compatible with different computers, programs and devices, but Microsoft's own WMA and WMA Pro formats can create better-sounding tracks with lower file sizes. Of these, WMA Pro is the most effective, but also the less widely supported by MP3 players. WMA Lossless and WAV Lossless are designed for creating a premium-quality archive of your music; the files will sound as good as the original CD, but they'll be large, so you won't be able to fit as many on the average MP3 player, if it's capable of playing them in the first place. In short, it's horses for courses, so make sure you back the right one before continuing with the ripping process.

Digital audio always involves trading off quality against file size. Choose 192Kbits/sec WMA/WMA Pro or 320Kbits/sec MP3 if you want the very best sound, have the speakers or headphones to do it justice, and don't care how big your files are; or go for 128Kbits/sec or 256Kbits/sec if packing more music into a smaller amount of memory – perhaps on an MP3 player – is your primary concern. Now, click the Rip CD button and copy the tracks from the CD to your hard disk in your chosen format.

**④  OVER-PROTECTIVE**  The first time you rip an audio CD, Windows 7 will ask whether you want to copy protect your music. This means the files will play only on your PC (not other computers) and on compatible secure devices. There's absolutely no benefit to this. Choose the "Do not add copy protection to your music" option and tick the box next to the disclaimer. There's no downside to doing so, and it will save you frustration later on when you can't copy tracks to other devices. Remember, of course, not to share copies illegally.

**HOW LONG?**
Exact timings vary, but Windows will rip a CD several times faster than playing it in real-time.

**HOW HARD?**
Ripping is effortless; checking track names and fiddling with audio formats are optional.

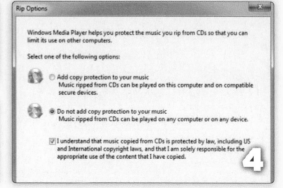

ADD A TV TUNER TO YOUR PC AND YOU CAN TRANSFORM IT INTO YOUR
FAMILY'S PRIMARY SOURCE OF ENTERTAINMENT, ALL THANKS TO MEDIA CENTER.

# Introducing Media Center

Windows Media Center has come a long way since its inception back in 2002, and in Windows 7 it's matured into a key attraction. At a quick glance, it might not look to have moved on a great deal since Vista, but look closer and it's both easier to use and more powerful than ever before.

**FRIENDLY FACE** Media Center's simple, friendly interface gives you access to TV, music, movies and photos at the touch of a button. If you're looking at the pretty screenshots and wondering where all the clutter and convoluted file menus have gone, well, you won't find any. Media Center has been designed to be intuitive and straightforward, whether you're using it at a desk with a keyboard and mouse or from the comfort of your sofa with a compatible Media Center remote control (see Tip, left). It's even more usable than in previous versions, with neat additions such as the new desktop widget giving rapid access to recently recorded TV shows at the press of a button.

Even if you forego a dedicated remote, it's also easier to navigate via mouse and keyboard, with Windows 7 bringing welcome improvements to the user interface throughout. A timeline at the foot of the screen lets you skip back and forth through video files, or even time-shifted TV programmes, and previously neglected or hidden-away features have been refined and made easier to access.

**HD OR NOT HD** Like its predecessors, Windows 7 Media Center has an MPEG2 video decoder built in, so it will play DVD movies right off the bat. With the assistance of a TV tuner it can also receive analogue, digital and – for the first time – satellite TV broadcasts. This time it also has support for DivX, XviD and the H.264 video format, which paves the way for receiving high-definition TV.

The current route to free HD content is a satellite dish and a DVB-S or S2 satellite TV tuner card to allow you to tune into Freesat's free-to-air services. But a clutch of HD channels are soon to be available on terrestrial Freeview HD, a forthcoming free-to-air service that only needs a standard aerial and one of the all-new DVB-T2 TV tuners.

**RAY OF HOPE** One mild disappointment is that support for Blu-ray is absent. If you have a Blu-ray drive and want to play HD movies, you'll have to budget for ArcSoft's TotalMedia Theatre 3 Platinum or CyberLink's PowerDVD 9 software. Both cost extra, but integrate seamlessly into Media Center's menu, so you can just pop in the disc and watch.

If you're wondering why you should choose Media Center over the more straightforward charms of a Sky+ box or hard-disk based PVR, then turn to p96, where we go into more detail about Media Center's considerable range of TV-related abilities.

turn to p96

## Tip

If you're looking to integrate a Media Center PC into your lounge, make life easier with a dedicated Media Center remote control and USB infrared receiver, available together for about £20. Dedicated shortcut buttons give rapid access to your media and put all of Media Center's functions within easy reach. Press the My Photos button, for example, and even if it wasn't already up and running, Media Center bounds into life and takes you straight to your photo library.

Welcome to Windows Media Center

The best way to experience TV on your PC.

Continue

# HOW TO...
# NAVIGATE MEDIA CENTER

**1** **MAIN MENU** Media Center's main menu is simplicity itself, split into six main headings: Extras, Pictures+Videos, Music, Movies, TV and Tasks. Scroll up or down to the category you want, then left and right to select from the available options. If at any point you want to return to the main menu, you can toggle back and forth by clicking the green button at the top left of the screen or, if you're using a remote, by pressing the actual green button. This doesn't interrupt the playback of TV, video files or music; audio continues to play in the background, and thanks to a nifty transparency effect, video is still visible behind the menu.

**2** **MUSIC** As long as you've made sure all your music is stored in your Windows 7 Music Library, Media Center will automatically present it as a quilt of CD covers that stretches across the screen. Music can be sorted by a range of criteria, such as album, artist, genre, composer and year of release, or you can just start typing a keyword to instantly find the music you're looking for. If you don't see your music, go to Tasks | Settings | Media Libraries, and manually add the directories where your music is located. This can be on local or network drives, so it doesn't matter where you store your music; it could even be on a NAS (network attached storage) device elsewhere on your home network.

**3** **VIDEO/PICTURE** Just like the Music option, the picture and video libraries tile your display with little thumbnails of your media files. Videos can be ordered by name and date taken – a handy option for camcorder users – while pictures can be sorted by name, date taken, embedded tags or their star rating (manually applied by you in Windows). You can now edit your pictures, too. Right-click an image (or press the Info button on your remote), select Picture Details and you can access basic editing tasks such as rotating and cropping, enhancing contrast or removing red-eye, as well as printing out images quickly. Any changes you make are saved to the original image file, though, so be careful before accidentally ruining your precious photos.

**4** **TV** The TV menu provides access to TV shows you've recorded, the TV guide, and live TV. You can also search Media Center's TV listings. If you like a particular actor, for example, you can find every upcoming film or TV programme that they'll be starring in. There have been plenty of other improvements here, too. Dab the up cursor – either on your keyboard or on your remote control – while watching TV and the new Mini Guide appears. This lets you browse through a reduced version of the TV guide without obscuring too much of the programme in the background.

**HOW LONG?**
Give yourself 20 minutes to fully explore Media Center's features.

**HOW HARD?**
Media Center is designed to be intuitive, and it is.

WHO NEEDS A SEPARATE, NON-UPGRADABLE PERSONAL VIDEO RECORDER WHEN YOUR CUSTOMISABLE PC CAN DO THE SAME JOB EVEN BETTER?

# Watching and recording TV

There are few things worse than sitting down to relax at the end of a long day only to find there's nothing but dross on TV. Get to grips with Media Center's comprehensive TV guide, movie listings and recording functions, however, and you can be sure there's always something worth watching.

**CENTER OF ATTENTION** Its predecessors were no slouch, but Windows 7 Media Center makes finding and recording the TV you want to watch an effortless experience. The TV guide shows what's on now and next at a glance, and stays up to date by downloading 15 days of advance listings every day. Want to record a single programme? Press the record button once. Want to record the whole series? Press it again.

If you'd like to know more about a programme before wasting hard disk space on it, you can bring up the information overlay. This provides a synopsis and, if you have a habit of missing the beginning of shows, also lets you know when it will be repeated. If all that isn't enough, you can also use the search feature to find programmes you want to watch by title, keyword, category, actor or director.

At the foot of this page you'll see one of Media Center's greatest additions: the Movie Guide. This presents forthcoming movies on TV as a browsable grid of covers. You can see what films are on now or next, select a movie

genre to search for, or just list all the films showing in the next 15 days. You need never miss a good film ever again.

With basic TV tuners available for as little as £30, it's easy and affordable to turn your PC into a lounge-friendly PVR (personal video recorder) that can eclipse the best set-top boxes and HDD recorders money can buy.

**TUNER SANDWICH** Delve beneath Media Center's glossy surface and much more has improved. It was previously all but impossible to connect more than two tuners at once, and you could only use one type, analogue or digital, not both. Windows 7 has moved with the times, and as well as supporting analogue, digital, satellite and cable tuners, it ups the ante by supporting up to four of each.

For most people, any of the many Media Center-compatible dual-tuner TV cards – USB, PCI or otherwise – will be a sensible initial setup. You can always add extra tuners later, and should you want to mix and match a digital TV tuner to receive Freeview while installing a satellite tuner to add Freesat's range of TV channels, you can. Or, pair two twin-tuner TV cards together and (as long as your PC can keep up) you can record programmes on up to three channels at once while freely channel-hopping live TV on the fourth tuner. The possibilities are almost endless.

## FAQ

**Q:** Are there alternatives to Media Center?
**A:** A Sky+, Sky HD or Virgin V+ HD box may seem a simpler option than setting up a Media Center system, and products such as the Wyplay Wyplayer, Popcorn Hour A110 and Western Digital WDTV all bypass the need for a PC – so Windows Media Center needs to work hard to compete. But, in fact, its potential is far greater. A PC can be upgraded as your needs grow and new technologies emerge: for example, by adding extra TV tuners, Blu-ray drives or multiple hard disks. And whereas most set-top boxes can be connected to only one TV, a Media Center PC can expand its reach via Microsoft's Xbox 360 console or other Media Center Extenders, easily delivering live and recorded TV, videos, photos and music to a whole house over your network. To make the very most of your media, press the green button and you won't look back.

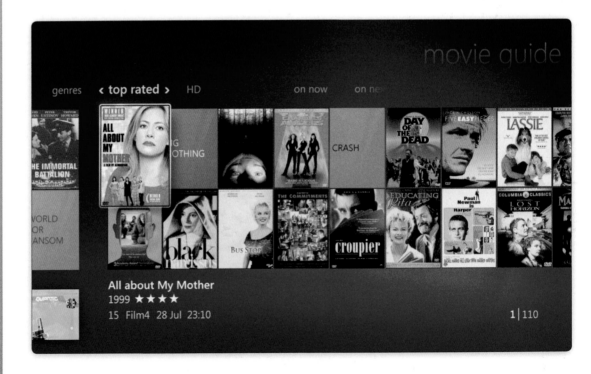

**All about My Mother**
1999 ★★★★
15  Film4  28 Jul  23:10                                    1│110

# HOW TO...
# ADD A TV TUNER

**(1) CHOOSE A TUNER** Whether you're installing your first TV tuner in a PC or adding a second, it's pretty simple. Windows 7 allows you to choose analogue, digital, satellite or cable TV tuners – up to four of each simultaneously. With the UK's analogue TV switch-off in progress, don't be tempted by a cheap analogue-only tuner; spend a little more on a dual tuner that will last. The extra tuner will allow you to record one channel while channel-surfing freely with the other, or record two channels at once while watching one of your recorded TV shows. As long as it has Media Center logos on the box, suitable drivers should be included.

You can run satellite tuners and digital tuners side by side (or any combination), but apart from the couple of new HD channels on Freesat, many of the channels will be identical. Bear in mind that Freeview HD begins rolling out in December 2009, and with one of the as-yet-unreleased DVB-T2 TV tuners (current tuners can only receive DVB-T), you'll be able to get HD through your rooftop aerial. We wouldn't recommend a cable (DVB-C) tuner yet: the UK setup process is incredibly finicky.

**(2) LOAD THE DRIVERS** If you don't already have a driver disc to hand, download the appropriate drivers from the manufacturer's website. Don't worry if there aren't any specific Windows 7 drivers, as Vista-certified drivers should work fine. Be sure to follow the installation instructions: usually it's necessary to install the drivers and then install the TV tuner afterwards.

If you can't find your driver disc or any suitable drivers on the internet, it might be worth installing the tuner anyway, and letting Windows Update search for driver files online; you might just be lucky. Once the tuner is successfully installed, fire up Media Center and go to Tasks | Settings | TV | Set Up TV Signal.

**(3) FIND TV CHANNELS** Once the setup process is in motion, Media Center leads you through a simple wizard. You'll need to enter your postcode and select your nearest transmitter, so you can download the appropriate TV listings, and then Media Center will start scanning for channels. Make sure your aerial is connected, then go for a cup of tea while scanning completes.

**(4) TROUBLESHOOT** Media Center should pick up about 92 services – that's the sum of the TV and radio channels on Freeview. If there are any missing, you might be struggling with a weak signal. Try a signal booster between the TV aerial and the tuner, and see if it helps. If so, go back to the end of step 2 and run through the TV signal wizard again to get all the channels.

**HOW LONG?**
You may want to spend some time choosing your kit, but it shouldn't take long to set up.

**HOW HARD?**
Dead-easy with a USB tuner; with PCI and PCI Express cards, you'll need to open the PC's case.

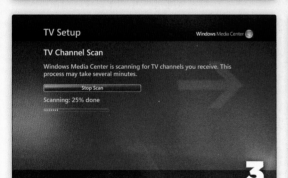

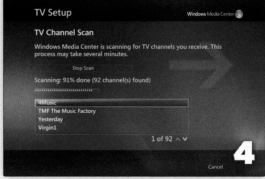

LIKE PREVIOUS VERSIONS, WINDOWS 7 COMES WITH A SELECTION OF GAMES. WE GIVE OUR VERDICT ON WHAT'S INCLUDED... AND WE'RE NOT OVERLY IMPRESSED.

# Windows 7's bundled games

Microsoft's decision not to release a Home Basic version of Windows 7 in the UK means everyone, whether they're running Home Premium, Professional or Ultimate, will get every Windows Premium Game installed as standard. Only those who buy a netbook with Starter edition miss out.

Starter edition does include old favourites – such as Minesweeper, Hearts and Solitaire – and they're all unchanged from Windows Vista. With simple gameplay and thousands of fans the world-over, there was no real need to revamp these classic titles for the new OS.

Also returning are Vista's Premium Games: Chess Titans and Mahjong Titans. Chess offers ten levels, a 3D chessboard and the ability to save a game in progress to continue later. It's also possible to choose the materials your chess pieces and board are made of and tweak graphical options to make sure Chess Titans will run on your PC, no matter how modest its specification. However, we're disappointed that there's still no option to record games so that you can learn from them, nor any sort of rating to see how you match up to the rest of the world.

Mahjong Titans offers a more polished experience. The classic tile-matching game can be played using six different styles of board and, thanks to impressive 3D graphics and plenty of sound effects, it's the best Mahjong we've played. Plenty of customisation is available: you can pick which tile set and background you use, and save your game so you can come back to it later if you're interrupted.

**ALL IN ONE** As in Vista, all the default games can be accessed through the Games Explorer, a simple window that gathers together all your installed games for easy access and updating. Handily, it will also gather together any third-party games you install, keeping all your titles in one place.

Younger users are catered for by Purble Place, a title specially designed for children that was first introduced in Vista. It's a colourful world full of sound effects and cute animation in a trio of kid-friendly games. The first, Purble Pairs, is a simple tile-matching game with three levels of difficulty, and the second, Comfy Cakes, is a fun cake-making challenge. The third, Purble Shop, is a simple guessing game featuring a cute potato head-style character.

While it's true that no-one is going to buy Windows 7 for its games alone, it's disappointing that Microsoft hasn't made more effort with its latest OS. Children will be far more entertained by games from the likes of www.bbc.co.uk/cbbc and www.nitrome.com, while adults could do worse than Call of Juarez: Bound in Blood – although serious Mahjong players might find it a bit tame.

## Tip

**Q:** Is there a new version of Microsoft's DirectX with Windows 7?

**A:** Yes, DirectX 11. This should enable more ambitious games by making it easier for developers to use multithreading, making full use of the multiple cores in modern processor chips. A technology called tessellation should make the surfaces of objects look more realistic too. However, to reap the full benefits, games developers must use new programming techniques, which may take some time.

There's something oddly familiar about Windows 7's games collection.

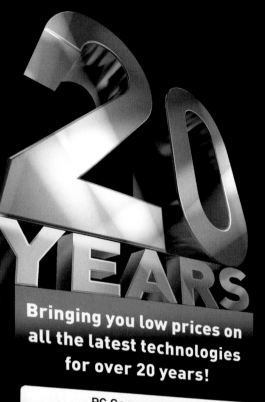

# dabs●com

**PRE-ORDER NOW AND SAVE**

**Ships 22nd Oct' 09**

**HURRY! STRICTLY WHILST STOCKS LAST***

**20 YEARS**

**Bringing you low prices on all the latest technologies for over 20 years!**

- PC Components
- Storage
- Memory & Upgrades
- Gaming & Gadgets
- Desktop PCs
- Software
- Cables & Accessories
- Printers & Multifunctions
- TFT Displays
- Laptops & Netbooks
- Cameras & Camcorders
- Networking & Communications
- Home Entertainment
- Telephones & Mobiles
- In-Car & Sat-Nav

## Order now and enjoy special introductory prices*

| Edition | Introductory Price | Post Promotion RRP |
|---|---|---|
| Home Premium | £64.69 INC VAT | £149.99 INC VAT |
| Professional | £149.99 INC VAT | £219.99 INC VAT |
| Ultimate | £159.99 INC VAT | £229.99 INC VAT |

## Your PC, simplified...

Windows 7 is the easiest, fastest, and most engaging version of Windows yet. Better ways to find and manage files, like Jump Lists and improved taskbar previews, help you speed through everyday tasks. Faster and more reliable performance means your PC just works the way you want it to. And great features like Windows Media Center and Windows Touch make new things possible. Get to know Windows 7, and see how it can simplify just about everything you do with your PC.

**Learn more about Windows 7**  **EPISODE 12**  **Watch Episode 12 of the Dabs VideoCast at www.dabs.tv**

# Buy online today at www.dabs.com/pcpro

TAKE A LITTLE TIME TO DIG INTO THE FEATURES OF THE NEW WINDOWS MEDIA
PLAYER AND YOU'LL BE SHOCKED BY JUST HOW MUCH YOU CAN DO.

# Streaming music and video

We've already seen how you can enjoy your music, movies, TV and photos on your computer using the new features in Windows 7's Media Player 12 and Media Center. You can even display media from your PC on your widescreen TV. But there's another way to enjoy your favourite content without having a noisy computer in the lounge. It's called media streaming, and allows your Windows 7 PC to serve up movies, recorded TV and music to a multitude of devices over your home network – or even across the internet.

Imagine being able to play the album you downloaded from Amazon or iTunes last night on your internet radio in the kitchen, without having to move your laptop or burn a disc; or to watch a programme you recorded on your PC in the UK in a hotel room in the US. That's the sort of thing Windows 7's streaming features make possible.

**EASY AS PIE** Streaming is much easier to use than it was in Vista. Fire up Media Player and you'll see it's one of the three main menu items at the top of the screen. To enable it, turn on streaming in the Stream dropdown menu, then select the third of the three options in that menu: "Automatically allow devices to play my media" (it's selected by default). It's as simple as that. Now connected devices that support UPnP media servers (or any device bearing the DLNA logo) will be able to share and play all the media that Windows Media Player 12 makes available over a local network. On the opposite page, we investigate how to stream your content over the internet too.

**PLUG AND PLAY** Windows 7 uses UPnP (Universal Plug and Play) media server technology to make its media library available to third-party devices, so when buying a streamer, look for the UPnP logo. Windows 7 also complies with DLNA (the Digital Living Network Alliance standard), which makes these products extremely easy to set up.

DLNA media streamers, such as the ZyXEL DMA1100P, bring another of Windows 7's new features into play: the ability to remote-control connected devices from your PC. It's called Play To. Rather than simply letting devices pull video or audio from your computer, this allows you to send content actively to them. With a DLNA Digital Media Renderer (DMR) device connected to your network, you can right-click a file – or several files – in Windows Media Player 12, select Play To, and pick from the list of connected devices. (See this in action on p92.)

The great thing about this feature is that it isn't just limited to music and video streamers. All sorts of products support the DLNA standard and can be used in a similar way. With a DLNA-compliant digital photo frame, for instance, you can send a photo from your computer at any time. With a digital radio, you can send tracks from your PC and even adjust the volume remotely.

## Tip

If you're looking to buy a media-streaming device and want to take advantage of Windows 7's advanced features, make sure your new box is DLNA-compliant. This is usually indicated by a logo on the packaging, but you can also check on the DLNA website at www.dlna.org

You can use Windows Media Player 12 to remotely control DLNA-compliant streamers such as the ZyXEL DMA1100P. And if that's gobbledygook to you, read the rest of this page to find out what it's all about.

# HOW TO...
# SET UP INTERNET STREAMING

While you were looking through the Stream menu (see opposite page), you may have noticed a couple of other options. These are the new additions to Windows 7's toolbox of media-streaming features: internet streaming and remote control.

The more exciting of the two is the former, which allows you to share media, not only around your home network but also over the internet. This creates the opportunity to listen to your music from anywhere without having to duplicate a massive collection of MP3 files, and also to watch home movies or even TV shows recorded using Media Center.

It works by linking the media collection stored on your PC to a Windows Live ID. As we'll see in this tutorial, it isn't a complicated process. Once you follow these four steps, you'll be able to access your music and movies wherever you are. And that also means you won't have to remember to load up the MP3 player before you go off on your travels.

**1** ACCESS ALL AREAS Fire up Windows Media Player and click the Stream option at the top left. Enable "Allow Internet access to home media". You'll need to link your Windows Live ID to Media Player before you can do anything else, so in the next window choose the option to "Link an online ID".

**2** SHOW YOUR ID A window should now appear prompting you to choose an online ID provider. Click "Add an online ID provider", then choose Windows Live on the following web page. This will take you to the page for the Windows Live Sign-in Assistant program; download and install this, taking care to follow the instructions correctly.

Now go back to the "Link online IDs" box, which should still be open; if not, press the Windows key and type "link online IDs", then press Return to launch the item when found. Click the link labelled "Link online ID", and in the next box enter your Windows Live username and password and hit Sign in.

**3** JOIN THE ASSOCIATION Windows 7 will take a few seconds to associate your ID with Windows Media Player. Once this is done, click OK, then in the Internet Home Media Access dialog box select the "Allow Internet access to home media" option and, finally, click OK once more.

**4** ANOTHER LINK IN THE CHAIN To link your second computer to the first, simply repeat these steps. The first computer's media library will now appear in the Other Libraries list in the left-hand pane of this PC's Windows Media Player 12 window, and vice versa.

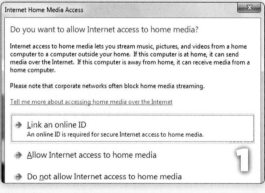

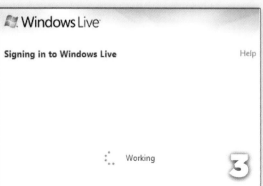

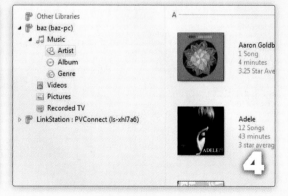

**HOW LONG?**
Barring complications, you could be ready to go in ten minutes.

**HOW HARD?**
There are a couple of obstacles, but anyone who can use a Windows Live ID can get this done.

THANKS TO WINDOWS 7, IT'S EASY TO PLAY PHOTO SLIDESHOWS, LISTEN TO MUSIC AND WATCH RECORDED TV WITH YOUR MICROSOFT GAMES CONSOLE.

# Using an Xbox with Windows 7

Millions of homes have an Xbox 360 console tucked under the living room television or in a teenager's bedroom. What many of them might not realise is that the console can be connected to a Windows 7 PC, turning it into a home entertainment centre as well as fine games machine.

That's because the Xbox 360 is one of the devices that Microsoft calls a Media Center Extender. This means you can use it to enjoy all the features of Windows Media Center – photo slideshows, music, live and recorded TV – as if you were sitting in front of your PC. It's particularly useful if you connect your Xbox console to a large HDTV set, because you can enjoy all the media stored on your PC on a far bigger screen. Conversely, if you have a Media Center PC connected to your living room TV, you can now watch all the shows on its hard disk from another room.

Another little-known fact is that you can stream BBC iPlayer shows downloaded on your PC to the Xbox. This, coupled with the Sky Player service due to arrive on the Xbox 360 in autumn 2009, essentially turns your console into a TV-on-demand service.

**JOIN UP** Both your Windows 7 PC and Xbox will need to be connected to your home network. To stream live or recorded TV, you'll need a strong wireless connection – or,

even better, an Ethernet cable – to your router, especially if you want to watch high-definition (HD) content. If your wireless connection isn't good enough (see opposite page) and you can't physically cable your devices, you might want to consider HomePlug Powerline adapters, which use your mains electricity circuits to transmit data.

It's worth noting that some antivirus programs can be overly fussy when you attempt to connect a Windows 7 PC to an Xbox 360. Keep an eye out for any pop-ups from your security software during the setup procedure, which might seek your permission to allow the console to connect. If you can't make the two devices see one another, check your security software's website for any special instructions on connecting an Xbox 360, such as opening firewall ports.

**TAKE CONTROL** While Microsoft does sell dedicated Media Center remote controls for the Xbox 360, offering a host of advanced playback controls, don't think you have to spend extra. The standard Xbox 360 controller is perfectly adequate for operating the Media Center features. By the same token, both wired and wireless Xbox 360 controllers can be used directly with your PC (the wireless version requires an extra USB dongle), which saves you investing in gaming joypads if you already have an Xbox.

## Tip

To watch BBC iPlayer shows on your Xbox 360, you need to download the special Windows Media Player files to your PC, not the standard iPlayer downloads. Go to www.bbc.co.uk/iplayer and click on the show of your choice. Just underneath the regular Download button, you should see a button that says More Downloads. Select Windows Media Player from this dropdown menu and save the file to the Videos folder on your PC. Once downloaded, the show should appear in the Xbox's video menu. Remember, iPlayer downloads are valid only for a limited time.

With an Xbox 360, you have a great way to play content from your PC on your TV, without having to copy any files or shell out for any extra hardware or software.

# HOW TO...
# USE AN XBOX AS A MEDIA PLAYER

**① PREPARE YOUR EQUIPMENT**  Switch on your PC and your Xbox 360 and make sure both are connected to your router, either via a wired or wireless connection. If you have an Xbox Live account, you should see a pop-up message saying you're logged in to it, assuming your internet connection is working. Alternatively, check you're online using the Test Live Connection facility in the setup menus. If your PC is connecting wirelessly, hover over the Wi-Fi symbol at the bottom right of the screen and check that the signal strength is either good or, preferably, excellent. If it's any weaker, try moving the PC closer to the router, or the Xbox may struggle to stream content from it successfully.

**② CONNECT TO MEDIA CENTER**  On your Xbox 360, go to the My Xbox menu and scroll right until you reach the Media Center option. Click on this and click Create a New Connection, and on the next screen write down the eight-digit code that's shown. Now click Continue. Your Xbox will tell you to visit www.xbox.com/setup on your PC and download some software. Ignore this – it's completely unnecessary with Windows 7. Back on your PC, all you need to is open Media Center, select Tasks and Add Extender. You'll now be asked to enter the code you were given earlier. The PC should now connect to the Xbox console.

**③ CHECK SIGNAL STRENGTH**  If the wireless signal between your PC and the Xbox is weak, you may now see a screen that helps you improve it. A sliding scale reveals whether your connection is strong enough for standard-definition television (SDTV) or high-definition streams (HDTV). If the connection is weak, try moving your Xbox or your PC closer to the router. Make sure no other devices on the network – such as mobile phones or network storage devices – are operating while you perform these tests. If the connection is still too weak, check you have the latest drivers for the wireless card in your PC: these can greatly improve the connection. If all else fails, you may have to resort to cables or an alternative such as HomePlug networking.

**④ START USING MEDIA CENTER**  Your Xbox should now be showing the same Media Center screen you see on the PC. The first time you use Media Center on the Xbox, performance can be sluggish as the console scours through all your photos, videos and music. Don't worry, it soon settles down. And don't fret about all those files filling up your Xbox's hard drive: the content stays on your PC while the Xbox streams it over the network. This does mean the PC has to be turned on. You can use it for other tasks at the same time, although not intensive ones such as video editing or 3D games.

**HOW LONG?**
Ten minutes should do it, unless you have to rejig things to get a Wi-Fi signal.

**HOW HARD?**
Easier than any game you'll play on the Xbox 360.

# IN THIS CHAPTER

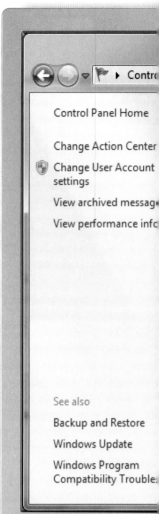

Staying safe

# STAYING SAFE IN

Windows 7 is the most secure Windows operating system yet, but that doesn't mean you can be complacent. Whether it's children let loose on vital files, malicious code invading your system or pure and simple hardware failure, a computer is always under threat. Luckily, there's a wealth of options to keep things running. Windows Defender will hold back

# WINDOWS 7

spyware, while the built-in Firewall keeps hackers out. Windows Backup goes from strength to strength, and User Account Control has developed from a perpetual annoyance into a useful way of keeping your PC safe from both accidental and intentional changes. So Windows 7 is pretty safe out of the box – and in this chapter we'll look at ways to make it even more secure.

# 8

## *Staying safe*

 CHILDREN CAN GET INTO ALL SORTS OF TROUBLE USING A PC, BUT WINDOWS 7 GIVES YOU WAYS TO LIMIT THE DAMAGE TO THEMSELVES AND THE COMPUTER.

# Introducing Parental Controls

Allowing your kids on the home PC is a crucial part of their education these days, but give any inexperienced user unfettered access and you're asking for trouble. Windows XP started the ball rolling by allowing multiple restricted accounts, and Vista introduced the concept of parental controls for individual users, building in features such as internet security and web filtering. In Windows 7, web filtering is now part of the optional Windows Live Family Safety application, which we look at on p108.

There are two main facets to Parental Controls: time limits and controlling access to applications. It all hinges on having multiple limited Standard user accounts as well as a full-blown Administrator account, as we explained on p38. Once you have at least one Standard account, and password-protected your Administrator account, you can start restricting what users can do. By default, a Standard user can't make changes that affect other accounts, so they can't erase your spreadsheets or crucial system files.

Parental Controls goes much further. You can restrict which games a user can play by setting a maximum age rating. Windows matches games you've installed against the ratings issued by the British Board of Film Classification (BBFC) and Pan European Game Information (PEGI) – 12, 15, 18 and so on. Alternatively, you can allow a certain age certificate, but bar particular games if they include content you find objectionable. For instance, you could allow games rated up to 15, but not if they include violence. You can also opt to block any game that doesn't have an official rating.

Finally, you can select individual games and say whether your children can or can't play them. Clicking the "Block or Allow specific games" link presents you with a list of the games currently installed: click Always Allow or Always Block. Similar controls are available for allowing or prohibiting users from accessing certain applications.

**GRANTING ACCESS** If a child attempts to launch a game or application that you've blocked, they'll get the opportunity to send you a message requesting permission to run it (or you can type in your password there and then).

Parental controls are just the start, though. We recommend you download Microsoft's Windows Live Family Safety application – it's free, gives much more control over what children can and can't do, and, as we show overleaf, it's also very easy to implement.

## *Tip*

It should go without saying that there's no substitute for being directly involved when it comes to kids and PCs. While Parental Controls and web filtering can help to limit access to unsuitable material, it's wise to minimise the time a child can use a PC without human supervision. Do check that your Administrator account is password-protected, and that your kids don't know the password. Without this, all your work setting up Parental Controls will be for nothing.

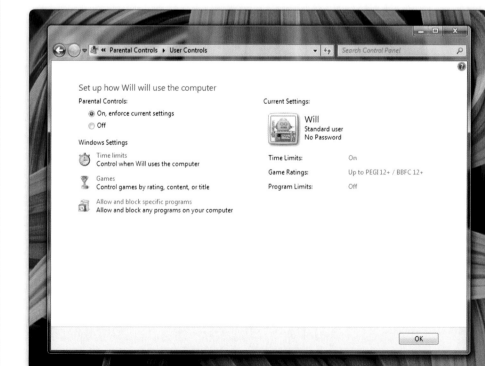

**To control what your kids get up to on your PC, it makes sense to set up an individual account for each of them, especially if they're of different ages.**

# HOW TO...
# SET UP PARENTAL CONTROLS

**(1) TIME LIMITS** This is where you set when and for how long a child (that is, a specified Standard user account that a child will be logging in as) can use a PC. The blue squares represent the hours during which this user account will be inaccessible. You can choose specific times for each day of the week, so you could allow an hour every school-day evening and then a few hours more during the weekend, blocking off the PC after bedtime and in the morning. To change a schedule, once you've dragged the mouse over a block of hours, simply repeat the process to revert them to free hours. By default, a new user account is free all the time.

**(2) CLASSIFIED INFORMATION** Click on Games in the main Parental Controls panel and you can choose which games each user will be allowed to load, based on their content ratings. The first question is whether a user is allowed to play any games at all; if so, your next task is to set which age ratings they can access. Remember, an age certificate is just the beginning – different games have different reasons for being awarded certain certificates. Windows 7 acknowledges this, and you can block games that have certain attributes, such as violence, bad language or sexual content. Keep track of the option at the top, which allows you to block games that don't come with a rating.

**(3) EXCEPTIONS** You can override the settings you made in step 2 by clicking "Block or Allow specific games". This presents you with a list of all the games currently installed on your system. Here, it doesn't matter what age or content restrictions you may already have set up: if you click Always Allow, this user will be able to load the specified game. The games that come supplied with Windows 7 are a tame bunch, and none is rated unsuitable for anyone over the age of three, but this is a good place to experiment with your settings.

**(4) BLOCKING APPLICATIONS** It's unlikely that you have many applications (as opposed to games or documents) on your PC that you wouldn't want a child to access, but by clicking Block and Allow specific programs, and then choosing the second option, you can see a list of those available and choose which to prohibit. You might want to block high-end apps such as Microsoft Excel as part of protecting your work content, or restrict programs that access the internet, such as web browsers, while allowing common applications such as Microsoft Word and essentials such as virus scanners. In the unlikely event that an application you want to block isn't in the list, click Browse at the foot of the screen and navigate to the program's application file (the file that its shortcut in the Start menu points to) to block it.

**HOW LONG?**
Five minutes; longer for lots of users or if you want to set up a complex barrage of controls.

**HOW HARD?**
Easy. If you get stuck, you could always ask a teenager to help. No, hang on a minute...

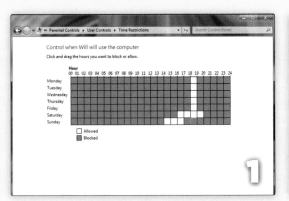

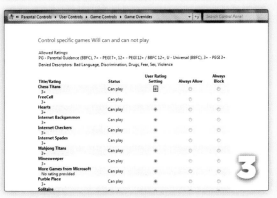

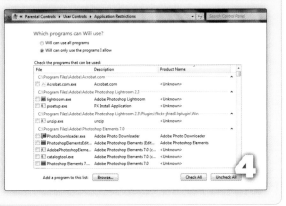

 THERE'S SOME DODGY STUFF ON THE INTERNET, BUT WINDOWS 7'S VERSATILE FILTERING AND MONITORING SYSTEM HELPS KEEP IT AWAY FROM YOUR KIDS.

# Windows Live Family Safety

Parental Controls help you ensure your kids don't spend their whole lives online, but when they are there's always a chance they could stumble across dodgy content or unsavoury characters. Enter the Family Safety tool, one of Microsoft's Windows 7 Live Essentials (see chapter 5).

It works using Windows Live IDs, so if you don't already have a free Hotmail or Live account you'll need to create one for yourself, as a parent, and for each child. Once Family Safety is installed, your child simply needs to sign in using the Family Safety applet in the Windows System Tray – either on your PC or their own – and they're protected.

**WEB FILTERING** Family Safety has three main modules, all configured through the Family Safety website. Web Filtering governs what children can access through a browser. The most restrictive setting locks them out of all web content except a shortlist of pre-approved "child-friendly" sites. For older kids, basic filtering opens up most of the web but excludes known pornographic or violent sites and pages related to hacking. You can set up a custom filter to restrict access to particular types of pages or block individual sites.

Web Filtering works at the operating system level, so kids can't get around it simply by installing a new web browser, for example. And it's versatile: if a child finds a site they want to access is blocked, you can enable it immediately for them by entering your parent password. If

you're not around, the child need only click a button to have an access request sent to you by email for you to review and respond to at a later point (or instantly).

**ACTIVITY REPORTING** The Activity Reporting module shows you which websites each user has visited. You can view details of every page to see exactly what your child has been browsing, or check which sites have been blocked. If you feel a blocked site is in fact appropriate, you can enable it. Activity Reporting also shows you which programs other than web browsers have been accessing the internet, so it can help you ensure no unwanted communications or data are flowing into or out of your home.

**CONTACT MANAGEMENT** The third major module is Contact Management. This lets you restrict who your child can communicate with. While we don't subscribe to the view that the internet is a terrible place full of terrible people, young children using email could get into some confusing situations. Again, if a child finds someone they want to contact is blocked, they need only click a button: you'll receive an access request, which you can approve or deny.

Note that one limitation of Windows Live Family Safety's Contact Management is that it works only with Microsoft services, such as Messenger and Hotmail. If your child uses a different system, such as Google's Gmail, Family Safety can't help you.

*Tip*

Double-click on the Windows Live Family Safety icon and a little panel shows (among other things) whether Activity Reporting is active. The user receives no other warning that their online actions are being recorded. If you're planning to monitor your child's online activity and investigate which sites they've been visiting, you may want to make this clear to them first – after all, nobody likes being secretly spied on.

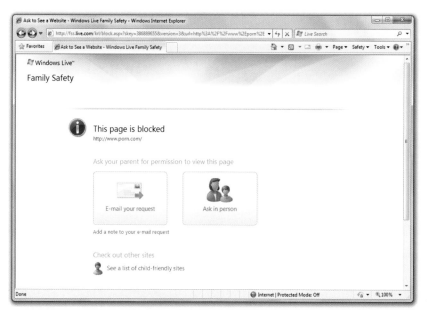

Family Safety will say no to resources it thinks aren't suitable for kids, but the final decision lies with you. If you're not on the spot to override the block with your password, your child can opt to send you an automated email that you can respond to online to give or deny permission instantly.

# HOW TO...
# PROTECT YOUR CHILD ONLINE

**(1)** **INSTALL WINDOWS LIVE ESSENTIALS** The Windows Live Family Safety tool is one of the Windows Live Essentials, so you'll need to install it via the Live Essentials installer. You can access this either from your PC or via Microsoft's Windows Live Essentials homepage – see chapter 5 for more information. Once Family Safety is installed, you'll find it in your Start menu under Windows Live. Run it, and the first thing you need to do is sign in as a parent. If you don't have a free Microsoft Hotmail or Live account, you can create one right now.

Once that's done, you'll be up and running. However, for Family Safety to be useful, you also need to create IDs for the children. You can do this on the Family Safety website; click the link to visit it. Note that if your children use their own computers to access the internet, you'll need to download and install the Family Safety client on their PC as well as your own.

**(2)** **CONFIGURE FAMILY SAFETY** At the Family Safety website, you can set up web filtering, activity reporting and contact management for each of your children by clicking on the relevant tabs down the left-hand side of the Family Safety website. You'll need to be logged in as a parent to do this. Remember to hit Save after making any changes to the settings.

**(3)** **MONITOR THE KIDS** Your child now simply needs to log in to the Family Safety client, on whichever PC they're using, and they can browse the web without supervision. If you've enabled Activity Reporting, you can later check which sites they've been visiting – and which particular pages within those sites – simply by returning to the Family Safety website, logging in (as yourself) and clicking on Activity Reporting in the left-hand bar. You can filter the access log by date, to make it easier to see new activity, by computer or by user account.

You'll also see a separate tab for Other Activity. It's worth checking this, as your child could be using software that isn't fully protected by Family Safety. Apart from the risk of exposure to unsuitable content, they could be illegally sharing files (for which you could be held liable), or might even be unwittingly hosting some type of networked malware.

**(4)** **MANAGE REQUESTS** You can also manage your child's access requests from this page. Click on Requests and you'll see full details of blocked web pages and contacts that your child wants to access. There's a simple dropdown menu that you can use to approve a page or a contact for everyone, or just for that child. Or, of course, you can say no.

### HOW LONG?
Ten minutes using the standard settings; longer to set up your own lists of contacts and websites.

### HOW HARD?
The Family Safety web interface is clear and simple to use, once you understand the way it works.

# 8
## *Staying safe*

# Introducing the Action Center

One of Windows Vista's most significant failings was how frequently its Security Center alerted users to supposed problems. Alarming little balloons would often pop up from the System Tray at the bottom right of the screen, and you'd have to stop what you were doing to dismiss them.

Well, the Security Center has been closed in Windows 7 and the Action Center opened in its place. The most obvious improvement is that you're no longer troubled by a constant stream of alerts: if the Action Center has something to tell you, it will sit quietly until you check it, with a little red flag to tell you there's something to see.

**WATCHING BRIEF** Think of the Action Center as a watchdog: it won't scan your system for viruses or spyware, but it will warn you if there's something wrong with the programs you've installed to do those jobs (see p114). If you don't like the way Action Center is giving you information, you can click Change Action Center settings and deselect certain messages. So if, say, Action Center is alerting you because you haven't backed up but you've already done so using a third-party application, you can uncheck the box and Windows will stop telling you about it.

Action Center monitors the Windows Firewall (see opposite page), User Account Control (p112) and Windows Update (p118). You can also monitor Windows Defender (p120) through its simple interface. And if your computer stops working properly and you're unsure why, you can view an archive of messages Action Center has already displayed to help you track down the problem.

At the bottom of the Action Center are two extra links: Troubleshooting and Recovery. Troubleshooting brings up a list of common steps you can take to get your PC healthy again, while Recovery gives you a gateway to System Restore, which we cover on p150.

Windows 7 turns the Action Center from something you saw every day into something you'll hardly ever have to look at, which is a mixed blessing – there are times when its messages are quite important, and some may feel Microsoft should have erred on the side of caution. Best keep an eye on that little icon in your Taskbar, just in case.

If you do encounter a problem, Action Center should be your first port of call. Not only will it let you know about gaps in your security setup, but it's also a good place to start when trying to track down everyday system niggles.

## *Tip*

◢ If you right-click on the Action Center flag (which sits in the System Tray area of the Taskbar at the foot of the screen, near the clock), you can troubleshoot a problem there and then. Unlike in previous versions of Windows, the troubleshooting tool actually works.

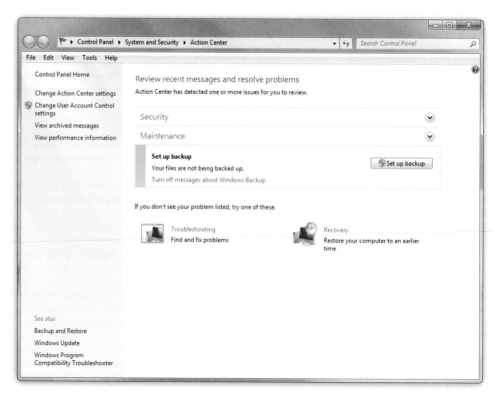

Double-click on the small flag sitting in your Taskbar, and Action Center will spring into view. It's well worth checking your security status, especially when a red flag is showing.

# HOW TO...
# CONFIGURE WINDOWS FIREWALL

Forget the criticisms you might have heard about Windows' built-in firewall. In Windows 7, it's now a decent tool that will help keep you safe from internet threats.

**1 WHERE ARE YOU?** When you connect to a new network, you're asked to define it as a Home, Work or Public location. This determines your networking features and firewall settings. The Firewall is more relaxed if you're at home or at work, as you're less likely to be sharing a network with nefarious characters than you might be at an internet café. Either way, you're told when an application tries to access the internet.

**2 FIREWALL CONTROLS** Access Firewall's controls by opening Control Panel and entering "firewall" in the Search box. To change an application's internet access, click "Allow a program or feature through Windows Firewall". This opens a list of all the apps that have accessed the internet through your system. By default, this screen is locked and you need to click "Change settings" at the top, which may prompt a UAC box (see p112). You can then start changing things. For instance, you might want to make an app available on a public network, or to block one altogether. It would make sense to clear both the Private and Public checkboxes, but instead use the Remove button below.

**3 ALERT!** You can make broader adjustments. Clicking "Change notification settings" doesn't just affect how often Firewall alerts you; you can also set it to its most paranoid. "Block all incoming connections, including those in the list of allowed programs" means your internet access is effectively shut off. This can be useful if you find yourself connected to a network but unwilling to let any data in or out, or if you have children and you simply don't want them to access the internet. Or switch off Windows Firewall altogether using the radio button at the bottom. You'll then be inundated with warnings (although you can disable them) until you turn it back on.

**4 MORE DETAIL** For the expert user, clicking on "Advanced settings" takes you to the heart of Windows Firewall. Not only can you filter connections by application, but also by network domain, regardless of that network's Home, Work or Public setting. You can also view the rules already created in far more detail. The default view allows you to choose only whether a connection is allowed. In the Advanced view, you can allow a connection only if it's secure, and also define precisely what you mean by secure. For added security and flexibility, you can also internet-enable applications depending on which user is logged in.

### HOW LONG?
Most people will be happy leaving Firewall as it stands. Fiddling with it still shouldn't take long.

### HOW HARD?
If you adjust settings, be sure you know what you're doing – it's easy to make mistakes.

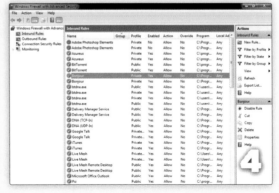

**8**

*Staying safe*

# Introducing User Account Control

Windows Vista may have been an improvement on XP, but one new feature nearly everyone hated was User Account Control. This irritating pop-up was designed to prevent users or applications making changes to your system on the sly, whether installing a new program, configuring something like the Firewall or simply changing the date.

Every time User Account Control was activated – and there were *plenty* of times – you'd see the whole Windows screen dimming while the all too familiar box popped up, preventing you getting on with anything else until you confirmed or denied what you were trying to do. Many people became so annoyed with User Account Control within a few weeks of starting to use Vista that they turned it off, rendering an important security improvement useless. Others failed to figure out how to kill it and just ended up swearing at it with monotonous regularity.

If there were those who felt nothing but gratitude to Microsoft for the daily – well, more like half-hourly – reassurance that their system was watching over them and protecting them both from malicious software and from their own foolish mistakes, they kept pretty quiet about it while everyone else was moaning vociferously. This was a

shame. User Account Control (UAC) was a good idea, in that it placed a real obstacle in the way of any malware that might be attempting to infect your PC: the only way it could get through would be for you to click Continue, which presumably you wouldn't, unless you'd got so accustomed to seeing UAC pop up that you'd stopped thinking about it.

It also forced anyone using a Vista computer to confirm their actions before installing a new piece of software from an unrecognised company, or making potentially damaging changes to settings. Generally, that was no bad thing. The trouble was, everyone who used Windows at any sort of advanced level was consistently bombarded with messages. Something needed to be done.

**BETTER BY DESIGN** While many people would have been glad to see the back of UAC altogether, it hasn't been removed from Windows 7. Instead, it's been redesigned. The most immediately noticeable difference is the reduction in the number of times UAC rears its head. It's still an occasional presence, but when you see it now there's usually a good reason. Installing applications, for instance, or renaming files, very rarely results in an instance of UAC.

*Tip*

 Don't let other users of your main PC have Administrator accounts. Making Administrator-level changes is far too easy, and you run the risk of others rendering your PC unusable. Give them Standard accounts instead – most people won't notice the difference, and UAC will prompt them to ask an Administrator when necessary.

Whenever you initiate an operation that could harm Windows – or a malicious program tries the same thing without your knowledge – the User Account Control dialog will appear to check that you really want the operation to be carried out. You can only proceed by entering an Administrator password.

This is partly because software developers have learned to optimise their applications to take account of UAC and behave in ways that don't cause it to appear. As we discover in the box on the right, UAC is also far easier to configure in Windows 7 than it was in Vista.

**SAME DIFFERENCE** You may see it less often, but the way UAC works essentially remains the same. Whenever a system-level change is about to be made by an application – whether you started it yourself or not – you'll be alerted. If you're logged into an Administrator account, you can either click Yes or No to dismiss the alert. But one of the key features of UAC is that you don't need to be logged in as an Administrator to perform Administrator-level actions. If a user with a Standard account attempts something potentially risky, they're prompted with a UAC box. If they have the Administrator password – or the Administrator is willing to enter it for them – they're allowed to continue.

As we've explained on p38, it's best practice with Windows to have all the users of your PC log in on Standard accounts. These are far more controllable: you can't, for instance, apply Parental Controls to an Administrator account, since by definition an Administrator can do whatever they like. It's even advisable for system administrators themselves – that's you – to use a Standard account for day-to-day computing. That way, you're not prevented from making system-level changes, but you're far less likely to make them by accident. Using a Standard account also means that if you leave your PC accidentally logged in, subsequent users can't take advantage.

**LIFE WITHOUT UAC** If you really can't be bothered with the UAC system, because you find yourself carrying out a lot of operations regularly that provoke warning boxes, you can turn it off. Should you decide on this rash course of action, simply open Control Panel, run the User Accounts utility and click on Change User Account Control Settings. You then drag the slide bar down to its lowest position and click OK, at which point the screen will dim one last time and you'll be asked if you really, really want to do such a thing. If you go ahead, you'll be prompted to restart.

Without UAC, you can still use the different privileges of Administrator and Standard accounts to protect your system, ensuring other users log in with Standard accounts and doing so yourself whenever you know you won't need to change system settings or install software. But you'll lose the extra security of UAC when running as Administrator, and, rather inconveniently, Standard users – including you, when you're logged in as such – won't be prompted to request your Administrator password when they try to carry out an operation that's blocked by the UAC dialog box. Instead, they'll receive a message saying they "must be a computer administrator" to perform this task, and they (or you) will have to save their work, log out and log back in as an Administrator.

Depending on how your PC is used, this could prove to be more hassle than putting up with UAC in the first place. It really isn't such a bad system after all.

# UAC IN ACTION

Windows 7's UAC shows four different prompts depending on what an application or user is trying to do. Fortunately, they have fairly self-explanatory logos. The quartered shield, reminiscent of a Windows logo, indicates that a function within Windows is trying to start. A question mark refers to an application that isn't part of Windows but has a valid digital signature. An orange shield with an exclamation mark means a program without a digital signature is trying to run, and you should check where it came from. A red shield with a white cross (not shown here) tells a Standard user they can't proceed without Administrator access.

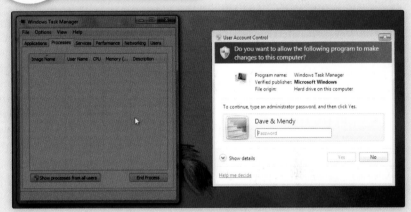

Other users may not be too keen on someone else (you) being in charge of their accounts and applications, but it's in their interest. When a user on a Standard account tries to access someone else's files, run a protected application or make a change to the system, they'll see this screen. At this point, you – the crucial person who knows the Administrator password – will need to authorise the action.

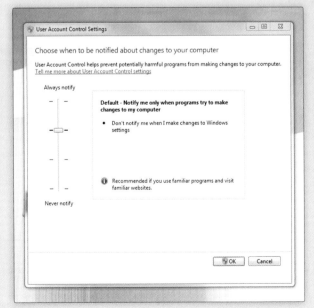

UAC is now far better behaved on its default settings, but you can make it more or less strict depending on how worried you are. To change it, click the Start button and type "uac", then click on Change User Account Control Settings. On the slider, the higher the bar, the more UAC will appear. The top setting notifies you whenever you or an application make a significant change. The second setting alerts you only when an application makes a change. A lower setting doesn't dim the screen and stop you working, and the final option turns UAC off – after questioning your sanity.

## 8

*Staying safe*

COMPUTER VIRUSES AND RELATED THREATS REMAIN VERY REAL, BUT SECURITY SOFTWARE CAN PROTECT YOUR PC AND YOUR DATA FROM INFECTION.

# Adding virus protection

Computer viruses are a fact of life, so it's important to understand how they can infect your computer and what you can do to protect yourself. The first point is that, technically, most infections these days aren't caused by viruses but by other types of unwanted software, some of which we'll examine below. So when we're talking about keeping your computer safe, it's clearer to say we're fighting "malware", a general term for all kinds of malicious software.

**WHAT IS MALWARE?** For your PC to be infected with malware, it must execute a piece of programming code designed to deliver an ill effect. An obvious way is if, for example, you're browsing the web and see an advert for a free music player. You download the file and double-click it, and instead of installing the software you wanted, it installs malware. Congratulations: you've just been tricked by a trojan (named after the Trojan Horse of legend).

You can avoid simple deceptions such as this by keeping your wits about you and not running software from untrusted sources: most web browsers will warn you before downloading executable files for precisely this reason.

But it isn't always that easy. Sometimes, hackers find ways to get your web browser to run malicious code automatically when you visit a website. Simply viewing the page causes your PC to become infected, even if you don't click any links or explicitly download anything. This type of malware is known as a "drive-by download".

If you think you can stay safe by steering clear of dodgy sites, think again. Unscrupulous hackers have been known to break into respected websites and plant their malware code on legitimate pages. One famous hack a few years ago saw an official website for the US Super Bowl giving malware to visitors. Plus, drive-bys have been contained in adverts that reputable sites accepted in good faith.

Perhaps the most alarming category of malware is worms. These programs reach out across the net and use technical tricks to implant themselves in the systems they find. Your PC is at risk from a worm attack any time it's connected to the internet, even when you're not browsing.

**WHERE DOES MALWARE COME FROM?** In the 1980s and 1990s, viruses were written by students and hobbyists who wanted to see how far their creations could spread. These days, most malware comes from criminal sources with far more nefarious intentions. Some can record your keystrokes and send details back to their creators; if you use

## Tip

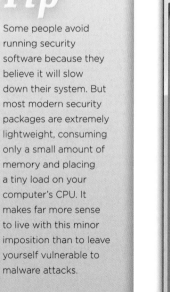

Some people avoid running security software because they believe it will slow down their system. But most modern security packages are extremely lightweight, consuming only a small amount of memory and placing a tiny load on your computer's CPU. It makes far more sense to live with this minor imposition than to leave yourself vulnerable to malware attacks.

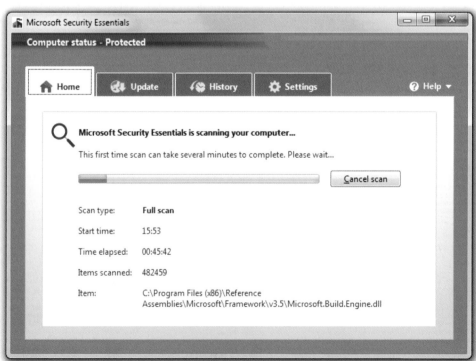

Microsoft's free Windows Security Essentials can scour your system and eliminate any trace of malware before it ruins your day.

Internet Explorer can't prevent you from getting infected, but it can remind you of the risks of downloading software. Note that "this file type" in the above alert simply means a program file – it isn't warning you of any specific problem with the content of the file in question.

online banking or access other confidential information, the danger is obvious. Other programs subsume your PC into a "botnet", a network of "robot" systems that can be remotely controlled. Typically, botnets are used to send junk emails from thousands of locations at once, making the original sender impossible to identify. Being part of a botnet can eat up your PC resources and clog up your internet connection, as well as helping to damage or inconvenience other users.

Today's malware creators don't want to create a stir; on the contrary, they want their work to go unnoticed so they can keep harvesting bank details and sending spam. So if your PC is infected, the odds are you won't know about it. That makes it all the more important to avoid infection.

**HOW CAN YOU PROTECT YOURSELF?** Windows 7 is the most secure edition yet. Many of the technical vulnerabilities that made previous malware infections possible have been firmly closed, so for the time being you're unlikely to be hit by a drive-by or a worm. However, that's bound to change as hackers find and exploit the inevitable vulnerabilities in the new operating system. That's why the first step to protecting yourself is to let Windows Update install new security enhancements as they become available (see p118).

The second step is to pay attention to the User Account Control requests that Windows 7 will periodically display (see p112). If UAC pops up unexpectedly, warning you that a program is trying to change your system settings, it's a fair bet that something dodgy is going on; you should deny the request and run a malware check.

The third step is to install security software and keep it up to date. The Windows Defender module that's built into Windows 7 can detect some types of malware. Microsoft's free Security Essentials package detects a much wider range of threats, and can leap in to warn you as soon as any type of malware is recognised on your PC. Ideally, you should consider investing in a third-party security suite, since these have many additional options to keep you safe: we list some of the choices available on the right.

# SECURITY SOFTWARE

Antivirus software isn't included with Windows 7, but there are plenty of security packages to choose from, some of them available for free to home users.

**VIRUS KILLERS** There are many security packages available for Windows 7; respected brands include Avira, BullGuard, Eset, Kaspersky and Norton. These companies all offer antivirus programs that can detect all types of malware using "behavioural analysis". That means they don't just look for known malware files; they determine whether a program is good or bad based on the changes it makes to your system. So, they can protect you even against brand-new threats that have never been seen before.

You can also invest in a more comprehensive security suite, which will include the standard antivirus module plus an enhanced firewall to prevent worms and other intruders getting into your system in the first place. Many packages also add protection against unwanted email, such as spam and phishing messages that try to trick you into giving away passwords and personal information. Some include parental control features, too. You'll notice that all these features are already built into Windows 7, but independent packages are typically more customisable and offer more features.

**WHY SUBSCRIBE?** Malware authors are constantly seeking new ways to sneak their evil code on to unsuspecting PCs. That means security software must be constantly updated to recognise these ever-evolving threats. Normally, when you buy a security package the price entitles you to one year of updates, although there are often reduced rates available if you pay for a number of years up front. If you don't want to spend the money, there are some free options. Apart from Microsoft's own Security Essentials, available from www.microsoft.com, Avira (www.avira.com) and AVG (www.avg.com/uk) are two well-known security developers that offer free antivirus products for personal use. They're not as sophisticated as the paid-for products, but you can use them for as long as you like and benefit from free regular updates.

As you might guess, not all security suites are created equal, and none can guarantee a 100% success rate. Check independent software reviews, such as those in PC Pro (www.pcpro.co.uk), to see which suites have a good track record and which might be more likely to let malware slip through the net.

## 8
### Staying safe

WINDOWS 7'S BACKUP AND RESTORE CENTER IS MICROSOFT'S MOST ADVANCED SO FAR, BUT BEWARE OF SOME LIMITATIONS IN THE HOME PREMIUM VERSION.

# Setting up Windows Backup

We all have files we couldn't bear to lose, from work documents to photo albums, music collections to TV shows. Windows 7 has a powerful Backup and Restore utility built in for precisely this reason, and all you need to run it is a spare hard disk, network drive, blank DVD or memory stick.

If you've used Vista's Backup tool or third-party software such as Acronis True Image (www.acronis.co.uk), you'll be familiar with how it works. The wizard-based utility takes copies of your chosen files – although, disappointingly, not system or program files – and compresses them all into one smaller file, then stores this in an external location.

When you need to retrieve files, the wizard allows you to browse through them and restore them to your hard disk. You also have the advanced option of browsing and restoring backup sets from any other Windows 7 PC, giving you a useful way to manage backups across several systems.

**SET UP AND FORGET** When you create a new backup task, Backup and Restore will either attempt to choose your backup files automatically or save and compress every file you select. Whenever the same task is run again, it will only add new or edited files, saving time and disk space. The

original file and folder structure is retained, which is vital for organised files such as a music collection.

Backup and Restore includes a comprehensive scheduler, so you can leave it to run automatically. It can be set to run monthly, weekly or even daily. If your PC is off at the specified time, the backup will run as soon as you log back on, and it runs in the background so as not to disrupt your work. Backup and Restore also includes options for managing the storage of backup sets, so you can delete old backups as well as setting the system to only store the most recent full backup if you're short on hard disk space.

**TOTAL PROTECTION** Users of Windows 7 Home Premium have a slightly limited version of Backup and Restore, but the Professional and Ultimate editions include an extra option that elevates it to a genuine all-purpose backup tool. It's the ability to image your entire hard disk, so should the worst happen you can boot from the install DVD and restore your system onto a new hard disk exactly as it was when it was imaged. It's a good idea to add this option to your backups every so often as a safety net, and it's enabled by default the first time you set up a backup task.

## Tip

Third-party backup software will generally add more features and flexibility, especially if you have Windows 7 Home Premium with its more basic functions. Acronis True Image Home 2010, for instance, adds continuous protection for your data and can even migrate all your data and programs from one installation of Windows to another.

## Tip

Backup and Restore also gives you the option to create a System Repair Disc. While not quite as comprehensive as a full system image, this DVD will at least allow you to boot in case of emergency, and includes all the Windows recovery tools you'll need to rescue your vital files. See p154 for more details.

This is the drive to which you're going to back up. Make sure you have enough free space for all your files. If there isn't enough room, click **Manage space** to free some up.

Windows 7 makes it simple to **restore** all your backed-up files or specific ones you need to retrieve.

Creating a **system repair disc** gives you an extra line of defence: should things go horribly wrong, you can use it to restore your PC to a working state.

You can see the time of your **last backup** and if it failed, along with the next scheduled backup time and its contents.

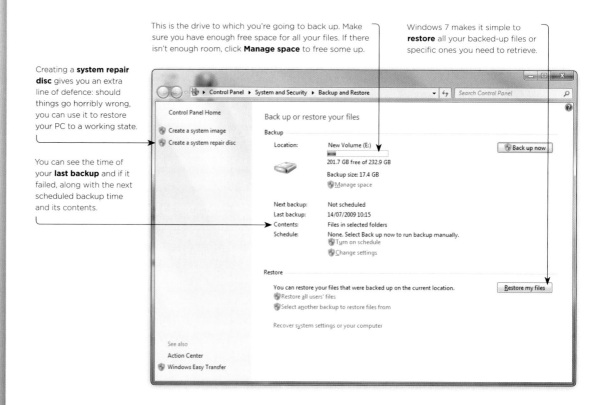

# HOW TO...
# BACK UP TO AN EXTERNAL DRIVE

 **RUN BACKUP AND RESTORE** To begin the process of setting up your backup, open the Start menu, go to All Programs | Maintenance, and click on Backup and Restore. In the window that appears, select "Set up backup". You'll be offered a choice of all the storage devices connected to your computer – internal and external hard disks, DVD drives, USB flash memory drives – as well as a button to choose a network location to back up to if you prefer. We'll choose an external hard disk. Windows will offer to select the files to back up, but you're better off ticking the option to pick your own.

 **CHOOSE YOUR FILES** Backup and Restore cleverly makes use of Windows 7's new Libraries, allowing you to quickly back up files of a particular type. You'll want to choose your Music, Pictures and Video libraries as well as the other key user account elements, such as Documents and Favorites. (If you have the patience, you should ideally set up separate backup tasks for your media and for your documents, and have them run at different intervals depending on their importance.) Then, if need be, browse through your main hard disk and add any other folders you'd like to protect. Finally, users running the Professional or Ultimate editions of Windows 7 can choose whether to add a full system image to the backup task.

**SCHEDULE THE TASK** Your new backup task will run immediately once it's set up, but you should also schedule it to run daily, weekly or monthly, so that you always have a safe copy of your important files. Before you save your backup task and exit, click "Change schedule". Then choose a day of the week as appropriate, and pick an hour of the day from the dropdown list. Whenever this time is reached, the backup task will automatically begin in the background, so you can continue working undisturbed. If your PC is off at the time, it will run next time you log on. Now that you've scheduled the task, click "Save settings and run backup" to begin your first backup. It may take anywhere from a few minutes to several hours, depending on the amount of data involved.

**RESTORE YOUR FILES** If you ever lose any files, it's now easy to restore them. Open Backup and Restore and choose the Restore option at the bottom. It should show any recent backups, or give you the option to locate one stored elsewhere. Restore the entire backup set (or full disk image), or browse through the files you've previously saved to choose which needs to be restored. Then start the restore process and sit back and wait for your vital files to find their way back to where they should be: safe on your hard disk.

**HOW LONG?**
Half-an-hour to several hours, depending on the amount of data.

**HOW HARD?**
It's easy – the wizard takes you through the whole process.

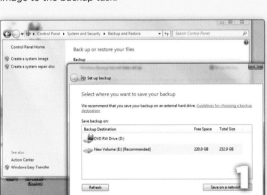

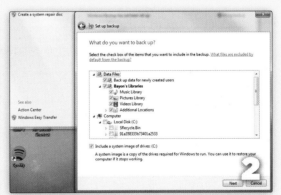

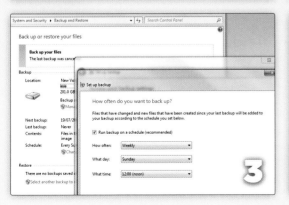

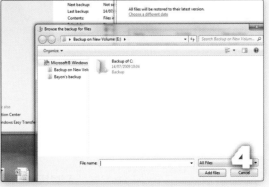

# 8

## Staying safe

IT'S IMPORTANT TO MAKE SURE YOUR SYSTEM HAS ALL THE LATEST SECURITY ENHANCEMENTS AND DRIVERS. WINDOWS UPDATE MAKES IT A BREEZE.

# Introducing Windows Update

Once upon a time, installing an operating system was a one-off job: you might run for years with the same system files. These days, computing moves much faster. Microsoft is constantly rolling out improvements, and Windows Update is your gateway to those often important system patches.

**WHY DO YOU NEED UPDATES?** The main reasons to keep your PC up to date are stability and security. An operating system as huge and complex as Windows 7 is bound to encounter occasional problems with combinations of hardware and software, and that's before you consider the cybercriminals actively seeking ways to break Windows 7's security so they can take over your computer (see p114).

Windows Update lets Microsoft fix a problem and push out the fix right away, so users always have the most stable and secure system possible. Keep an eye on the updates as they arrive and you'll see a regular stream of security enhancements. In fact, some of the most damaging malware infections of the past few years exploited weaknesses that, for Windows Update users, had already been fixed.

As a welcome side-effect, Windows Update can improve performance by making sure you have the latest versions of the correct drivers for all your hardware. Alongside the critical fixes, it will also deliver "recommended" updates such as new Help files or upgraded device drivers.

**AUTOMATIC INSTALLATION** When you start Windows 7 for the first time, you're prompted to configure updates. The default is to download and install key updates automatically. This is a great idea from the point of view of keeping your PC up to date, but sometimes after an update is installed Windows needs to be restarted, which can be inconvenient. So you may prefer to let Windows download updates, but hold off installing them until a time of your choosing. Or you can avoid checking for updates altogether. If you take one of these paths, Action Center will warn you that you're not as safe as you could be. Carry out your own regular checks or you'll be vulnerable to emerging security risks.

If you install Microsoft Office or other Microsoft applications, you'll also be given the option to turn Windows Update into a more general Microsoft Update centre. It's worth doing this: Office, too, could be exploited by crooks to gain access to your information unless you keep your security patches up to date.

## Tip

Windows is far from being the only piece of software that can benefit from regular updates. You'll find many non-Microsoft products, such as Mozilla Firefox and Apple iTunes, have their own built-in updaters. Use them regularly to ensure everything on your system is running with maximum security and efficiency.

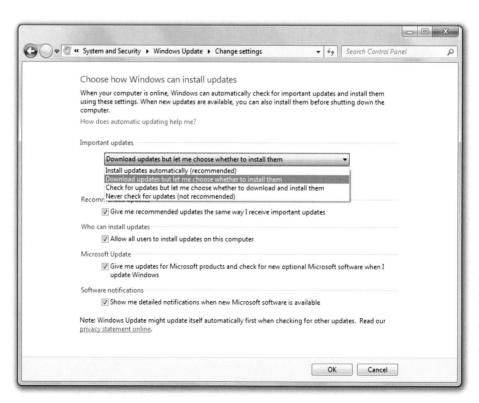

Windows Update can be set to wait for your say-so before installing updates, but it's safest to let it apply patches automatically as soon as they're available.

Since the beginning of time,
they have been on opposing sides...
One is swift and light while
the other is powerful
and invulnerable...
But against all odds,
they have now joined forces.

## The advanced Internet security solution is born.

Trend Micro Internet Security is a light yet powerful no-compromise solution that offers protection for your home network. The solution monitors all system entry points (Internet connection, wireless networks, USB flash drives, etc.), identifying threats before they occur. It authenticates websites and protects your online purchases. With Trend Micro, your system is fully protected!

Download a free trial version at:
**www.trendmicroupdate.com**

# 8
## Staying safe

ALTHOUGH WINDOWS 7 COMES WITHOUT BUILT-IN VIRUS PROTECTION, IT DOES INCLUDE WINDOWS DEFENDER TO SAFEGUARD YOUR PC AGAINST SPYWARE.

# Introducing Windows Defender

Windows Defender is a small but fully functional application that protects your PC from spyware. Spyware and viruses are similar things, but spyware is explicitly designed to take information from your PC and send it over the internet.

Windows Defender works in two main ways: by periodically scanning for files it knows to be dangerous, and by scanning everything that comes into your PC and trying to match it against its spyware definitions.

**DETECTING SPYWARE**  Defender keeps itself up to date via Windows Update (see p118) and by periodically downloading new spyware definitions. When it detects a suspicious file, it presents four options. If you're quite sure the program that's attempting to run is legitimate, choose "Always allow", so you won't be bothered by the same message again. If you're fairly sure it's okay, choose Ignore. The program will be allowed to install, but, should it then attempt to mess with important Windows settings, you'll get a second warning. You'll also be warned if the same software is still running when you next boot up Windows.

If you suspect the file is spyware, you can prevent it from running and store it in the Quarantine area, where it will be unable to cause harm. While it's in this virtual jail, you can restore or delete it at any time. If you're certain it's spyware, just choose Remove to delete it permanently.

When a program you've allowed to run attempts to change a Windows setting, you get two options: Permit or Deny. If you find yourself constantly clicking Permit, you can add the program to the "Allowed items" list.

**REAL-TIME PROTECTION**  Defender uses "agents" to check that Internet Explorer hasn't been tampered with, as well as keeping an eye on Windows add-ons, services, drivers and apps that behave oddly. Internet Explorer is a favourite target of spyware, but Defender will stop malware changing settings such as the homepage, proxies and toolbars.

Like most antivirus programs, Defender can scan your whole system for threats or look in individual folders. You can exclude folders, to save time, by adding their locations to the list at the bottom of Defender's Settings.

By default, Defender is accessible to every user of your PC unless you untick "Allow everyone to use Windows Defender". You'd only disable it for your own account if you'd installed a third-party antispyware program instead.

## Tip

It can be hard to know if a program is spyware or not. If in doubt, check the website you downloaded it from. Is it the official website for the program you want? Most antivirus programs scan for spyware too, so if Defender flags up a suspicious file, seek a second opinion by running your antivirus scanner on it. If both claim it's spyware, it probably is. Delete it, even if it promises free access to pictures of naked celebrities.

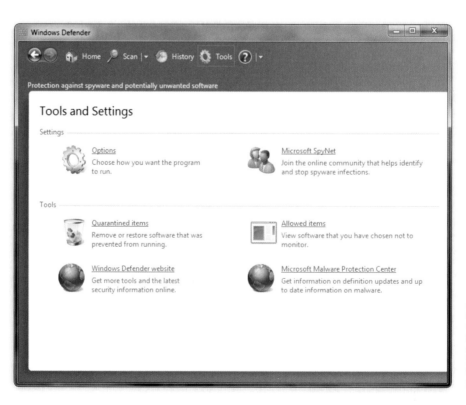

As long as you remember that it's only designed to detect a narrow range of threats, Windows Defender is a useful built-in element of your security system.

# HOW TO...
# FIND SPYWARE WITH DEFENDER

**1** UPDATE WINDOWS DEFENDER Before you use it to scan your system, first ensure that Windows Defender itself is up to date, so that it has the best chance of finding the latest spyware. If you have Windows Update set to download and install updates automatically (see p118), you may find it's already updated Defender to the most recent version available, and you can proceed with scanning straight away. Alternatively, to update from within Windows Defender, click the tiny triangle next to the Help icon in its toolbar and choose "Check for updates" from the menu that appears.

**2** PERFORM A SCAN To run a quick scan of your computer, click the Scan icon in Defender's toolbar. This checks the places in your system where spyware is most likely to hide. If you suspect you know where a piece of spyware is, you can tell Defender to look in one place, which is faster: click the triangle next to the Scan icon and choose "Custom scan...". For the most thorough search, choose "Full scan", which checks every file. It will slow down your other programs, so it's best done when you're not using your machine.

**3** DEAL WITH THREATS If the scan finds anything untoward, it will tell you how many possible spyware files it's detected and display a

one-button option to delete these threats immediately. If you don't care what they are and just want rid of them, click the Remove All button at the bottom right of the window. If you want to find out more and check Defender's diagnosis before erasing files that might have been misidentified, click the link labelled "Review items detected by scanning".

Each file identified as spyware by Windows Defender now has a list of possible actions displayed next to it. Choose from Remove, Quarantine or Allow (the last is for programs you're sure are legitimate). In our example, we want to move the suspect files to Quarantine to give us time to figure out what's wrong with them. If you choose the same course of action, make sure you then click "Apply actions" and not "Clean system" at the bottom. Once you've dealt with the spyware, you'll probably be asked to restart the computer.

**4** REVIEW DETECTED FILES At any time, you can review all the files detected so far. Open Defender's main window and click the Tools icon in the toolbar at the top. Choose "Quarantined items" and look through the captured files. Click any of these once, and a short description of it appears below. Tick the box next to any file you want to delete, then click the Remove button at the bottom right to erase it permanently.

**HOW LONG?**
It only needs a few clicks, but a full scan can take a little while to complete.

**HOW HARD?**
Defender is pretty simple to use – just think twice before clicking Remove.

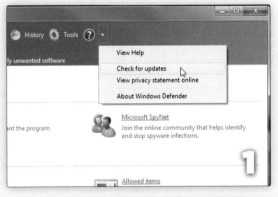

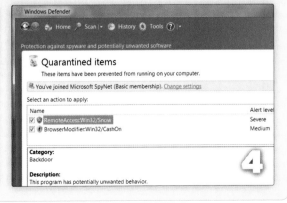

# IN THIS CHAPTER

**9**

*Laptop computing*

# WINDOWS 7 ON

With sales of laptops overtaking those of desktop PCs, Microsoft has stuffed Windows 7 full of features that make it easier to use on the move. In this chapter, we'll take you through some of the key enhancements that have been designed with laptops in mind, including 3G dongle support – which can allow you to surf almost anywhere, even if you don't have access to a wireless

# YOUR LAPTOP

internet hotspot – and the revised Tablet PC features. We've also come up with some top tips to extend your battery life, from simple power-management tweaks to more advanced options that could dramatically increase your time between mains sockets. In short, if you want to get the most out of your laptop in Windows 7, the following pages are essential reading.

# 9
## Laptop computing

# Introducing Sync Center

The Sync Center is the one-stop destination for keeping all your files up to date on all your computers and devices. After all, with the potential for hundreds of gigabytes of data to be scattered everywhere on your home network and on mobile devices such as smartphones, it isn't practical to keep everything in sync manually.

Sync Center comes to the rescue, ensuring two or more versions of the same file stored in different locations are matched with each other. If you add, delete or modify a file on one computer or device, Sync Center can mirror this on the same file in the other locations that you choose to sync with, whenever you choose to sync.

**HOW IT WORKS** The most common type of synchronisation will be for mobile phones (see opposite) and files on your network – or, if you own one, a network-attached storage (NAS) device that connects to your router. If you set up a homegroup (see p86), this makes it easy to keep files synchronised between your various PCs.

The simplest way to set up a new sync is to browse to a folder on your network and right-click on it. Then choose the "Always available offline" option. Windows 7 will churn through all the documents in that folder before telling you that it's finished and the files are ready. We suggest you

then create a shortcut to that folder by dragging it to the Favorites category in the left-hand panel of the Explorer window; this makes it much easier to find.

When you start a sync, Windows 7 compares the same files in different locations, determines if any have changed (including files that have been added or deleted), and works out which version of each file to keep, then copies that file to the other locations you selected. It's seamless.

By default, as you'd expect, Sync Center keeps the most up-to-date version of a file and overwrites the older versions with this. If the same file has been modified in two different locations, you have what's known as a "conflict". Sync Center won't try to guess which is the "right" version, but will ask you which version you want to keep and which you want to update.

**WHAT YOU CAN SYNC** You can sync any type of file, including music and photos from an MP3 player, photos from a digital camera, and contact or calendar information if your mobile phone supports Sync Center.

Not all devices support it, and unfortunately, the only way in which to find out is to plug in your device, install any software that came with it, and see if it then appears in the list of new sync partnerships within Sync Center.

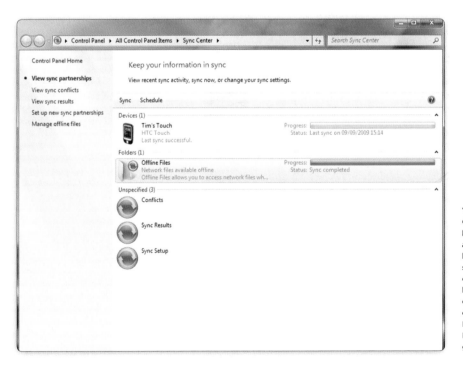

Windows 7's Sync Center automatically keeps selected files and folders up to date between multiple storage locations and devices. It's especially handy with portable devices, although only those based on Microsoft's Windows Mobile operating system get the full benefit.

# HOW TO...
# SYNC A WINDOWS MOBILE

The Windows Mobile Device Center, part of Sync Center, lets you configure how your phone syncs with Windows 7. You can sync contacts, appointments, email, tasks, notes and more, as well as music and documents.

**1** **OTHER PHONES NEED NOT APPLY** Windows 7 has a clear bias to Windows Mobile phones; if you own a Nokia or Sony Ericsson, for example, your options will be limited to transferring data to and from its memory, and the only way you can synchronise with Outlook is to use the software that came with your phone. If you have a Windows Mobile, you can do much more.

**2** **SET UP YOUR DEVICE** The first time you connect a new Windows Mobile phone, you'll see two options: "Set up your device" or "Connect without setting up your device". Clicking the latter will take you to an Explorer window where you can view the contents of your device, plus any storage cards.

Windows 7 doesn't include the Outlook email program as standard, so you'll need to install a version on your computer if you want to sync email, calendar and contact information. Click "Set up your device" and you'll see a list of checkboxes where you can decide what to sync. Some – but not all – categories have additional settings, and a link will appear when you tick the box.

Click Sync Settings under E-mail, for example, and you can choose whether to download attachments larger than a specified size, as well as how far back in time to sync emails. Click Save once you've made all your settings and you'll be taken back to the Home page of the Mobile Device Center, where a sync automatically starts.

**3** **PROGRAMS AND MEDIA** You'll also notice more options have appeared. The Programs and Services tab lets you access your device's Add/Remove Programs Control Panel, and there's also a link to the Windows Mobile website for updates and help. The Pictures, Music and Video tab lets you import media from your phone, and you can choose where to put the files on your PC. You can add media to your Windows Mobile phone from Media Player by using the last option here.

**4** **ADVANCED SETTINGS** Roll your mouse over the Mobile Device Settings tab and you'll see "Change content sync settings" – where you can alter the settings you made in step 2 – and also "Manage a Partnership". This lets you choose what happens if there's a conflict when syncing: items are replaced on either the device or on the host computer. If you make most of your changes on your PC, you'll want to set this to "Replace items on device".

**HOW LONG?**
If you leave the settings at their defaults, ten minutes should do it.

**HOW HARD?**
Like many tasks in Windows 7, it's quite easy once you know how.

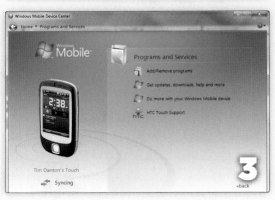

# Introducing Mobility Center

Only available on a laptop or Tablet PC, Windows 7's Mobility Center is a central hub for tweaking the most common mobile settings. It's a small window with a variety of tiled options, most of them familiar. To get advanced options for each tile, you just need to click the icon in the top-left corner and you'll be taken straight to the relevant Control Panel page.

**SIMPLE OPTIONS** The first box adjusts the system volume, and also offers a checkbox to mute the speaker. This is of limited worth, as it's simpler and quicker to click the speaker icon in the System Tray, or indeed use the hardware controls or keyboard shortcuts that are likely to be on your laptop.

A similar System Tray shortcut handles power options, but if you prefer to use the Mobility Center there's a useful quick-select box that allows you to choose the preset Power Saver or High Performance modes, rather than the default Balanced.

You can enable or disable your wireless connection from the next tile, and it displays the usual five green bars to let you know the signal strength. Clicking the bars takes you to the pop-up window that normally appears when you click on the network icon on the taskbar, so you can connect to any available networks, or open the more comprehensive

Network and Sharing Center. Again, however, we'd question the point of this when you can just click on the Taskbar.

When not on the move, many laptop users prefer to connect to a home or office monitor. With Mobility Center running, plug a display into a vacant video port and click the "Connect display" button. You'll be given the option to duplicate or extend the display or use the monitor alone (switching off the laptop's screen). Tablet users get an extra option to change the orientation from landscape to portrait.

**ADVANCED OPTIONS** The final two standard tiles may be less familiar. The first is a link to the Sync Center. Windows 7 users can use this to keep files up to date between their PC or laptop and other mobile devices; in the Professional and Ultimate editions you can also sync PCs, laptops and devices across a network.

The final tile lets you turn on the extremely handy Presentation mode, which changes the power settings to disable the screensaver, adjust the system volume and switch the current display background to something more appropriate. The system will always stay awake, and system notifications are turned off. These settings can be tweaked by clicking the icon. The only disappointment is that there isn't an option to temporarily hide all your desktop icons.

Click on any of the icons to access advanced settings.

Windows' preset power profiles can be accessed quickly from here, although the System Tray icon is equally convenient.

The Mobility Center is expandable, so more options may be added by your laptop's manufacturer.

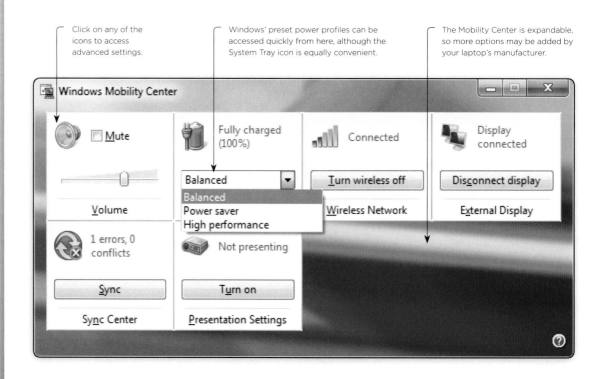

# Access, store and share your files from anywhere, for less than your daily latte.

Make humyo your office away from the office with our secure online workspace. Store, backup, access and even share vital files and folders with customers, remote workers or partners. We're Europe's largest independent online file storage and sharing business with over 300,000 customers worldwide, so you know you're in good company.

Accessible from any computer, you'll never be more than a few clicks away from your digital office, and all for a lot less than you'd think.

**Visit business.humyo.com now and register for our free 30 day trial or call us on 0845 862 0927**

humyo.com™

*access your life*

# 9

## Laptop computing

ALMOST EVERY LAPTOP COMES WITH WI-FI, BUT ONLY A 3G MODEM LETS YOU ACCESS THE INTERNET WHEN YOU'RE NEITHER AT HOME NOR IN A HOTSPOT.

# Using 3G in Windows 7

Walk into the Carphone Warehouse and you'll be blitzed by mobile broadband offers. This is a completely different proposition to Wi-Fi, which comes built into most new laptops to allow them to connect to your home wireless router and public wireless hotspots such as those in coffee shops. 3G data services work via the same networks as mobile phones, and are dominated by the same companies: 3, O2, Orange, T-Mobile and Vodafone. You sign up to a contract, either monthly or pay-as-you-go, to pay for broadband on the move just like you pay for your mobile phone. The connection is made with a small USB stick, or "dongle", that plugs into your laptop and contains a network SIM card and receiver.

**3G DONGLE SOFTWARE** The software you need to install your dongle will be included on the stick itself. Plug it into one of your laptop's USB ports and it will automatically ask if you want to install it, then launch and configure itself.

With this done, whenever you connect your 3G dongle (they're not usually compact enough to be left plugged in all the time) the software will automatically launch. It's normally crammed with options for configuring your 3G connection. Typically, you can customise and monitor your connection, check the speed that it's running at, and see how long you've been connected and how much of your monthly data allowance you've used up. A

more detailed breakdown is often available, so you can see exactly where you're using up the most megabytes. There will be dozens of advanced settings, too, from updating and connection options to extra services such as text messaging.

**MANAGING 3G IN WINDOWS** Most users won't need to tinker with the advanced options, and often it's faster to manage your 3G connection using Windows 7's built-in network connections manager instead, in the same interface you use to handle Wi-Fi connections. To do this, click the wireless internet icon in your Taskbar and click on your mobile operator's network when it appears. If it fails to show, you can click the Network and Sharing Center link, which displays your internet connection and also gives you access to numerous other connection management tools.

To explore more settings, right-click your 3G connection and click Properties, or select the Manage Network Connections link to open a menu containing all of your connections: Windows 7 now groups them together, whether they be wireless internet, 3G or a wired network. Once your dongle has been installed, its security settings can also be handled by the Windows 7 Network and Sharing Center, so you won't need specialist software to get online.

3G reception is now widely available in urban areas, but when you're out of range your laptop should still connect anywhere within the cell network, at a lower speed.

## Tip

3G can be excellent value these days, but do compare tariffs carefully and read all the small print. All "pay monthly" deals place a limit on the amount of data you can transfer, with automatic charges for every megabyte beyond this. And think twice before using your 3G dongle when abroad: "roaming" charges can very quickly add up to tens or even hundreds of pounds for what may seem fairly light usage.

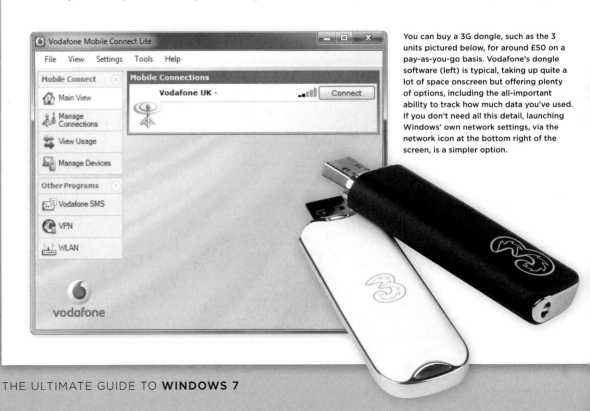

You can buy a 3G dongle, such as the 3 units pictured below, for around £50 on a pay-as-you-go basis. Vodafone's dongle software (left) is typical, taking up quite a lot of space onscreen but offering plenty of options, including the all-important ability to track how much data you've used. If you don't need all this detail, launching Windows' own network settings, via the network icon at the bottom right of the screen, is a simpler option.

# PC PRO

## THE UK'S NUMBER 1 MAGAZINE FOR IT ENTHUSIASTS AND PROFESSIONALS

# 3 ISSUES FOR £1

PC Pro is the biggest and most respected IT magazine in the UK. **Discover why for just £1.** Our hardware and software reviews and always unbiased and written by industry experts. If we recommend a product, it's worth buying. It's simple as that. Stay ahead of the latest developments in the world of IT with PC Pro. Each issues is packed with:

- **News and reviews**
- **Group tests**
- **PLUS! Each month you'll receive a DVD packed with free software**
- **Hard-hitting features**
- **Real world advice**

## Find out more with for 3 issues for £1

Right now you can claim the next 3 issues for just £1! It's a 100% risk free offer because if after 3 issues you're not completely satisfied you can write to cancel your subscription and you won't pay any more than the £1 already debited.

### YOUR GREAT DEAL

- 3 issues for £1
- If you're not satisfied, simply cancel and **pay no more than the £1** already debited
- **FREE delivery** to your door
- **Save up to 33%** on the shop price if you continue your subscription
- Get every issue **before it hits the shops**

# CALL NOW ON 0844 844 0031

Order securely online at www.dennismags.co.uk/pcpro entering offer code G0906PRM or return the invitation below

---

## PC PRO 3 ISSUES FOR £1 OFFER [UK ONLY]

☑ **YES! Please start my subscription to PC Pro with 3 issues for just £1.** After this, my subscription will automatically continue by Direct Debit at the LOW RATE of £19.99 every 6 issues. I understand that if I'm not completely satisfied with PC Pro, I can write to cancel my subscription and pay no more than the £1 already debited.

**YOUR DETAILS** - Please complete in BLOCK CAPITALS

MR/MRS/MS _____ FORENAME _____

SURNAME _____

JOB TITLE _____ COMPANY NAME _____

ADDRESS _____

POSTCODE _____

DAYTIME PHONE _____ YEAR OF BIRTH _____

MOBILE NO. _____

E-MAIL _____

**Direct Debit Payment** - £19.99 every 6 issues - Saving 33% on the shop price

*Dennis* **Instruction to your Bank or Building Society to pay by Direct Debit** ●**DIRECT** **Debit**

Please complete and send to: Freepost RLZS-ETGT-BCZR, Dennis Publishing Ltd, 800 Guillat Ave, Kent Science Park, Sittingbourne ME9 8GU

Name and full postal address of your Bank or Building Society

To the manager: Bank name _____

Address _____

Postcode _____

**Originator's Identification Number**

| 7 | 2 | 4 | 6 | 8 | 0 |

Ref no. to be completed by Dennis Publishing

Account in the name(s) of _____

**Branch sort code**

**Bank/Building Society account number**

Signature(s) _____

Date _____

**Instructions to your Bank or Building Society**
Please pay Dennis Publishing Ltd. Direct Debits from the account detailed in this instruction subject to the safeguards assured by the Direct Debit Guarantee. I understand that this instruction may remain with Dennis Publishing Ltd and, if so, details will be passed electronically to my Bank/Building Society.

Banks and building societies may not accept Direct Debit instructions for some types of account

You will be able to view and amend your subscription details online at: **www.subsinfo.co.uk**

**PLEASE RETURN TO:**
Freepost RLZS-ETGT-BCZR, PC Pro Subscriptions,
800 Guillat Ave, Kent Science Park, Sittingbourne ME9 8GU

Offer Code: G0906PRM

# 9

## Laptop computing

# Extend your battery life

Windows 7 offers a trio of power plans that can help to either maximise your laptop's performance or to conserve power, depending on which is important to you. When the Power Saver plan is selected, for instance, your screen is dimmed, the processor is reined in, and other unnecessary services are halted to help your battery last longer. The High Performance plan goes to the opposite extreme, letting all components do their utmost regardless of power usage.

For most people, the Balanced plan strikes the right, well, balance – upping processor power if needs be, but reducing it to a low level when it isn't being pushed. To switch between these plans, simply click on the battery symbol at the bottom right of the Taskbar. You'll initially be presented with the two choices of Balanced or Power Save, but clicking "More power options" shows others – although you may still need to click on the small downward arrow next to "Show additional plans" to reveal the High Performance option and any custom plans you add.

**TWEAK ADVANCED SETTINGS** The three default power plans also have further options that give you more control over your PC's power usage: click "Change plan settings" to access these. At their simplest, these control when the display is switched off and when the computer goes into Sleep mode, but clicking "Change advanced power settings" opens up a new world of tweakery. The list of variables is vast: you can turn off your hard disk after a certain period of inactivity, for instance, or selectively suspend USB ports that aren't being used to stop them draining a trickle of power. You can also tweak your processor, specifying minimum and maximum levels of CPU activity, so that when you don't need all of your system's capability you can throttle down the chip to prevent it draining excessive battery power.

Many of these options can be set to different levels depending on whether your laptop is plugged in or running on the battery, so there's no need to limit your computer's performance when you're on the mains.

**REDUCE SCREEN BRIGHTNESS** Whether your laptop is a tiny 8in netbook or a mammoth 17in desktop replacement model, a screen running at full brightness is a huge power drain. Turning down the brightness a few notches is one of the most efficient ways to instantly increase your battery life. It's easy to do: most laptops have shortcut buttons on the keyboard to raise and lower brightness, and Windows 7's power management screen also has a slider for this.

## Tip

A useful setting, found on the Power Options homepage, is "Choose what closing the lid does". This should normally be Sleep, as closing the lid is the instinctive action when you've finished working; when you open it an hour or a day later, it will spring back to life without having run down the battery. However, if you like to listen to music tracks with the lid shut, for example, you'll want to change this to Nothing.

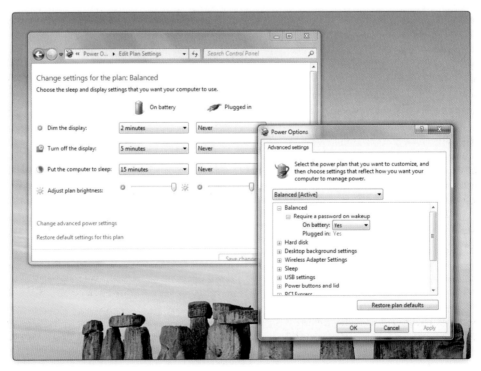

Windows 7 provides three default power plans; you can customise these, for example, to vary how your laptop behaves depending on whether it's plugged in or on battery power, or create your own power plan from scratch. Go to Create a Power Plan in Control Panel to add a custom plan.

**SPRING CLEANING** If you're more confident messing around with your computer, it pays to do some laptop housekeeping every so often, because keeping your system clean and tidy can actually help to conserve battery power.

More often than not, unscrewing the bottom of your machine (see, we said you'd need to be confident) will reveal the fan that keeps your processor and graphics chip cool, and some further careful screw removal will let you pry the fan itself away from its mounting. This will allow you to gently clean dust away from the fan and its vents (usually on the side of the machine), which will improve your computer's efficiency and, therefore, make it use less energy: a dusty PC will need to work harder because of the hotter, more claustrophobic conditions created inside its case.

**DISABLE WIRELESS AND BLUETOOTH** The wireless transmitters and receivers inside your laptop draw plenty of power, and if you're not online, they're sitting there draining the battery for no benefit. Some laptops include a hardware switch for turning Wi-Fi on and off, while others use a shortcut key (such as <Fn+F8>). If you know you won't be using wireless networking any time soon, however, you can disable them altogether.

To do this, you'll need to access the Device Manager: a tool that lists, and helps you interact with, all the hardware installed in your PC. To find it, simply open the Start menu and type "device manager" into the search box, then press Return when it appears at the top of the list. When it opens, navigate to the Network Adapters submenu and open that: it shows your laptop's wireless card, Ethernet adapter and any 3G or Bluetooth radio components you may have. Right-click the wireless icon and select Disable to turn off the device and stop it using energy. When you need to use it, just go back and enable it again.

**TURN OFF UNNECESSARY SERVICES** Your computer loads dozens of services and applications when it's booted up, but how many of them do you use? If you have ten icons sitting in the System Tray but never interact with any of them, chances are you have applications and services running that you don't need, and every one of these wastes additional processing power.

To halt applications that you don't need, type "msconfig" into the Windows 7 search box to open the System Configuration menu. The Services tab lists the dozens of small applications that run in the background of your machine: tick the Hide All Microsoft Services box, then disable any others that you don't need. The Startup tab lists all the applications that load when your laptop boots, so simply untick those that are unnecessary. It's easy to reverse this – you just need to go back into System Configuration and re-tick the boxes.

**KEEP YOUR SYSTEM ORGANISED** It may seem trivial, but keeping your PC organised and its hard disk defragmented can make it run more efficiently, which has an effect on both processing power and battery life. Windows 7's disk

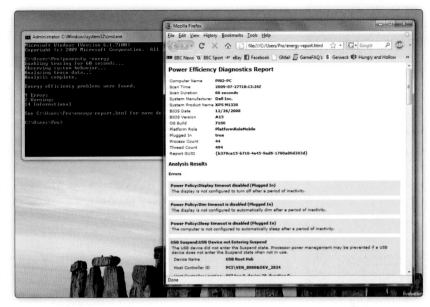

Although it's a bit geeky to use, Powercfg can find extra ways to reduce power consumption.

Turning off devices you won't be using ensures they're not drawing battery power unnecessarily.

Windows loads dozens of small apps whenever your laptop starts up. Removing those that aren't essential can reduce the load on the CPU and thus save energy.

defragmenting tool reorganises files on your hard disk to make them easier for the system to find and faster to access. Type "defragmenter" into the search box to find this tool, then open it and select "Analyze disk" to see if your hard disk could benefit from a little spring cleaning. If you do opt to defragment, this time-consuming operation will be performed in the background, so you don't need to stop working while it's tidying up your PC – although, ironically, it will use up the battery faster while in progress.

Third-party software can also be useful in the fight against clutter. Applications such as the *PC Pro* award-winning CCleaner (www.ccleaner.com) will scan your system for redundant Windows Registry entries, cluttered caches and memory dumps, then hunt down and delete the offending items. The result? A laptop that spends less time churning through pointless files and more time being useful, meaning that you can do more work while expending less energy – and for longer, too.

**DELVE A LITTLE DEEPER** If you're comfortable using the command prompt, a little-known tool called Powercfg could help pinpoint areas where your battery is using up power unnecessarily. To use this, load the Command Prompt by typing "cmd" into the Windows 7 search box and clicking the first item that appears. When it's loaded, type "powercfg -energy" (with the minus sign, but without the quotation marks) into the box and press Return. The software will run for 60 seconds and then generate a report, which is saved into the root folder of the active user account.

This detailed breakdown of your laptop's energy usage should highlight dozens of ways in which you could trim your power consumption and increase your battery life, as long as you're prepared to get into the nitty-gritty of adjusting various settings. It may be a last resort but, if you're trying to extract every possible second from your battery, it could provide the extra boost you need.

# 9

## Laptop computing

## Tip

If you'll excuse the pun, this is a TIP tip. On the Touch Interface Panel, go to Tools | Options to tweak the interface. You can choose where the panel docks, to ensure it doesn't block any icons or programs you need; select the thickness of ink and the length of the pause before entering characters; and change the strikethrough gesture from the new "scratch out" back to the old-style Z pattern.

TABLET PC TECHNOLOGY IS BUILT INTO WINDOWS 7, SO THERE'S NEVER BEEN A BETTER TIME TO THINK ABOUT SWITCHING TO TOUCHSCREEN INPUT.

# The Tablet PC advantage

Tablet PCs are laptops with built-in touchscreens, meaning they can be operated by a stylus rather than with a keyboard and trackpad. Microsoft introduced a redesigned Tablet PC section in Vista, and it's been tweaked, refined and revitalised in Windows 7.

Windows 7's Tablet PC interface revolves around the Tablet Input Panel, or TIP, which is used for all stylus interaction and docks tidily at the side of the screen when it isn't needed. While some touchscreen computers still have a keyboard, the idea is that you no longer need it, so one of the TIP's functions is to let you enter text with your stylus. It's been trained to analyse your handwriting for more efficient text entry with, hopefully, fewer mistakes – and it learns more about your writing as time goes on.

The stylus also takes the place of the mouse – just tap directly on the icon or menu you want to select or open – and Windows 7 continues Vista's tradition of making this easier. Hover the stylus over the desktop and a dot appears to show exactly where it's located; tap an item and a small ripple appears, with a right-click producing a stronger circle.

These functions are built into the core of Windows 7, so you won't even need Aero to use them – handy if you're running a stripped-down edition that doesn't include the Aero effects, or you've disabled them to help a slow PC cope.

**WHAT'S NEW** While the basic core of the TIP has remained largely unchanged from Vista, Microsoft has been busy making it more intuitive. Even more styles of handwriting should be recognised, and a new Smart Correction feature makes correcting mistakes far easier than it ever was.

Elsewhere, it's possible to enter a URL and then visit that web page, and new visual effects make the touch keyboard simpler to use. Predictive text can suggest which word or even phrase should come next in your sentence, and mathematical equations can now also be input.

**FLICKS AND GESTURES** Gestures are more advanced stylus functions that can replicate key presses and other often-used commands. Gestures can be used instead of tab, backspace and spacebar, for instance. A quick flick can scroll a web page up or down, or even copy and paste. These functions can be customised in the Pen and Input Devices section of the Control Panel, which also lists many other gestures. Flicks can be set to one of eight directions and several sensitivity levels, and a practice mode is available.

Also worth investigating are Sticky Notes and Windows Journal: the former creates small notes on your desktop, and the latter is for longer jottings. Journal files can be converted to regular text and are fully searchable.

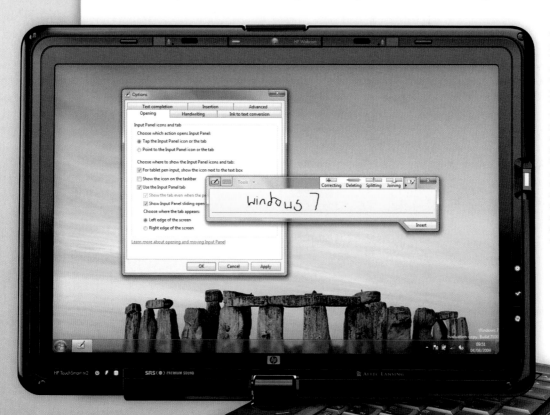

The latest touchscreen laptops, such as HP's TouchSmart tx series, offer completely new ways to interact with your computer – and Windows 7 is ready to take full advantage. But you don't have to own a touchscreen to use some of Windows 7's touch-based features. Add a graphics tablet (from companies such as Wacom) to any PC and you can use the same flicks and gestures as if you were working directly on the screen.

# HOW TO...
# USE HANDWRITING RECOGNITION

The Tablet Input Panel may not immediately impress, but it can be quickly trained to recognise your style of handwriting – and, like at school, it's simply a case of copying out words and letters with your pen.

**1** **START TRAINING** Go to Start | All Programs | Accessories | Tablet PC and open the Tablet PC Input Panel. Rather than beginning to write, go to the Tools menu and choose Personalise Handwriting Recognition to begin training Windows 7. Later you can teach it to recognise specific errors, or switch on automatic learning to have it analyse your scrawl as you write, but it's best to start with "Teach the recognizer your handwriting style". You'll be asked whether you'd like to enter full sentences or letters, and led through options that take advantage of Windows 7's improved training and recognition algorithms.

**2** **EASY AS A, B, C** The wizard will guide you through eight screens that cover a range of commonly used letters, numbers and characters. The first deals with digits, the second punctuation, and so on. Simply input your letters into the yellow boxes below the characters, working your way through each stage and letting Windows learn your writing style. Unlike with handwriting recognition systems of the past, you're not expected to write in a special way; stick to your usual script and let the software get the hang of it. Once you've filled in every stage, you'll be returned to the main screen.

**3** **JOINED-UP THINKING** Now you've trained the system to recognise individual characters, it's time to move on to full sentences. Choose the relevant options and you'll be presented with a similar interface, but with randomly selected sentences to copy rather than letters and numbers. Again, you should write the words exactly how you would on paper. There are 50 sentences to complete, but you can exit at any time and the training database will still be updated.

**4** **TROUBLESHOOTING** The final option can target specific problems, such as words or letters that Windows 7 frequently misreads when you write them. If you know which word or particular character is proving problematic, you can type it and then write it four times to allow the system to store it in its database. Alternatively, some written shapes may be interpreted to be several different characters - for example, "0", "o" and "O". Once this stage is complete, you should notice an immediate improvement in the accuracy of recognition, but make sure automatic learning is activated to help the system refine its database as time goes on.

**HOW LONG?**
Ten minutes for basic training, but up to an hour to refine the system.

**HOW HARD?**
Training is a no-brainer – you just have to copy out text from the screen.

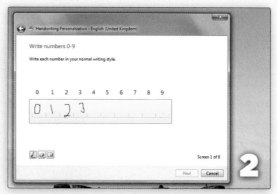

BITLOCKER HELPS BUSINESS USERS KEEP DATA SECURE ON LAPTOPS USING FULL DISK ENCRYPTION, BUT BITLOCKER TO GO TAKES IT ONE STEP FURTHER.

# Introducing BitLocker To Go

BitLocker first appeared in Windows Vista, designed to allow complete and secure encryption of an entire hard disk. This essentially meant that even if your laptop was stolen, no-one could access any of the data on its hard disk without the correct password, and if the drive was removed from the laptop it was unreadable. BitLocker is still included in Windows 7 – notably, only in the Ultimate and Enterprise editions – but Microsoft has now tackled the missing piece of the security puzzle. Standard BitLocker can only protect fixed system disks, which arguably leaves open the main pathway for sensitive data falling into the wrong hands: USB flash memory drives.

That gap is filled by the new BitLocker To Go. In security-conscious firms, system administrators can now stipulate that USB flash drives can only be used after BitLocker has been enabled. Local authority departments throughout the land should take note. A potential benefit for users is that this offers a responsible alternative to banning USB drives altogether, which can be highly inconvenient.

**PASSWORD PLEASE** Encrypting a drive using BitLocker To Go is simple (see opposite), but think carefully when choosing your BitLocker To Go password. When someone is trying to break into the data on the drive (and that's the eventuality that all this fuss is about in the first place), the strength of the password becomes hugely important: much more so than with, say, a webmail account, where people are locked out after three wrong attempts. If someone has

nabbed your drive, they can leave their cracking software running 24 hours a day doing a brute-force attack on your password – that is, trying every combination of letters and numbers – until they hit the right one. The longer and more complicated the password, the better.

BitLocker To Go is perfectly happy with spaces in its password, so you can use phrases. A totally nonsensical phrase is a good idea, since it's long, unique and easy to remember. "I made 12 biscuits, and watched EastEnders!", for example, is a phrase that no human being has probably ever uttered before (so it won't be in hackers' dictionaries) but is easy to memorise once you've thought of it.

Never use proverbs or film quotes, since they'll be cracked in a jiffy. It has to be something you've made up, and ideally containing numbers as well as characters such as exclamation marks or question marks. When you set up

BitLocker in Windows 7 requires a TPM 1.2 chip in your PC before it can encrypt system drives, but you don't need it to use BitLocker To Go.

**For earlier versions of Windows,** the built-in BitLocker To Go Reader enables access to a drive (with the password); this is offered when the drive is connected if AutoPlay is on. Users can read files but can't write to the drive.

BitLocker To Go on a flash drive, it will stipulate a password of at least eight characters and not allow anything shorter – but we'd recommend a password at least double that length.

**THE RECOVERY KEY** Once you've entered a password, Windows will also generate a recovery key and offer to save it to a text file and print it. The key itself is a 48-character string that you can use to unencrypt the drive without the password if it's ever forgotten. Remember that BitLocker uses strong encryption, so if you do forget the password, the recovery key is the only possible way of ever getting your data back. If there's any chance at all you'll forget the password, make sure the key is both saved to a file and printed. Don't carry the printout with the drive.

**EASY ACCESS** Once your USB drive is encrypted, there's a neat feature you can make use of. If you head to Control Panel | System and Security | BitLocker Drive Encryption, you'll see that the encrypted drive appears with a padlock icon, and there's an option to Manage BitLocker. Click it and, among the obvious options like changing the password, there's also the option to "Automatically unlock the drive on this computer". Click this, and your system will remember the password, allowing you to use the flash drive with this PC (and only this one) without having to enter the password every time you plug it in. So you can use the drive as if it wasn't encrypted, but if it goes astray your data is safe.

**VISTA AND XP** Although BitLocker To Go is Windows 7-only, you can still access encrypted drives on other Windows PCs, including any edition of Vista or XP. When Windows 7 converts a disk, it creates an unencrypted area on the drive containing a program called the BitLocker To Go Reader. Double-click this (or choose it from the AutoPlay menu) and you'll be prompted to enter the password for the drive. This opens a window showing the drive's contents. You can then view and copy contents from it, but note that you can't write files back to it, or edit existing files on the disk.

**FULL-STRENGTH BITLOCKER** We've concentrated on BitLocker To Go here, but what about encrypting your whole system drive using BitLocker? First, go to Control Panel | System and Security | BitLocker Drive Encryption. The resulting window shows every drive on the system; just click Turn on BitLocker to prepare the drive as required.

Note that your PC must have a TPM 1.2 (trusted platform module) on its motherboard for this to work. These are now common on business laptops, but rare in consumer models. Fortunately, you don't need it for BitLocker To Go.

# HOW TO...
# USE BITLOCKER TO GO

**① TURN ON BITLOCKER** Connect the drive you want to encrypt, and open the Computer view. Right-click on the drive and select "Turn on BitLocker". The BitLocker wizard starts up, and after a brief pause you'll be asked to enter the password you want to use. Make sure this is a strong password, for the reasons we explain on the opposite page, but one you can remember.

**② SAVE RECOVERY DATA** Once you've entered a password, the wizard will offer to save and/or print the recovery key file. Do both. The recovery key is your only alternative to the password should you ever forget it; without both, your data would be gone forever. Before the drive can be protected, the whole structure has to be encrypted. This takes roughly ten minutes for every gigabyte of capacity on the drive, so make sure you don't need anything from it in a hurry before you start.

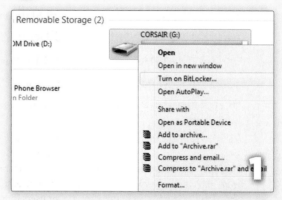

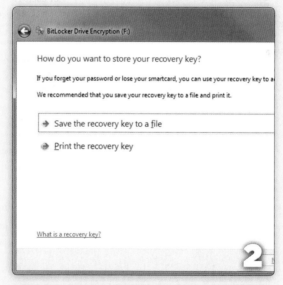

**③ FINISH UP** Once the encryption process has begun, pay attention to the warning in the progress box and don't remove the drive without pausing. We'd also be on the safe side and avoid trying to copy any files to or from it either. When the process is complete, the drive will work as before, but all files will be securely encrypted as they're written to it. If you take the drive out, when you re-insert it you'll see a dialog box asking for the password. As soon as you enter it, you're away again.

# IN THIS CHAPTER

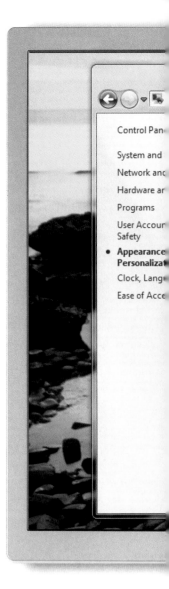

# 10
*Fine-tune Windows 7*

# FINE-TUNING W

Windows 7 is designed to be easy to use right out of the box, but it also offers a huge number of ways to make the operating system work exactly how you want. In this chapter we look at the Control Panel and the many settings it offers, letting you customise features as diverse as the appearance of your screen, your security settings, your hardware drivers and the way your PC

Panel ▸ Appearance and Personalization ▸                    ⌄  ↻    Search Control Panel    🔍

**Personalization**
Change the theme | Change desktop background | Change window glass colors
Change sound effects | Change screen saver

**Display**
Make text and other items larger or smaller | Adjust screen resolution
Connect to a projector | Connect to an external display

**Desktop Gadgets**
Add gadgets to the desktop | Get more gadgets online | Uninstall a gadget
Restore desktop gadgets installed with Windows

**Taskbar and Start Menu**
Customize the Start menu | Customize icons on the taskbar
Change the picture on the Start menu

**Ease of Access Center**
Accommodate low vision | Use screen reader | Turn on easy access keys
Turn High Contrast on or off

**Folder Options**
Specify single- or double-click to open | Show hidden files and folders

**Fonts**
Preview, delete, or show and hide fonts | Change Font Settings | Adjust ClearType text

# NDOWS 7

connects to a network. We examine how to measure
performance: is everything in your system running
as well as it should, and how can you keep it fast and
responsive? Finally, we explore the latest accessibility
options, including High Contrast and the Magnifier.
It's all designed to make sure anyone – young or old,
novice or expert – can get the very best from Windows.

**Q:** Is there an easy way to collect together my most commonly used Control Panel items?
**A:** Drag any link or icon out of the Control Panel window to make a shortcut that you can place on your desktop, in a folder, in your Favorites list, on the Taskbar, or anywhere else you like.

**Q:** Can messing with Control Panel damage my computer?
**A:** No, but if you change things carelessly there's a small risk you might disable important features – you could lose your network access, or end up staring at a blank screen. Since most settings don't have an Undo, proceed with caution. If you're at all uncertain, use System Restore (see p150) to take a snapshot of your system before you change any settings.

# Introducing Control Panel

The Windows 7 Control Panel lets you change hundreds of aspects of your computer's behaviour and appearance. This isn't just a feature for die-hard tweakers: even if you're a novice, you're sure to find settings and options here that will help you make your PC behave just how you want. You'll find a link to the Control Panel in the right-hand pane of the Start menu, or you can simply navigate to Computer in Windows Explorer and click Open Control Panel in the bar along the top of the window.

The default Control Panel view is divided into eight main categories of settings, which we'll discuss below. Beneath each heading are links to some of the most useful tasks.

When you click on a category, the main categories move over into the left-hand pane, while the main window shows the various configuration options for the category you chose. These appear in the same format, with shortcuts underneath that link directly to common tasks. The actual categories are a bit loose, so some settings appear under more than one: Power Options, for example, can be found under both System and Security and Hardware and Sound.

You can also access all of Control Panel's features by clicking the dropdown menu and switching from the Category view to one of the icon-based views. Many options can also be accessed from the relevant places within the Windows interface, and anything you can find in the Control Panel can be located with Windows Search (see box, right). Consider the Control Panel simply a handy central repository where you can find all your settings in one place.

A full explanation of all of the settings would fill a book in itself, but here's an overview of the categories.

**SYSTEM AND SECURITY** This category is designed for when you want to check or change something about the day-to-day functioning of your PC – for example, you want to know how much memory it has, or modify your Windows Update settings. You can launch tools such as System Restore or the hard disk defragmenter from here, and configure BitLocker encryption if it's included in your edition of Windows 7.

**NETWORK AND INTERNET** From here you can access the Network and Sharing Center, which holds all the options you need to configure your home network and internet connection. You can set up HomeGroup (see chapter 6), and change various settings relating to your web browser.

**HARDWARE AND SOUND** Look here if you want to change the way your hardware works: for example, you can set up

The Network and Internet category takes you to the Network and Sharing Center, where you can alter all Control Panel settings related to your network and internet connection.

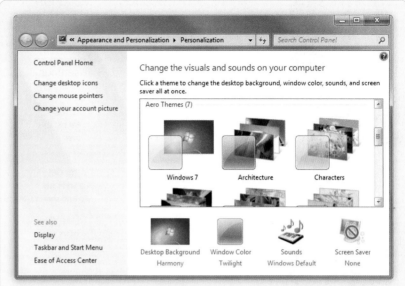

System and Security contains the core settings that govern how your Windows PC works, including how long it waits before going to sleep, when it backs up your files, and how Windows protects you from malware. You can also sort out your hard disk here.

**ALTERNATIVE ROUTES** Control Panel shows your system settings in one place, but in everyday use you won't need to visit it often, because most options can be accessed directly from the relevant part of Windows 7. For example, if you want to tweak your desktop, right-click on the background: the menu that opens will contain direct links to Screen resolution, Gadgets and Personalization. If you want to configure your Taskbar, right-click on it and select Properties. The same thing works with the Start button and numerous other elements of Windows.

If you want to tweak your network settings, right-click the networking icon in the System Tray at the bottom right of the screen. From here, you can open the Network and Sharing Center and take control of everything to do with networking.

When you're in a hurry, you can use Windows Search to jump straight to the setting you want. Either use the Search box at the top right of the main Control Panel window, or just open the Start menu and search from there. If you do this, your results will be divided into sections, one of which relates to Control Panel.

For example, if you type "display" you'll see a shortcut to the main Display Properties page, followed by shortcuts to relevant configuration tasks. All the main Control Panel windows, and many of the most common settings, can be accessed in this way, so you can find the setting you want simply by typing one or two words.

multiple monitors or change the way your computer uses its speakers. You can also manage printers, MP3 players and other peripherals from here, and set what happens when you insert removable media such as a DVD or a flash drive.

**PROGRAMS** If you want to uninstall a program, or tell Windows to open a particular program when you double-click a certain type of file, this is the place. You can also add or remove Windows components and Gadgets (see p34).

**USER ACCOUNTS AND FAMILY SAFETY** In this category, you can create and modify accounts for multiple users – useful if several people use your computer, or if you want to share files and folders over your home network (see p89). You can also access Windows 7's Parental Controls and manage any passwords that Windows has memorised.

**APPEARANCE AND PERSONALIZATION** This brings together various settings that affect the way you interact with your

computer. Links to Display and Gadgets reappear here, and you can customise the way the Windows Taskbar and Start menu behave. You can also set Ease of Access options (say, to make text larger for anyone with impaired vision), along with cosmetic settings such as those that control your desktop wallpaper, screensaver and system fonts.

**CLOCK, LANGUAGE AND REGION** This is one of the most self-explanatory categories. You can set the date, and tell Windows which time zone you're based in. You can also change regional settings, such as your keyboard layout, the format you use for dates and times, and the language in which you prefer to read system messages.

**EASE OF ACCESS** This final category reveals the same Ease of Access settings that are found in the Appearance and Personalization category, plus speech-recognition options, so you can set up Windows 7 to be controlled without using a mouse or keyboard.

WINDOWS 7 IS DESIGNED TO WORK SEAMLESSLY, BUT IF PROGRAMS ARE STILL SLOW OR REFUSE TO RUN THEN THERE ARE TOOLS TO FIND THE CAUSE.

# Keeping an eye on performance

Windows 7 has tools to help you track your computer's performance and isolate which, if any, of the components in your system are struggling. What's more, with a little know-how you can monitor your applications and see which ones are hogging resources. Using that knowledge, you can make decisions about which applications you might ditch and which parts of your PC might be due for an upgrade.

**ARE YOU EXPERIENCED?** The Windows Experience Index is effectively an internal benchmark, running a sequence of tests on your PC to assess the key system components. The index breaks these down into five categories – Processor, Memory (RAM), Graphics, Gaming graphics and Primary hard disk – and awards each a score from 1.0 to 7.9. The lowest of these scores, rather meanly, is your Base score.

The Experience Index is of particular interest to gamers. Before Vista, deciding whether a game would run or not meant checking its recommended specifications against your system, component by component. The Experience Index does all this work for you, as games now list their required Index scores in the Windows Games Explorer, and you can easily compare them with your own results. It's a shame more game publishers don't print these scores where they would be most useful: on the box.

**PERFORMANCE ART** When you need to dig deeper, click on "Advanced tools" in the Performance Information and Tools dialog box. Performance Monitor helps you analyse system bottlenecks over time. It logs data and presents it on a graph. By default, it tracks just one metric, "% Processor Time" – the percentage of time the processor is busy. This should rarely exceed 70% on most PCs. Press the "+" button above the main graph window to select Counters for other aspects of processor performance plus memory, network and hard disk statistics. The list is long, so the trick is to be sparing. The more Counters you select, the more convoluted and hard to read the graph becomes.

Add the Counters you want, then click on the left-hand pane and go to Action | New | Data Collector Set. Run through the wizard, giving your log a name and a location. Leave the "Run as:" option set to <Default>, then choose "Start this data collection set now". Click Finish. Performance Monitor works in the background, collecting the requested performance data for your log. To check it at a later date, start Performance Monitor, then click the View Log Data icon, second from left above the graph. Browse to your saved log, then open it to check it out.

The second advanced tool is Resource Monitor, which we run through in detail on the opposite page.

## Tip

If you're not a gamer, don't despair about a low Graphics or Gaming graphics score in the Windows Experience Index. Provided you're not intending to watch high-definition video or blast aliens in Crysis, it isn't the end of the world for everyday use.

**BioShock**

Check how well this game will perform on your computer:

| | |
|---|---|
| Recommended | 2.0 |
| Required | 1.0 |
| Current System | 5.6 |

Learn more about these scores

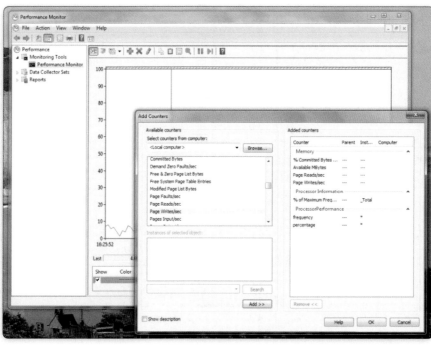

Windows 7's Performance Monitor lets you automatically log a wide variety of system statistics over time, so you can spot where and when problems might be occurring. Interpreting the data it produces can be a rather time-consuming job in itself.

# HOW TO...
# USE RESOURCE MONITOR

As an everyday tool, Resource Monitor may be more useful than Performance Monitor. Not only does it give you at-a-glance information on how heavily your PC's core components are being utilised, it also shows which applications are hitting them hardest.

**1** **GET AN OVERVIEW** The Resource Manager window is split into five tabbed areas. The Overview tab allows you to monitor CPU, disk, memory and network usage at the same time; the small square gauge on each bar provides the most basic data, or you can click on each bar to expand it and get a more detailed view of which processes are using most resources. You'll find the resource hogs at the top of the list, and less demanding apps or processes near the bottom. Meanwhile, the graphs on the right show resource utilisation peaking and dropping as applications load, quit and do whatever you ask them to in between.

**2** **DRILL DEEPER** Clicking on a tab drills down to provide even more detailed information. If you want to select a specific process to watch – for example, to see how much CPU power the Google Chrome web browser is using – click on the checkbox next to it in the CPU pane. This will filter out all Services not connected to the processes in question, and give you

a firmer idea of what resources the program as a whole is running. Note, too, the blue line in the CPU total graph and the blue meter in the CPU bar. If you allow Windows to dynamically control CPU speed, usually for power-saving reasons, then the blue bar and line track what percentage of your CPU's processing power is actually available for use at that specific time.

**3** **SPOT THE HOGS** The Memory and Disk tabs work along similar lines. The Physical Memory pane in the former tells you exactly how much of the actual RAM installed on your PC is in use at that moment. If most of the bar is green and orange, it might be time to invest in some more RAM. Disk Activity, meanwhile, shows which applications are thrashing the hard disk.

**4** **WATCH THE TRAFFIC** Finally, Network Activity allows you to track how much of the available bandwidth between your PC and the network is being used, and which applications are using it. Not only is this a good way to spot if some errant program is tying up your whole connection – even streaming media apps and large downloads should struggle to do that – it's also a good manual check if you suspect dubious programs are streaming large amounts of data upstream. See anything you don't recognise? Google it and find out what it is.

**HOW LONG?**
The results are instant; understanding them can take a little more time.

**HOW HARD?**
These aren't tools for beginners, but nor do you have to be a PC genius to fathom how they work.

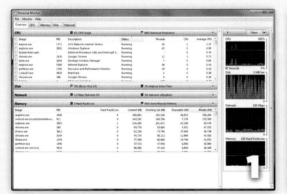

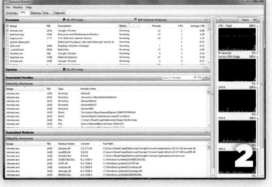

THERE ARE BENEFITS TO USING SLEEP RATHER THAN SHUTTING DOWN FULLY, AND YOU CAN SAVE POWER BY ENSURING YOUR PC SLEEPS WHEN NOT IN USE.

# Shutdown and sleep

The most obvious way to switch off Windows is to use the "Shut down" button to the bottom-right of the Start menu. On most systems you can also instigate a shutdown by simply pressing the power button (hold it for five seconds to force a shutdown without saving any data).

Click on the arrow to the right of the "Shut down" button and you'll see more options for closing down your Windows session. "Switch user" and "Log off" will both take you back to the logon screen so a different person can use your PC — the difference being that "Log off" closes down all your programs first, while "Switch user" leaves them running so you can switch back to your own desktop later. "Lock" hides your Windows desktop so it can't be accessed without your password. "Hibernate", meanwhile, saves the current state to your hard disk and shuts down.

**SLEEP MODE** But it's the bottom option – "Sleep" – that's the most interesting. When you send your computer to sleep, it remains switched on but suspends all programs and cuts the power to most of its components to almost zero. It also powers down the hard disk and any fans in your computer, and sends a "sleep" message to your monitor, causing the screen to go blank. A sleeping computer looks very much like it's switched off.

The big difference is that, when you start up again, you don't need to wait for Windows to reload. Your operating system is already present in RAM – in a suspended state – and can spring back to life in a few seconds as soon as you move the mouse, press a key or do something else to let your PC know you want to use it. Clearly, most of the time, sleep is more convenient than a full shutdown.

One warning about sleep mode: although the computer may appear to be switched off, there's still power running through its circuits. If you install or remove hardware – such as a new graphics card or a RAM module – while the computer's asleep, you risk damaging it. Always make sure your PC is fully switched off before you open the case: we suggest you unplug it from the mains, and if it's a laptop you should remove the battery too.

Windows 7 can automatically put your PC to sleep if it detects you're not using it (see opposite), so you get the convenience of a PC that's always available for use while drawing much less power than if you simply left it switched on all the time. A system that draws 200W from the mains when fully powered-up is likely to consume only a few watts in sleep mode – barely more than if it was switched off altogether.

## Tip

If you get into the habit of always using Sleep, rather than powering down, it's easy to go for days and even weeks without needing to restart Windows. That's great, but sometimes when you install a new application or a Windows Update, the installation can't complete until you reboot. In such cases, you should let the system restart as soon as you get a chance — if the latest updates aren't fully installed, the security and stability of your system could be at risk.

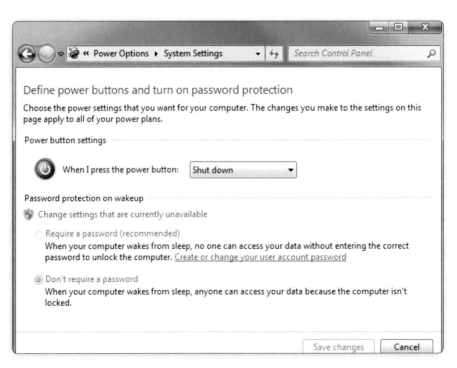

You don't have to make do with Windows 7's default power settings. You can change what pressing the power button does, for instance, and if you're worried that others may use your PC while you're away then force it to require a password when it wakes from Sleep mode.

# HOW TO...
# SET POWER OPTIONS

Windows 7's default settings will send your computer to sleep after 30 minutes — but you can customise numerous settings, and work with multiple power plans to make your PC behave exactly as you want in different circumstances.

**① POWER OPTIONS** You'll find Power Options in the Control Panel, under "System and Security". In the left-hand pane are some simple options to adjust settings such as when the display is turned off, and how long the computer will sit idle before going to sleep. The main pane is dedicated to power plans. You'll see two pre-configured plans listed, named "Balanced" and "Power saver". A third plan, "High performance", is hidden by default. Your PC manufacturer may have included additional plans too. You can customise these plans to suit your preferences, but we suggest you create a new plan for your personal settings. To do so, click "Create a power plan" in the left-hand pane.

**② CHOOSE A TEMPLATE** Windows will ask you which of the existing power plans you want to use as the basis for your new plan. This is just to save you time — whichever option you pick, you'll be able to tweak all its settings later. The "Power saver" plan is designed to keep electricity consumption low at the expense of speed. "Balanced" lets your computer run at

full speed when it needs to. "High performance" keeps full processor power available all the time.

**③ SET BASIC OPTIONS** On the next page, you can set how long Windows waits before turning off the monitor and putting the computer to sleep. Choose these intervals and click "Create" to start using your new plan. You'll now see your new power plan listed in the main Power Options window. If your priorities change at a later date, you can always come back to this page and switch back to one of the predefined plans — or create more plans of your own.

**④ SET ADVANCED OPTIONS** You can take more control over your power settings. Click on the "Change plan settings" link to the right of your new power plan, then click "Change advanced power settings". The window that opens lets you configure many additional settings, such as how long Windows should wait before spinning down the hard disk, and whether Windows should sleep or shut down when you press the power button. Some of these settings require a certain degree of technical understanding: if you're not sure what a setting does, click on the "?" icon in the top-right of the window to open Windows Help. This should help you decide whether or not to change a particular setting.

**HOW LONG?**
If this is the first time you've configured power options, allow 15 minutes.

**HOW HARD?**
It's easy to change settings, but some of the options available to you are quite technical.

## Tip

 When a laptop PC is in sleep mode, it's still drawing a small amount of power from the battery — so you could come back to your laptop after a break and find it dead. One solution is to enable "Hybrid sleep", available under "Advanced power options", which will force it to hibernate if your battery runs low.

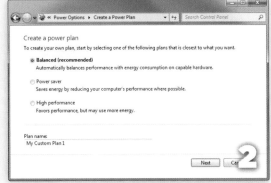

WINDOWS 7 IS MUCH MORE RESPONSIVE THAN VISTA, BUT WE HAVE A FEW TIPS TO MAXIMISE ITS SPEED AND HELP TO KEEP IT RUNNING SMOOTHLY.

# Making Windows 7 faster

A sure-fire way to make a computer faster is to upgrade it by adding memory, a faster hard disk or a more powerful processor. However, in many instances you can speed up your PC for free, without taking it to pieces first. All you need to do is tailor the software side – specifically, the operating system – so that you can apply the maximum resources available to the tasks you want to perform.

**COPE WITH LIMITED MEMORY** We'd recommend a minimum of 1GB of RAM for Windows 7, and if at all possible 2GB or more. A shortage of RAM is the single biggest factor that will make your PC seem slow – far more so than a slow processor. When Windows runs out of RAM, it uses the hard disk as a fall-back area to store data (known as virtual memory). But the hard disk is much slower to access than memory, leading to a dramatic performance decrease.

Microsoft offers one remedy in the form of ReadyBoost. This is an option you'll see every time you plug a USB flash memory drive into your system, and tells Windows to use the flash memory as system memory before resorting to the hard disk. If you have a decent-sized flash drive – in our view, that means 1GB or larger – then it's worth experimenting to see if it does make any difference to performance. Keep your expectations low.

RAM is fairly cheap to add, but if you don't relish the thought of opening up your PC, and ReadyBoost doesn't make a difference, you can at least try to make as much of your RAM as possible available to programs by ensuring it isn't tied up doing things you're not bothered about.

Click the Start orb to show the Start menu, then right-click on Computer and select Properties. The System Properties window will appear, but we want to delve further, so click on "Advanced system settings" in the left pane. The traditional-style System Properties window will appear, with a tab called Advanced. Click on Settings in the Performance area, then choose "Adjust for best performance".

Click OK and prepare for a shock, as Windows 7 turns into a hideous retro monster! The gradients, curves and fripperies of the Aero interface disappear, to be replaced by an old-school angular appearance that predates even XP, looking more like Windows 98. All of Windows 7's advanced features are still available: they're simply now clad in very drab clothes – which take up fewer system resources.

To see how much of a difference is made by this (or any other performance-boosting measure), you can use the Task Manager to monitor system resource usage, as seen on the opposite page. To open Task Manager, right-click on any clear part of the Taskbar and select Start Task Manager.

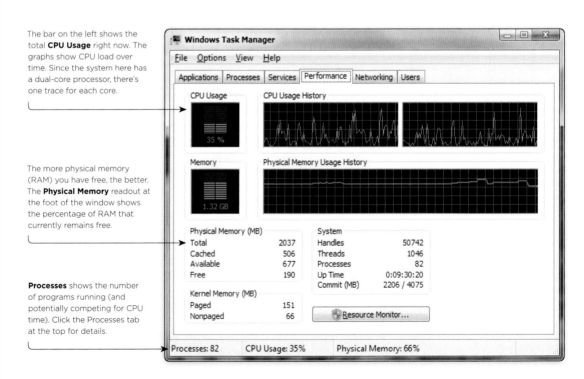

The bar on the left shows the total **CPU Usage** right now. The graphs show CPU load over time. Since the system here has a dual-core processor, there's one trace for each core.

The more physical memory (RAM) you have free, the better. The **Physical Memory** readout at the foot of the window shows the percentage of RAM that currently remains free.

**Processes** shows the number of programs running (and potentially competing for CPU time). Click the Processes tab at the top for details.

**CHECK BACKGROUND TASKS** The second way to speed up a PC is to make it spend less time doing things in the background that you didn't know it was doing anyway, and don't care if it doesn't. This can help both to reduce RAM usage and to free up the processor, boosting speed.

In a complex modern operating system there are always dozens of programs running in the background, even on a brand-new PC with a clean installation of Windows 7. If you don't believe us, see for yourself. Click the Start orb, and in the Start menu's Search box type "services", then press Return. After a short pause, you'll be presented with a fearsome-looking list of services.

A service, in this context, is a housekeeping task that runs in the background. On a completely fresh installation of Windows 7 Ultimate edition there are 116 of these, with just under half of them – 52, to be exact – activated and consuming system resources by default.

A note of caution: we're showing you the Services list as an illustration only. Don't alter or disable Services, or your PC may be rendered unbootable. This is under-the-bonnet stuff, and dropping a spanner into an engine is rarely a good way to tune it. We'll show you a safer route.

**PRUNE STARTUP ENTRIES** That route is via one of the hidden applications that don't appear in Windows 7's Start menu. It's called the System Configuration tool, and you can get to it by typing "msconfig" into the Start menu. If User Account Control asks you to confirm your actions, click Continue, and the tool's unassuming main window will then appear. Another word of warning at this point: don't fiddle with this utility indiscriminately, because it can still be dangerous.

What you *can* fiddle with are the program entries you'll see on the Startup tab. On a clean Windows 7 install, there'll only be a few items, primarily Windows Defender and a couple of cryptic ones labelled "Microsoft Windows Operating System". The programs listed here are non-critical background tasks – as opposed to Services, which are often critical – that are set to start up when Windows starts. If you come back to this window after a month or two, when you've added some software of your own, you'll probably find there are many more entries here. This is because a lot of third-party software is written by arrogant people who think their program needs to be running whenever Windows is running. But a lot of the time they're wrong.

To get your PC starting up and running faster, uncheck all the program names you recognise but don't want clogging up your system all the time. Or throw caution to the wind, hit Disable All and see what happens. Unlike with Services, you can't mangle your system to the extent that it won't boot. On the other hand, bear in mind that programs such as Windows Defender need to load at startup in order to be effective, so by turning them off you're opening up your PC to all the internet-borne baddies that Windows 7's security software was put there to guard against in the first place. It only takes moments for malware to strike.

The beauty of the System Configuration tool is that to reinstate a startup program, you just have to recheck

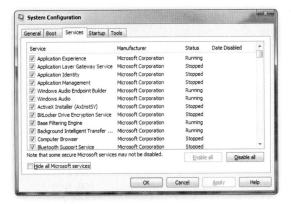

The safe way to eliminate some of the unnecessary chaff that can find its way onto your system is with the System Configuration tool. Any changes you make in the Startup tab are completely reversible – but avoid meddling with the settings in other tabs.

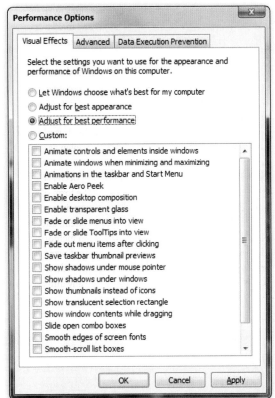

If you're low on memory, you can turn to the Performance Options dialog box. Beware, though, that when you choose "Adjust for best performance" and hit OK, your new operating system will look like Windows 98.

the box next to the program's name; or, if you want to revert to exactly how things were before you started fiddling about, simply click Enable All and then restart the computer. It's worth noting that you can perform the same trick from within Windows Defender, but the System Configuration tool is a quicker and less fussy method.

Tailoring your background tasks in this way can free up your PC's processor and memory subsystems to concentrate on servicing the foreground task – the one you're concentrating on at any given moment, and the one that will make you angry when you have to sit around twiddling your thumbs waiting for. The end result is that your system should seem to work faster, even though the hardware is exactly the same as before. Remember to revisit this technique every couple of months to clear up new detritus that's accumulated.

WINDOWS 7'S ENHANCED ACCESSIBILITY SETTINGS AIM TO MAKE THE NEW OPERATING SYSTEM A BETTER EXPERIENCE FOR EVERYONE.

# Introducing Accessibility Settings

As Windows has developed, so Microsoft has laboured to make it more accessible and easier to use. Anyone with visual impairments, hearing problems or conditions affecting our manual dexterity can have a hard time using a computer in the conventional way, as can those with conditions that affect writing ability or cognitive functions.

Windows 7 builds on the features provided by XP and Vista to overcome these difficulties, while providing enhanced versions of some core accessibility tools. With these, even people with severe impairments can work, communicate, learn and be entertained using their PC.

These tools and features can be found in the Ease of Access Center in the Control Panel, which has been configured to provide almost instant access to the main accessibility features while offering guidance to users who may not know which tools and options can help them.

For newcomers, the best place to start is Recommendations. You're asked five questions relating to your eyesight, dexterity, hearing, speech and reasoning (for example, whether you find it difficult to concentrate or remember). The program responds with a sequence of actions that you can opt in or out of by clicking a checkbox.

Alternatively, a series of "Explore all settings"

options below offer tasks described in plain English, phrased to achieve precise goals such as "Make the computer easier to see" or "Make the keyboard easier to use".

**VISION ON** For those with visual impairments, Windows 7 offers several useful options. Some are small but effective, such as enlarging the size of text and icons. Others include switching to the simplified white-on-black High Contrast theme and turning on the Narrator and the Magnifier.

The former gives an audio description of the active window, menu items and key presses, although in practice its approach can be confusing, and the American voice slips into such unnatural practices as describing our full stop as a period. Use the settings to control what announcements it makes, however, and the Narrator can be a useful tool.

The Magnifier is more useful to those with less severe vision defects, and has been improved since the version seen in Vista. There's just one spot of bad news: the High Contrast theme doesn't enable the Aero Glass graphics technology, and without Aero Glass you lose not only many of Windows 7's more exciting visual flourishes, but also the Magnifier, which is now powered by Aero Glass. Irritatingly, this means that you can't use two of the operating system's most useful accessibility features at the same time.

## *Tip*

If you're stuck for the right speech command, just say "What can I say?" and you get a full list of the available commands, plus when and how to use them.

Windows 7's accessibility tools include enhanced speech control. If your command isn't immediately recognised, you can have user interface elements automatically labelled with numbers, so that you can quickly select the one you want.

The High Contrast mode is still available, but now fails to work with the Magnifier – frustrating, if you need both features.

Both speech recognition (dictating text) and speech control (telling the PC what to do) are now easier to use and more accurate, with sensible workarounds to ensure you can make yourself understood.

**IN TOUCH** Users with hearing difficulties lose out on audio alarms and any other audio feedback used by Windows 7. Luckily, the "Get visual indications for sound" option replaces all those beeps and sirens with graphical equivalents, such as a flashing caption bar or window. There's also an option to get text captions for spoken dialogue, although this works only in programs that support it.

Finally, there's help for those who have trouble using a keyboard or a mouse. Along with options such as Sticky Keys – where you can press keystroke combinations in sequence rather than simultaneously – Windows 7 offers keyboard and mouse filters designed to intelligently assist your movements and weed out rogue clicks and presses. There's also a revised onscreen keyboard for users who work only with a mouse or other pointing device, plus improved speech control and recognition. The onscreen keyboard has a basic predictive text feature, with likely words appearing in easy-to-see slots above the virtual keypad.

Meanwhile, speech recognition goes beyond mere dictation – good as this is – with a speech control system that works on the principle of "say what you see". Speak the name of a button or menu item, for instance, and it should be selected. If that fails, just say "show numbers", and Windows covers active areas of the current window with numbers by which you can then refer to them.

Mention the number of your chosen option, and Windows clicks on that button or link. Such systems used to take hours to train and configure, but Windows 7 makes the process relatively quick and easy, and – cleverly – a series of tutorial and training exercises help you learn the system at the same time as training it to recognise your voice.

# HOW TO...
# USE THE MAGNIFIER

The Magnifier is a useful tool for anyone who has difficulty reading text on screen. It enlarges the specific area that you need to see so that it becomes easily legible, without reducing your screen resolution.

**①  ZOOM FOR IMPROVEMENT** If you run through the Ease of Access recommendations or pick an option such as "Make the computer easier to see", starting up the Magnifier will be one of the suggested actions. However, you can also switch it on by visiting the Ease of Access Center and clicking the Start Magnifier button in the Quick Access box at the top of the window.

**②  THE BIGGER PICTURE** By default the Magnifier works in full-screen mode, enlarging the whole of the current section of the display, with the view shifting as you move the pointer towards the edge of the screen. Clicking on the magnifying glass icon on the screen opens up the streamlined toolbar. The plus and minus keys adjust the level of zoom.

**③  THROUGH THE LENS** Click on the Views dropdown menu to change how the Magnifier operates. In Lens mode, seen here, it behaves like a traditional magnifying glass, enlarging the area under the lens, which moves along with the mouse pointer. Click on the Options button in the toolbar to increase or decrease the height or width of the lens according to your needs. Making it shorter but wider can help, for instance, when you're reading or writing a long text document.

**④  ENJOY THE VIEW** Switching to Dock mode moves the Lens to a specific area of the screen, although it still operates on the area surrounding the pointer by default. However, by clicking on the Options button you can command the Lens to track the current keyboard focus or the text insertion point in, say, a Word or Excel document. The Dock mode gives you all the advantages of large screen real-estate, while ensuring you can still see exactly what you're typing.

A few keyboard shortcuts will make your time with the Magnifier even easier. Press the Windows key and hit the plus or minus keys to zoom in and out; or hold <Ctrl+Alt> and press F, L or D to switch between full screen, Lens and Dock modes respectively.

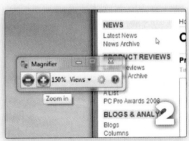

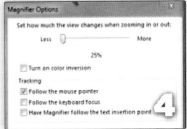

# IN THIS CHAPTER

# 11
*Solving problems*

# SOLVING SYSTEM

By now you'll appreciate that there's lots of great new stuff in Windows 7 – not least improvements to stability and security that should mean an even more hassle-free experience in everyday use. But that's not to say nothing will ever go wrong. Fortunately, there are also new tools to help if it does. In this chapter, we point out the essential Control Panel settings; show

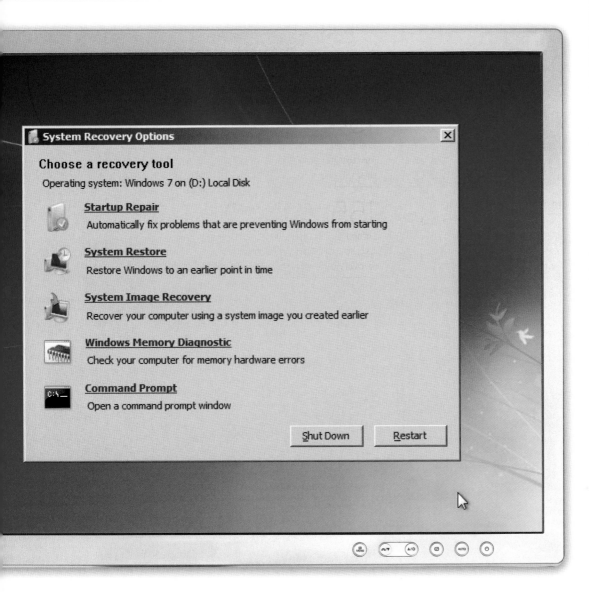

# PROBLEMS

you how to fix a compromised PC with System Restore or use Advanced Boot Options to get into a machine that won't start up; and explain how to make a System Repair Disc that can help rescue your computer when all else fails. You'll also see how Remote Desktop lets you control your Windows 7 PC from anywhere on the internet, just as if you were sitting in front of it.

# Troubleshooting Windows 7

Windows 7 makes it easy to install and configure software and hardware, and to remove it again if necessary. All the same, every so often things just don't work as they're supposed to. We can't give you specific help with the millions of software packages available, but we can show you some basic tools built into Windows that could save the day when a program – or Windows itself – starts misbehaving.

We'll start with the Troubleshooting section of the Control Panel. To open it, look under the System and Security heading in Control Panel and click "Find and fix problems". The first entry in the list that appears (pictured below), Programs, is specifically concerned with software compatibility. Windows 7 largely supports applications written for older versions of Windows, but it does bring new security features and upgraded components, so occasionally older programs may not work as expected. If you've come across one, click "Run programs made for previous versions of Windows", then choose your app from the list. Windows will try to apply the right settings to make it work, and in our experience it usually succeeds. (See p52.)

Below this, the Hardware and Sound options scan your hardware and drivers and try to repair anything that isn't working, be it an internal device, a printer or an audio component. Even if Windows can't get a recalcitrant device going, it can often tell you what you need to do to fix it.

You'll also find troubleshooting wizards to help you with networking problems and Windows 7's Aero desktop effects. And finally, under System and Security, there are a few general tools to help you keep Windows running as it should.

**SYSTEM RESTORE** Control Panel can help with the day-to-day running of your PC, but what if something goes badly wrong when you're installing new software or making a major change to your system settings? The good news is that Windows automatically takes a snapshot of your system before applying such changes, so if you later find that the new program or configuration is causing problems, you can easily roll back your system to its previous state. See the panel on the opposite page for more information about System Restore.

**ADVANCED BOOT OPTIONS** If the Control Panel can't help you, and System Restore doesn't do the trick, you could try a more advanced approach. Reboot your computer and then quickly, just before the Starting Windows screen appears, press the F8 key on your keyboard. You'll see a menu listing Advanced Boot Options. Some of these options demand technical expertise, so don't select anything you're not sure about. To get out of this menu, use the down cursor key to

## FAQ

**Q:** I want to run System Restore, but if I roll back my computer to last week, won't I lose the files I've created and edited in the meantime?
**A:** No. Like it says on the tin, System Restore is designed to roll back the operating system, not your files. It won't touch anything in your personal Libraries, nor anything it recognises as a personal data file (such as word processing documents or MP3 files). If you're anxious, back up your files onto an external hard disk or USB flash drive before running System Restore.

In the **Control Panel**, click the link labelled "Find and fix problems" to open this collection of system trouble-shooting options.

If you're having trouble with **older programs** after upgrading to Windows 7, click here to fix them.

Make sure this box is ticked to **update your troubleshooting options** on an ongoing basis with the latest advice.

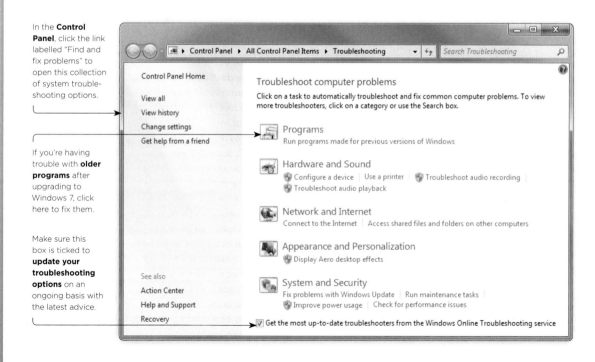

The Hardware and Sound section of Control Panel lets you check the settings and drivers for each of the hardware components of your system, including built-in and external multimedia accessories.

scroll down to Start Windows Normally at the bottom of the screen, then press Return.

If you're having trouble with your display settings, for example, choose "Enable low-resolution video (640x480)". This will launch Windows with basic screen settings, ensuring you can see what you're doing while you make any adjustments you need to. When you next reboot, the settings you've chosen will take effect.

Another useful option is Safe Mode, which loads Windows with a minimum of hardware support and system components. This gets you into the system if a rogue driver is preventing startup, for example, and lets you configure and uninstall software and drivers that are inaccessible in normal use. Again, reboot and the system goes back to normal, with the changes you made while in Safe Mode.

Another way to help deal with situations where the PC won't boot up is to create a system repair disc, as explained in our guide on p155.

**PROBLEM STEPS RECORDER** If none of these approaches can solve your problem, the maker of your PC or software should be able to offer technical support. But how do you tell them exactly what the problem is? In the past you simply had to describe it as best you could, but with Windows 7's Problem Steps Recorder you can show them.

The tool itself is hidden away in the depths of the Control Panel: the easiest way to find it is to open the Start menu and type "record steps". Press Return to launch it.

Once the recorder is running, just click Start Record, then do whatever you need to do to reproduce the problem. The recorder will start recording the activity on your screen, along with any mouse clicks; if you want to comment on something you're doing, simply click on Add Comment to drop in a note at the appropriate point. Optionally, you can also highlight an area of the screen to illustrate your comment.

When you hit Stop Record, your actions will be saved in an archive, with pictures and a full technical description, which you can easily send to a support engineer to help them diagnose your problem.

# USING SYSTEM RESTORE

Windows creates a restore point whenever something makes a significant change to your system: for example, when you install a new application or new hardware drivers, or when the system is updated via Windows Update. If you like, you can also create your own restore points, so that you can later revert your PC to a known state. To do this, simply select "Create a restore point" from the Control Panel.

By default, restore points are kept for 90 days before being deleted, although if they start to take up too much hard disk space the oldest ones are erased to free up space as needed. You can change how much space is permitted from the System Protection tab of System Properties: click the Configure button to access these settings. If you're very low on hard disk space, you can also disable System Restore altogether from here, but we certainly don't recommend that – it's far too useful to give up.

In System Properties, choose where restore points are stored (if you have more than one hard disk) and how much disk space they're allowed to consume.

**POINTS OF VIEW** When you launch System Restore, Windows will suggest you roll back to the most recent restore point. It will show you when that point was created, and provide a description of the action that triggered its creation (for example, "Installed Microsoft Office"). This is the action that will be undone if you proceed, along with any other changes you may have made since. If you want to know in more detail what changes will be reversed, click "Scan for affected programs" and you'll see a list of drivers and software packages that will be removed. If you need to go further back in time, you can click the link labelled "Show more restore points" to choose an earlier state. When you're ready, click Next to apply the changes. Windows needs to restart to apply a System Restore, so first save your work in any open programs. When the PC reboots, it's as if your last installation or system change never happened (but see FAQ, opposite).

**RECOVERY POSITION** Don't confuse Windows 7's System Restore with the "recovery" software that may have been provided with your PC. Such software typically reverts your machine to exactly the state it was in when you bought it – wiping out all your files and settings. This is a last resort if your PC goes haywire, or a way to prepare it before passing it on to a new owner.

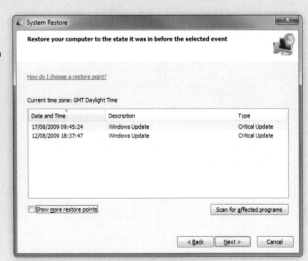

System Restore lists each available restore point along with a brief description of the action that prompted its creation. To go further back, click "Show more restore points". The maximum number of restore points depends on the amount of disk space allocated to System Restore.

# Introducing Remote Desktop

In chapter 6, we discussed using HomeGroup to share files and printers over a home network and over the internet. But sometimes you don't just want to access data, you need to change settings on a remote PC, or run a program installed on it. Windows 7 makes it possible to operate one computer from another, but only if the computer you want to access is running the Professional, Enterprise or Ultimate edition.

**WHAT IT DOES** Remote Desktop shows you the desktop of a different Windows PC on your own, and lets you control that computer just as if you were sitting in front of it. You can connect to any other Windows computer in the world, as long as it's switched on, awake, and accessible over a network. That last part is usually no problem in a home environment, but if the computer in question is on a different network (say, it's a PC at your office), you'll probably need to request access from the Administrator of the other network. You may also need them to tell you the internet address of the computer you want to connect to. Another big problem comes if you want to access your home PC over the internet and it connects via a router: see our guide at www.pcpro.co.uk/links/win7router

The remote PC itself must be running Windows 7 Professional, Enterprise or Ultimate (although the one you connect from can have any edition of Windows 7). And it must be specifically configured to accept Remote Desktop Connection requests, since these are switched off by default. You'll also need to know the username and password of a user account on the remote machine, and that account must have permission to log on remotely (see opposite).

**WHAT IT DOESN'T** Remote Desktop may let you use a PC as if you're sitting in front of it, but if someone else is sitting in front of it then they won't be able to use it at the same time; they'll just see a logon screen showing that you're busy using the PC. This means you can't use Remote Desktop to demonstrate a procedure to someone else. If that's what you want to do, you can use either Microsoft's Live Mesh (see p72) or the Windows Remote Assistance tool, which you'll find in the Start menu under Maintenance.

With Remote Assistance, you simply generate an "invitation", either in the form of an email code or a 12-character password, and pass it on to a friend or colleague. With this code, they can then connect to your desktop, see what you're doing and take control of the system (with your permission). It's very helpful for troubleshooting and collaboration, but both computers need somebody present to send and receive the invitation.

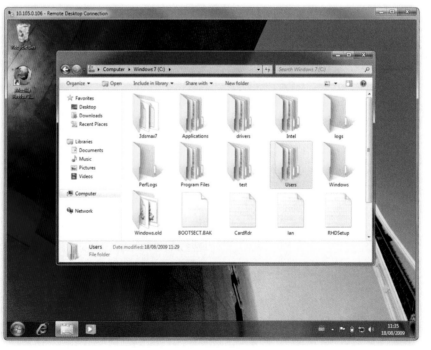

With Remote Desktop you can operate one PC from another, whether it's on the same network or elsewhere on the internet. You can do this from a PC running any version of Windows 7, including Home Premium, but the PC you're going to control must have the Professional, Enterprise or Ultimate edition, and you (or someone with Administrator access to it) must set it up first to accept Remote Desktop connections.

# HOW TO...
# GET REMOTE DESKTOP WORKING

**(1) ENABLE CONNECTIONS** Before you can control a PC remotely, you need to configure it to accept Remote Desktop connections. Search for "Advanced system settings". In the Remote tab at the top right, you'll see settings for both Remote Assistance and Remote Desktop. (If you don't, your edition of Windows 7 doesn't support incoming Remote Desktop connections.) By default, Remote Desktop is set to not allow connections. If you want to connect from a PC running Vista or Windows 7, select the bottom option. If you want to connect from Windows XP, choose the middle option.

**(2) SELECT USERS** When you now try to connect to this PC via Remote Desktop, you'll need to provide a valid username and password. (Blank passwords aren't allowed.) If you type in the name and password for an Administrator account on this PC, you'll be allowed in; but Standard users need permission to connect remotely. To grant this permission, click Select Users, and in the next window that opens click Add. In the dialog box that appears, you can type in the name of a Standard user to grant them remote access.

**(3) CONNECT** Now try to connect from your other PC. The icon for opening a Remote Desktop Connection can be found in the Start menu under Accessories. Run it and type in the name of the remote computer, such as BEDROOM-PC. (If you know your IP address, such as 212.100.242.151, then you can also enter this. However, as most people connect to the internet via a router, you'll need to set up port forwarding to connect to the PC in question. We cover this at www.pcpro.co.uk/links/win7router.) Hit Connect and, if everything is working as it should, you'll be asked for your remote username and password. Windows might complain that no "trusted certifying authority" has confirmed the identity of your remote PC; click Yes to proceed. Finally, you'll see the remote desktop appear in full-screen view. You can click in the bar along the top of the screen to shrink it into a window if you prefer.

**(4) OPTIONS** The next time you launch Remote Desktop Connection, try clicking the Options dropdown menu before hitting Connect. You'll see all sorts of settings you can change, including what the screen looks like and how the keyboard behaves. You can also configure which hardware on your own PC will be available to the remote PC when you're connected. By default, sounds are routed out of your speakers rather than through those connected to the remote PC (which would be pointless in most circumstances), and you can print from the remote PC directly to your local printer.

**HOW LONG?**
Allow ten minutes to configure user accounts and settings on both PCs.

**HOW HARD?**
Once you understand what you're doing, and if your two PCs can communicate across the network, it isn't difficult.

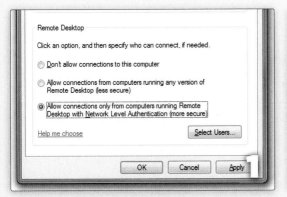

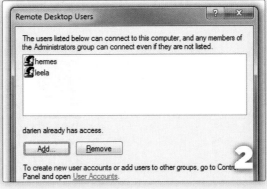

IF THINGS GO VERY WRONG, YOUR PC COULD GET SO MESSED UP THAT IT WON'T EVEN START. WINDOWS 7 COMES WITH TOOLS TO GET YOU BACK ON THE ROAD.

# Repairing a broken system

It doesn't happen often, but a PC that won't start is a real pain. If you do end up in this situation, there are several steps you can try that may resolve the situation.

If your computer used to work and is suddenly refusing to boot, the question is: what's changed? If you've added (or removed) a piece of hardware, try removing or replacing it to see if that cures the problem. If so, it could be physically faulty, or there may be a problem with its driver.

**BOOT OPTIONS** If that doesn't help, your first port of call should be the Advanced Boot Options menu. As we mentioned on p150, you get here by pressing F8 before the Starting Windows prompt appears. If there's a problem with your graphics card, you may be able to get into Windows by using the cursor keys to move down to the option labelled "Enable low-resolution video (640x480)". If the problem is with another driver, Safe Mode may work. If you can get into Windows this way, you can use System Restore to roll back your PC to a working state, or try updating hardware drivers or software to see if this helps.

If none of these methods gets you into Windows, another possible approach is to select Last Known Good Configuration from the Advanced Boot Options. This is similar to System Restore, but much cruder: it simply tries to boot the computer using the same drivers and settings that were used last time Windows started up successfully. That means there's a chance it will get you into Windows, from where you can perform more sophisticated troubleshooting.

**STARTUP REPAIR** If you still can't boot up, your next step is to try Windows' built-in Startup Repair tools. If you can get to the Advanced Boot Options, you can run this directly from the menu; if not, you can boot from the Windows 7 installation DVD and, from the title screen, select "Repair your computer". If you bought a PC with Windows 7 preinstalled, you may not have an installation DVD; in that case, you'll need to create a recovery disc to run Startup Repair. Obviously, you can't do this if you can't get into Windows, so it's a good idea to plan ahead and create the disc now, as explained opposite. (You may, at a pinch, be able to start up from a Vista install disc, although tools such as System Image Recovery may not work properly.)

If none of this works, as a last resort you may have to reinstall Windows 7. If you do this from an original Windows 7 installation disc, your personal files will be preserved in a folder called Windows.old. If you reinstall from a PC manufacturer's recovery partition, your entire hard disk will be overwritten and your files will be gone.

*Tip*

◢ Before delving into Windows' startup repair options, make sure the problem really is with your hard disk. If there's a DVD in your optical drive, or if you've left a USB flash drive or external hard disk connected, the problem could simply be that your PC is trying to boot from that drive instead, and naturally failing to find your Windows installation on it. Remove any such items and try again.

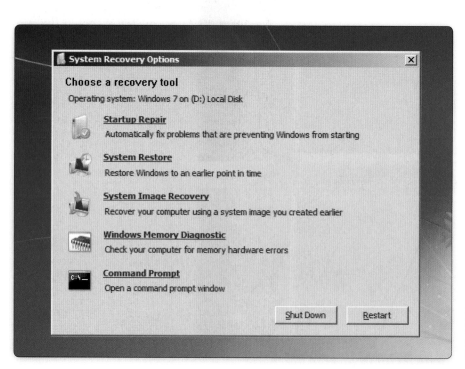

Even when all seems lost, Windows 7 provides emergency tools that may be able to bring your system back to life.

# HOW TO...
# USE A SYSTEM REPAIR DISC

**(1) MAKE A REPAIR DISC** Creating a recovery disc is easy. You'll find an icon labelled "Create a system repair disc" in the Start menu under Maintenance. Click this and you'll be prompted to select your CD or DVD drive. Insert a blank CD or DVD and click Create; the files will be written, and within a few minutes you'll have a disc you can boot from in case of emergency.

**(2) REPAIR ON STARTUP** When you need to use Startup Repair, boot from your new disc by inserting it into the drive before starting the PC. Alternatively, launch the process via the Advanced Boot Options menu or from the Windows 7 installation DVD, as described opposite. You may need to choose a username and type its password before your main options appear.

The menu offers five options. The first is Startup Repair: choose this and Windows will automatically scan your hard disk for operating system installations that might have become inaccessible (this can happen if, for example, you've used maintenance software that's changed the way your computer starts up). Once the Startup Repair process finds Windows 7 on your hard disk, it will try to rebuild the startup sequence so as to make Windows accessible again. In many cases, this is all that's required: hit Restart once it's finished and you may find Windows is restored to perfect working order.

**(3) SYSTEM RESTORE** From this window you can also launch System Restore or System Image Recovery. We've already covered System Restore on p150: this tool may allow you to revert your PC to a working condition by undoing the changes associated with installing software or drivers. System Image Recovery takes a more drastic approach: it will completely restore your PC to an earlier state, obliterating any changes or new files created since then. To use this, you must previously have created a system image within Windows. You can do this from the Control Panel, under System and Security. Images can be saved to an external hard disk, a DVD or a network drive.

**(4) MEMORY DIAGNOSTICS** If your system has stopped working without your making any changes, it's possible there's a problem with your PC's memory. The fourth Startup Repair option, Memory Diagnostics, will test your RAM for errors. If any are found, it's best to remove or replace the faulty module.

Finally, you can open a command prompt from which you can run advanced tools with full access to your hard disk. If all else fails, try opening this and entering **bootrec /fixmbr** followed by **bootrec /rebuildbcd**. These commands write new Windows startup code to your hard disk and just might get your PC working again.

**HOW LONG?**
Creating a recovery disc takes only a few minutes, but saving a system image or testing your RAM could take hours.

**HOW HARD?**
These procedures aren't difficult, but there are quite a few options to work your way through.

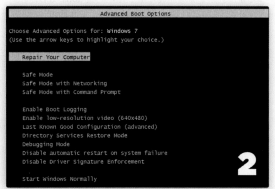

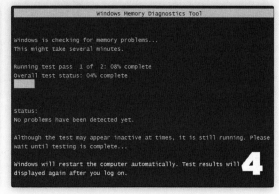

# 12
## *Glossary of terms*

# Windows jargon explained

**32-BIT/64-BIT** Refers to either the processor or the operating system. See p14 for more information.

**802.11** The name of the official standard that governs aspects of wireless networking and hardware. 802.11b, 802.11g and 802.11n denote the three types of consumer wireless connections. 802.11b is the oldest and slowest, 802.11g is faster, and 802.11n is the latest and fastest type, now becoming the norm for all new equipment. Officially, 802.11n has only just been ratified, which is why you may see some manufacturers refer to it as "draft-n".

## A

**AERO** The new look of Windows originally introduced in Vista and enhanced in Windows 7, including transparent window frames (see Aero Glass), live previews of windows (Aero Peek), a 3D carousel of your open windows (Flip 3D), the ability to snap windows to positions within your desktop (Aero Snap), and the option to minimise all windows apart from the active one by giving it a good old shake (Aero Shake). See p48 for full details.

**ADSL (ASYMMETRIC DIGITAL SUBSCRIBER LINE)** The most common form of broadband internet connection, working over traditional phone lines at speeds of up to 8Mbits/sec, or 20Mbits/sec where ISPs have installed new equipment at the local exchange. The alternative is cable broadband, available only from Virgin Media in the UK, available at speeds of up to 50Mbits/sec in cabled neighbourhoods.

**AERO GLASS** A subset of the Windows Aero theme, Glass is the effect that makes windows translucent. Not included in Windows 7 Starter edition, and may be disabled in other editions when the PC's processing power is insufficient.

**APPLOCKER** Unique to Windows 7 Ultimate/Enterprise, AppLocker is a feature aimed at large businesses that want to control exactly what applications can be installed and run by users on its PCs.

## B

**BIOS** The Basic Input/Output System configures your motherboard at startup and boots your PC. It's stored on a flash memory chip on the motherboard; its settings can be accessed by holding a specified key during startup.

**BITLOCKER / BITLOCKER TO GO** BitLocker and BitLocker To Go are only found in the Ultimate and Enterprise editions of Windows. BitLocker, introduced with Vista, offers a way to encrypt an entire hard disk, making it virtually impossible for laptop thieves to access the owner's data. BitLocker To Go is new to Windows 7 and applies the same principle to external disks, such as USB flash drives.

**BLU-RAY** The successor to DVD, storing up to nine hours of high-definition video or 50GB of data on a disc.

**BREADCRUMB BAR (OR BREADCRUMB TRAIL)** Introduced in Windows Vista, this is a way of showing you which folders you've navigated through in Windows Explorer to reach your present location.

## C

**CPU (CENTRAL PROCESSING UNIT)** Also known simply as a processor, the CPU is the component that interprets and executes computer programs. Common CPUs in personal computers include Intel's Pentium and Core series and AMD's Athlon and Sempron ranges.

## D

**DESKTOP** The primary working area of Windows, visible whenever your screen isn't covered by application windows, and home to Gadgets and shortcut icons.

**DEVICE STAGE** A new feature of Windows 7, Microsoft introduced Device Stage to make managing devices such as printers and MP3 players easier. The Device Stage for each device shows a picture and shortcuts to settings and controls, such as a scanner's settings. Theoretically, manufacturers could also provide shopping links here for consumables such as printer inks. See p54.

**DIRECTX** A set of Windows extensions from Microsoft to accelerate games and other performance-hungry software by allowing them to use your PC's graphics hardware to the full. DirectX 11 is introduced in Windows 7.

**DUAL BOOT** It's entirely possible to run two operating systems on one computer, for example if you wish to keep Windows XP to run ageing games but use Windows 7 as your main environment. As we explain on p24, you don't even need two hard disks to make this work.

**DVB-T (DIGITAL VIDEO BROADCASTING – TERRESTRIAL)**
A standard used by Freeview digital TV in the UK and supported by digital TV tuner cards and USB sticks for PCs. DVB-T2 tuners will support HD (high-definition) TV on their release in late 2009.

# F

**FAT32** A hard disk format used by older operating systems such as Windows 98 and also devices such as USB flash drives. Contrary to earlier announcements, Windows 7 can still access FAT32 drives, but the NTFS format is now standard and more reliable.

**FIREWALL** Software or hardware designed to protect networks and PCs from hackers, or from malicious software that they control.

**FIREWIRE** Also known as IEEE-1394 or iLink, this is a high-speed method of connecting external devices such as MiniDV camcorders. It's an alternative to USB 2, but more popular on the Apple Macintosh than in the PC world.

**FLASH MEMORY** A type of RAM used in USB memory drives and the memory cards for digital cameras. Flash memory retains its data even when power is removed.

**FULL-DISK ENCRYPTION** Any computer can encrypt data, but to prevent a potential hacker gaining any access to a hard disk, companies use a technology called full-disk encryption. In partnership with a dedicated processor embedded on a PC's motherboard (in what's called a Trusted Platform Module), this means the only way to access the disk is to know the password. BitLocker, only included with the Ultimate/Enterprise edition of Windows 7 and Vista, is the brand name of Microsoft's full-disk encryption technology.

# G

**GADGETS** Small, usually single-purpose programs that live on the Windows 7 desktop.

**GIGABYTE (GB)** 1,024 megabytes when referred to in the context of RAM; 1,000 megabytes in the context of hard disks. No one said this would be easy.

**GPU (GRAPHICS PROCESSING UNIT)** The chip in your PC, either built into your motherboard or onto a graphics card, that handles 3D games, as well as driving your screen display.

# H

**HARD DISK** A form of reliable, cheap magnetic storage that usually holds all of the data stored permanently within your PC.

**HDCP (HIGH DEFINITION CONTENT PROTECTION)** A form of DRM (digital rights management) used to ensure that PCs and related equipment can play, but not copy high definition (HD) media such as Blu-ray movies.

**HDMI (HIGH DEFINITION MULTIMEDIA INTERFACE)** A connector designed to carry video and audio signals between high-definition devices.

**HDTV 720I, 720P, 1080I, 1080P** The High Definition film and television standard, allowing greater resolution and picture detail. The numbers refer to the number of horizontal lines in a picture, and whether those lines are interlaced (i) or progressive (p). Higher numbers are better, and "p" is better than "i".

**HOMEGROUP** New in Windows 7, HomeGroup is Microsoft's name for a technology that allows you to quickly and easily share files and devices between all the PCs and laptops on your home network, even if the printer (for example) is connected to a different PC.

# I

**INTERNET EXPLORER** Microsoft's web browser. Windows 7 includes Internet Explorer 8, which is undoubtedly its best web browser yet. However, it has strong competition from Mozilla Firefox and others (see p78-83).

**ISP (INTERNET SERVICE PROVIDER)** A company that provides internet access to end users.

**IP ADDRESS** A number assigned to a PC on a network to allow it to be identified, so that incoming data can find its way to the correct computer.

# J

**JUMP LISTS** One of the best new features introduced in Windows 7, Jump Lists is Microsoft's term for the dozen or so documents that spring to life when you right-click on a program icon on the Taskbar. Software makers can add extra features to Jump Lists too; for instance, Microsoft's Media Player lets you access playback controls straight from its Jump List. See p32 for full details.

# L

**LIBRARIES** A new concept introduced with Windows 7, there are four different types of Library: Documents, Music, Pictures and Video. The idea is that, even if you store your music in several different places on your PC or network, you can access all of it from the Music Library. It's an odd concept, but it works. See p36.

**LIVE MESH** A free Microsoft service (for now) for sharing and synchronising documents across the net. See p72.

# 12

## Glossary of terms

**LIVE PREVIEWS** An element of Windows Aero, these allow you to see what's happening in a window or application by hovering the mouse pointer over its icon in the Taskbar.

**LOCAL** Describes a folder, file or resource that's stored within or connected directly to the PC you're using, rather than on a network or another computer.

## M

**MEDIA CENTER** Microsoft's simple-to-use program for viewing photos, video and TV (and for listening to music). Designed to work with a remote control, but can also be controlled via the mouse and keyboard. At its most powerful in a PC with a TV tuner (see p96).

**MEDIA CENTER EXTENDER** A device, most notably the Xbox 360, that can take all the music, video and TV stored on your Windows 7 PC and transmit it directly to the television or hi-fi that the Media Center Extender is itself attached to.

**MEDIA STREAMING** See streaming.

**MULTITOUCH** The capability for a computer or another interactive device (most famously, Apple's iPhone) to translate two or more finger touches into a command. For example, pinch two fingers together on a Windows 7 touchscreen PC running Photo Gallery and the picture will zoom out. Keep one finger down and rotate the other, and the image will rotate with you.

## N

**NTFS (NEW TECHNOLOGY FILE SYSTEM)** A hard disk format used in Windows NT, 2000, XP, Vista and Windows 7. The successor to FAT.

## O

**OEM (ORIGINAL EQUIPMENT MANUFACTURER)** The manufacturer of an entire PC or an individual component. You can buy so-called OEM versions of equipment and software, including Windows, which are cheaper but will come without manuals or technical support.

**OPTICAL DRIVE** A catch-all term for CD, DVD and Blu-ray disc drives.

## P

**PARENTAL CONTROLS** Software components to monitor and control how your children use your computer. It can restrict access to specified times, websites and applications. Windows 7 has basic parental controls built in, and you can download more advanced controls via Windows Live Family Safety (see p108).

**PARTITIONS** Artificially segregated areas of a hard disk. If you create two partitions, it's possible to install two different versions of Windows (or any other operating system), one on each partition.

## R

**RAM (RANDOM ACCESS MEMORY)** A high-speed form of memory holding the data and documents that you're currently using. The contents of RAM is lost when the PC is switched off (except in the case of flash RAM).

**READYBOOST** A method of using USB flash drives to boost the speed of PCs with less than 1GB of RAM. Frankly, we don't think it's much use.

## S

**SAVED SEARCHES** Folders that contain a set of user-defined search results, which update dynamically as files matching the criteria are added.

**SKYDRIVE** Not to be confused with Live Mesh, Windows Live SkyDrive is a free Microsoft service that gives you 25GB of online storage. See p70.

**START MENU/ORB** Pressing the Windows key on your keyboard will launch the Start menu. It's a simple way to access programs installed on your PC, and settings via the Control Panel. You can also click the "Start orb", the circular shape containing the Windows logo that sits at the bottom left of your desktop by default.

**STREAMING** If you want to listen to a piece of music stored on one computer on another, the simplest method is to "stream" it. Rather than copy the file and save it on the new PC, this process sends the music bit by bit; when you've finished listening, any information is automatically deleted from the receiving PC. If you ever watch videos on websites such as the BBC's, this uses a similar technology.

**SYSTEM RESTORE** A feature that allows you to "roll back" Windows to a saved set of settings. By default, Windows 7 will take a snapshot of settings each time a major change occurs, such as the addition of a new piece of hardware.

**SYSTEM TRAY** A small area at the right of the Taskbar that's used to show volume settings, network status, and other applications that are running in the background.

## T

**TABLET PC** Most commonly refers to slate-style mobile computers that don't include a keyboard and instead rely on a touchscreen with handwriting recognition for navigation and data input. Can also refer to laptops that include a touchscreen in addition to a keyboard.

**TASKBAR** Arranged by default along the bottom of the screen, the Taskbar is home to the System Tray and Start orb, as well as the Taskbar buttons of programs that are currently running. In Windows 7, you can also pin favourite applications here.

**TCP/IP (TRANSMISSION CONTROL PROTOCOL/INTERNET PROTOCOL)** A set of protocols used to transmit data over networks; the fundamental protocols at the heart of the internet.

# U

**UAC (USER ACCOUNT CONTROL)** Controversial measure introduced in Windows Vista and improved in Windows 7. The UAC box should appear only when a program requests permission to make a major change to Windows.

**USB (UNIVERSAL SERIAL BUS)** A "plug and play" interface for connecting the vast majority of peripherals to a PC.

**USB 2** The fastest form of USB currently available, running at speeds of up to 480Mbits/sec. Also known as Hi-Speed USB. "Full-Speed" USB, or USB 1.1, runs at a much slower 12Mbits/sec.

# W

**WAN (WIDE AREA NETWORK)** A network that extends over a large geographical area, as opposed to a LAN (local area network). A broadband modem's external connection (to the internet) is referred to as a WAN.

**WEP (WIRED EQUIVALENT PRIVACY)** A common, but flawed, method of encrypting the data sent over a Wi-Fi connection. It gives fair protection but can be broken by a determined eavesdropper. See WPA.

**WI-FI** The generic term for wireless networks and connections based on the 802.11a, 802.11b, 802.11g and 802.11n standards.

**WINDOWS DEFENDER** The anti-spyware software provided free with Windows 7.

**WINDOWS EXPLORER** The built-in way to browse your files (and your network) in Windows. Not to be confused with Internet Explorer, which is used for web browsing.

**WINDOWS LIVE ESSENTIALS** A collection of downloadable software that Microsoft offers free to Windows owners. Includes Windows Live Mail, Live Messenger, Live Photo Gallery and Movie Maker. See chapter 5.

**WPA (WI-FI PROTECTED ACCESS)** A very secure method of encrypting the data transmitted on a wireless network. The WPA2 standard is even tougher again.

# The Ultimate Guide to Windows 7

## EDITORIAL

**Editor**
Tim Danton  editor@pcpro.co.uk

**Managing Editor**
Adam Banks

**Production Editor**
Priti Patel

**Sub Editors**
Steve Haines, Simon Petersen

**Design and layout**
Adam Banks  adam@adambanks.com

**Contributors**
Stuart Andrews, David Bayon,
Jon Bray, Barry Collins,
Darien Graham-Smith, Mike Jennings,
Sasha Muller, Dave Stevenson

Stuart Turton made the tea.

## LICENSING & SYNDICATION

**International Licensing**
Winnie Liesenfeld  +44 20 7907 6314

**Syndication**
Jasmine Samra  +44 20 7907 6132

## ADVERTISING & MARKETING

**Advertising Manager**
Ben Topp  +44 20 7907 6625

**Digital Production Manager**
Nicky Baker  +44 20 7907 6056

**MagBook Manager**
Dharmesh Mistry  +44 20 7907 6100

**Marketing Manager**
Claire Scrase  +44 20 7907 6113

## MANAGEMENT  +44 20 7907 6000

**Publishing Director**
Ian Westwood

**MD of Advertising**
Julian Lloyd-Evans

**Production Director**
Julian Lloyd-Evans

**Newstrade Director**
Martin Belson

**Chief Operating Officer**
Brett Reynolds

**Group Finance Director**
Ian Leggett

**Chief Executive**
James Tye

**Chairman**
Felix Dennis

# Index